LANGUAGE POWER

100 THINGS YOU NEED TO KNOW TO MAKE LANGUAGE WORK FOR YOU

NORBERT SCHMITT

Edited by Dorothy Zemach

Illustrations by Will Mitchell

Cover concept by DJ Rogers

Published in the United States of America by Wayzgoose Press

ISBN: 978-1961953086

CONTENTS

PART 3
LANGUAGE AND GENDER

PART 4
LANGUAGE MANIPULATORS

PART 5
THE LANGUAGE OF TEXTING, COMPUTERS, AND THE INTERNET

PART 6
HOW YOUNG CHILDREN LEARN THEIR MOTHER TONGUE

PART 7
LEARNING TO READ AND WRITE (LITERACY)

PART 8
THE BEST WAYS TO LEARN A SECOND LANGUAGE

TIPS FOR READING THIS BOOK

This book is written for everyone interested in language. To make it as useful and as accessible as possible, I have used the following style:

- I do not assume you have any specialist knowledge about language or linguistics.
- I have written the book based on the latest academic research, but I have mostly used everyday language in my explanations, rather than an academic style.
- Each section answers a specific language question, often with examples, diagrams, checklists, or activities. The sections end with a "**Power Point**" that gives a brief summary of the key ideas.
- I suggest websites that offer interesting additional information for most topics. The websites are at the end of each section. These websites all worked at the time of publishing, but I ask your understanding if any have disappeared by the time you read this.

- Many issues in language are related, and so I have cross-referenced other sections with the (§) mark if they contain relevant related information (e.g., §8 = see also Section 8).
- Although the book is about the way language works in general, it is written in English, and so will highlight English in its examples and discussion.

PART 1

INTRODUCTION

1

EVERYONE USES LANGUAGE: KNOWING HOW IT WORKS CAN GIVE YOU AN EDGE

Why should I read this book?

Listening to the morning weather report on the radio. Reading the news to see what is happening in the world. Reading traffic signs on the way to work. Writing reports for your company. Checking the Internet for a nice present for your brother's birthday. Filling out forms to sign up to a new streaming service. Talking with your children's teachers about their needs. Having a conversation with your friends, parents, or aging grandmother. Reading a novel before going to sleep.

From the minute you wake up until the minute you fall asleep, you use language. Even when not actively reading, writing, listening, or speaking, you use language to think, and often to daydream. It is the essential tool that makes you human. It is the most complex thing you will learn in your lifetime. Knowing about it and using it effectively is a great asset that can make your life better, more enjoyable, and potentially more profitable.

Language affects everyone, and like many other people, you may have wondered about some of the following questions:

- Do men and woman really communicate differently?
- When should my child start talking?
- What is the best way to help my child learn to read?
- How might my elderly father's language deteriorate as he ages?
- How did that salesperson talk me into buying that car?
- My spelling is not great. Am I dyslexic?
- I would like to learn a second language. What is the best way of doing this?

These are issues that relevant to most people, but where can you find the answers? There is plenty of research to answer questions like these, but it tends to be written in academic books and journals, which are often not very accessible unless you are a language specialist. I have compiled state-of-the art research on 100 language questions that I believe are relevant and useful in everyday situations. I then summarized the answers in plain English, in a concise format that I hope you will find both appealing and useful.

After reading this book (or the sections you are most interested in), you will understand how to make language work better in your life. At the very least, I hope it will have been an enjoyable and enriching journey. If you become particularly fascinated by certain topics, I list websites that provide additional information in an easy-to-understand manner. Many of the sections have a quiz or activity to help you engage with the information in the section.

To start out, and to have a bit of fun, try the quiz below to see how much you already know about language, particularly English. The answers are at the end of the section.

Language Quiz

1. ____ of the ten million most visited Internet web sites are in English.

a. 26%
b. 38%
c. 64%
d. 78%

2. When would you normally expect your child to begin speaking their first words?

a. 4 months
b. 12 months
c. 16 months
d. 24 months

3. TRUE/FALSE: Texting on phones is ruining young people's ability to use language properly.

4. What is a *weasel word*?

a. part of animal language
b. a misleading word used in advertising
c. an insult used by young people
d. a word of unknown origin

5. Four of the following have been shown to help delay dementia and language loss. Which one has NOT been reported to help?

a. eating a healthy diet
b. doing exercise
c. moving to a warmer climate
d. learning to do new things
e. learning a second language

6. TRUE/FALSE: The key to success in learning a second language is going to a school that offers effective teaching of grammar rules.

7. What is *phonics*?

a. language used to discuss music
b. a term for how loud you speak
c. a way to improve pronunciation
d. a method to teach reading

8. Are the following real words? *cyberbullying; e-waste; hyperlocal*

9. At what age do children begin to learn gendered (male/female) language?

a. 1 year old
b. 2-3 years old
c. 4-5 years old
d. 6-8 years old

10. TRUE/FALSE: Learning a second language will set children back in their first language.

Answers and sections with further information

1. c. Almost two-thirds (64%) of the most popular Internet sites are in English. Russian-, Turkish-, and Spanish-language sites are far behind (4%-7%). (§2: See Section 2 for more details)

2. b. First words typically appear by about one year of age. (§43)

3. False. People are well capable of being proficient in both texting and more formal writing styles. (§39)

4. b. A *weasel word* is a vague word used in advertising and politics. (§13 & §14)

5. c. Moving to a warmer place may help you feel better, but there is no evidence that it delays dementia. There is evidence for the other four things. (§70)

6. False. A more important thing is the amount of meaningful language exposure the school provides. (§55)

7. d. Phonics is a method of teaching reading that stresses the relationships between the sounds of a language and its written letters or symbols. (§51)

8. Yes. Even though they may not appear in many dictionaries, they occur thousands or millions of times on the Internet. (§83)

9. b. Children start showing masculine/feminine behavior and language as early as 2-3 years. (§26)

10. False. Learning a second language is likely to *help* their first language, and other areas like literacy and mathematics as well. (§59)

2

ENGLISH IN TODAY'S WORLD

I know that many people are speaking and learning English around the world. But is it really the "World Language"?

There are over 7,000 languages in the world today, with English being by far the most important for global communication. This is quite amazing when you consider that English started out quite small, with only around 4 million speakers in 1500. This steadily increased through population growth to 6 million by 1600, 8.5 million by 1700, and 20-40 million by 1800. After that, English rose to prominence on the back of its speakers' industrial, financial, and cultural strength, first with the British Empire, followed by US influence.

By 1900, English had exploded to 116-123 million speakers, and it is now estimated that there are over 370 million native speakers worldwide.[1] This puts it third in number of native speakers behind Mandarin Chinese (921 million) and Spanish (471 million). But what makes English so special is the number of people who speak it or are learning it as a second language (around 978 million). Combining native and second language speakers, this totals over 1.3 billion people, which is far more than for any other language.

The reason so many people from so many countries are learning English is simply that it is the most useful way of communicating across national borders. If a Japanese engineer wants to work with a Brazilian chemist, they will probably converse in English. If a Chinese academic wants to write a research paper with a Dutch professor, they will probably write it for a journal published in English. Brazilian and Saudi businesspeople may well negotiate in English. English has become the *lingua franca* (common language) for all sorts of everyday international communication. It makes sense that governments want their citizens to learn this valuable professional tool, and so the vast majority of countries now teach English as a subject in their schools.

Although it is difficult to get precise figures about the use of English worldwide, and some of the available data is a quite old, the following estimates of English use are interesting, and illustrate its global reach:

- Around 22% of books published annually are in English.
- Most of the content on the Internet is in English. 64% of the ten million most visited web sites are in English, with the next largest percentages being Russian (7%), followed by Turkish and Spanish (4%).
- 32% of daily tweets are in English, with Japanese at 19% and Spanish at 8%.
- In 40 of the 55 countries for which cinema data was available in 2009 (73%), at least 7 of the top 10 most-viewed films were in English. In 21 countries (38%), all of the top 10 films were in English. The top 20 most-viewed

feature films in theaters globally during 2012 and 2013 were all in English.

- Many world institutions use English as their language, or as one of their languages; for example, the Olympics, the World Bank, and the United Nations.
- The official international language for both aviation and maritime use is English (§73).
- English is main language of communication in the scientific community. About 93% of all the academic journals listed in *Scopus* (a database of academic publications) are published in English.
- Over two-thirds of employers in countries where English is not a native or official language report that English is important for their business.
- Huge numbers of people are learning English as a second language worldwide, and this is illustrated by the very large numbers of people taking tests of English proficiency every year. For example, the International English Language Testing System (IELTS) test is taken annually by around 3 million people in more than 140 countries.

Despite its international reach, English remains remarkably consistent in its written form across the world, mainly because there is an accepted version used in most publishing, sometimes called 'Standard English' (§79). This allows written English to be understood by a wide variety of readers all across the world, both native speakers and English as a Second Language (ESL) users. But spoken English is much freer to change, and so varies considerably worldwide, especially in pronunciation.

There are numerous varieties of English (like American, British, and Singaporean English), and even more dialects (regional versions like New York, California, Merseyside, and Cockney

English) (§91). Despite this diversity, these varieties and dialects differ relatively little in their grammar. Their vocabularies do vary somewhat, but the most noticeable difference between varieties/dialects of English will almost always be the pronunciation, rather than the language itself.

Power Point: English is now the world language.

1. This is an interesting website which gives information about the languages of the world and the number of people who speak them.

https://www.ethnologue.com

2. The First Site Guide website gives a range of information of about global Internet use.

https://firstsiteguide.com/internet-stats

3

LANGUAGES IN THE UNITED STATES

I speak a second language. Am I unusual? What are the main languages spoken in the US?

There is an impression that the United States is a strictly monolingual country, with English being the only language of consequence. While English is obviously the dominant language, it would be a mistake to think of the US as a completely monolingual country. Being a melting-pot nation, there is a wide range of languages spoken in America. In fact, the US Census Bureau reports that at least 350 different languages are spoken in US homes. The 2019 census estimated that 78% of people spoke only English, while 22% also spoke languages other than English. This was an increase over the 2000 (18%), 1990 (14%) and 1980 (11%) figures for languages other than English. Among these, Spanish is the most common, followed by Chinese. The top 10 languages other than English from the 2009-2013 time span are as follows (with millions of speakers).

1. Spanish (37.5)
2. Chinese (2.9)
3. Tagalog (1.6)
4. Vietnamese (1.4)
5. French (1.3)
6. Korean (1.1)
7. German (1.1)
8. Arabic (.9)
9. Russian (.9)
10. Italian (.7)

Tagalog (Filipino) is the national language of the Philippines, and is often spoken in large metropolitan areas. There were also around 364,000 speakers of native North American languages (§87), with Navajo having the greatest number of speakers (167,000).

It is important to note that the majority of people speaking the above languages also speak English. This means that there is quite a lot of bilingualism in the US. This was confirmed by a 2013 Gallup poll where 34% of adult Americans said that they could hold a conversation in a language other than English. Of these, 60% said they could do it in Spanish, 18% in French, and 12% in German. But this conversational ability in a second language varied depending on a number of factors. Age made a difference, with younger people far more likely to be bilingual:

18-29: 52%
30-49: 36%
50-64: 27%
65+: 21%

Region also mattered:

Western US: 40%;
East: 38%;
South: 34%;
Midwest: 25%.

In addition, more education led to more second language ability. While only 26% of those with a high school education or less were bilingual, 40% of university graduates were, and 46% of those with Masters degrees or doctorates. This unsurprising result highlights the importance of students continuing to pursue second language education. The Modern Language Association carried out a survey of the classes that students were taking at over 2,500 US colleges and universities in 2016. It found that 7.5% of students were studying a foreign language. This is less than half the number from the early 1960s: 16.2-16.5%. But since 1974, the figures have been quite steady, only fluctuating between 7.3%-8.8%. So while we are down over the very long term, at least the percentage of students studying foreign languages has been stable over the last 50 years.

However, in terms of the total number of students studying languages, the picture is much brighter. About 1.4 million students were enrolled in language courses in 2016, up from 877,000 in 1980. By far the most popular language was Spanish (50% of all foreign language enrollments), with French also attracting a large number of students (12%). The top 10 languages studied and their percentages were:

1. Spanish 50%
2. French 12%
3. American Sign Language 8%
4. German 6%
5. Japanese 5%
6. Italian 4%

7. Chinese 4%
8. Arabic 2%
9. Latin 2%
10. Russian 1%

It is interesting that American Sign Language (§87) was #3 on the list, but perhaps this should not be surprising given that the 2019 census data shows that about 3.6% of the US population (over 11 million people) report having hearing difficulty. Based on earlier 1997-2003 data and different definitions of deafness, the Gallaudet Research Institute estimated that 13% of people in the United States were deaf or hard of hearing (ranging from 2% aged 3-17 to 29% aged 65 and over).

The Gallup poll also asked how important it was for Americans to speak a second language. 20% thought it was essential, and 50% thought it was important, with 28% saying it was not important. While 70% of respondents saw value in knowing second languages, nearly everybody thought that it was essential or important for immigrants living in the US to learn English (96%).

Power Point: Bilingualism is alive in the United States. There are hundreds of languages being spoken in US homes in addition to English. Between one-fifth and one-third of Americans are able to converse in a second language. But the percentage of students studying languages other than English at university remains stubbornly low at under 10%.

1. This is the US Census website with language data from 2009-2013 given by nation, state, county, and large city.

http://www.census.gov/data/tables/2013/demo/2009-2013-lang-tables.html

2. The first website summarizes the Gallup poll, and the second from the Modern Language Association gives more details about the 2016 survey.

https://news.gallup.com/poll/163895/say-essential-immigrants-learn-english.aspx

https://www.mla.org/content/download/110154/2406932/2016-Enrollments-Final-Report.pdf

PART 2

LANGUAGE AND PERSUASION

GETTING WHAT YOU WANT AND NEED

4

HOW CAN I BE MORE PERSUASIVE WITH MY LANGUAGE?

I need to convince my colleagues to support the new company work plan. How do I persuade them?

The various sections in this unit the book will give you advice on how to be more persuasive in a number of specific situations, but this section will start by giving basic hints about how to be more persuasive in general.

Pick your battles. If you are always pushing your ideas and products, you can come across as aggressive and overbearing. Save your persuasion for the things that really matter. If you advocate less overall, you may be more successful for the selected times that you choose to.

Listen to others and build a connection with them. You know what you want to say, but you cannot be effective unless you carefully take in what others are saying. This has at least three benefits.

First, you can evaluate how others are reacting to your message. Second, you can identify specific objections to what you are saying, so you can formulate rebuttals or refine your argument. Third, you can listen for points of agreement, which can then be built on. This last point is especially important, because it is crucial to create a connection with those you are trying to persuade. If someone has no emotional involvement with you or your ideas, it will be easy for them to dismiss your argument. Be considerate and likeable, and search for common ground and shared objectives. Once this groundwork has been laid, others will be much more receptive when you do begin to argue for your position.

Give a little. Try to make the people you are persuading feel like they are also winning. Emphasize your agreement on points of common ground, and give in on issues that do not really matter. This includes giving credit where it is due. When others make valid points in opposition to your views, you should acknowledge this and engage with those points. By giving others credit for their facts and views, they will be more likely to return the favor and be more open to your argumentation. People like to be valued, and giving subtle compliments can also help warm them to your position (*I can see you have thought about this*).

Establish credibility. This can be done in two ways. The first is to confirm your own qualifications for the issue/product you are advocating for. Depending on the situation and how well you know the people you are trying to persuade, this might be done by citing your title, education, number of years of experience in the field, etc. The second is by providing evidence for your position. Anecdotal evidence can be effective in getting your big ideas across in a comprehensible way that connects with the average person (*On the way to this meeting, how many of you were caught in a traffic jam? This shows that the road system is overstretched*). However, persuasion on most weighty issues will require more rigorous evidence, often from research (*A report by INRIX and the Texas A&M Transportation Institute shows that the average rush-hour commuter wasted 42 hours per year stuck in traffic congestion*). People like being given reasons to be convinced, so *'because'* phrases can be influential (*We should consider changing to the new system because* ...).

Make you points and then leave it. People dislike going around in circles and hearing the same arguments again and again. Build as much common ground as you can, make your case, close the conversation, and then back away and allow the person time to think things over. If they were truly receptive, they may persuade themselves that you were right. If not, then a more extended effort at persuasion would probably not have been successful anyway.

Use persuasive language. The language you use can help you achieve the above aims. Words like *we, our,* and *your* (or especially the person's name) can project the feeling of inclusiveness and belonging. Using words like *important, significant,* and *crucial* gives the sense of substance and importance. Emotive language can make people feel more positive, engaged, and interested (e.g. words like *beautiful, talented,* and *intelligent*). Humor is also a good way to create a connection with the people you are talking to. 'Active voice' sentence grammar (e.g. *I'll give you three good reasons to support this idea*) is simpler and more direct than 'passive voice' (e.g. *Three good reasons to support this idea will be given*), and so is easier to understand and potentially more persuasive. The human mind likes to think in terms of patterns, and three is smallest number that represents a pattern. Thus, the *Rule of Three* is often suggested as a useful organizing principle, such as in the example words in this paragraph and the three benefits in the Listening/Connecting paragraph above.

Body language. Your verbal language needs to match your body language to be convincing. For example, it is no good to say "I'm happy to stay and talk some more" with your face in a grimace and your whole body pointing towards the door. Albert Mehrabian (UCLA) studied how people interpret messages about feelings and attitudes when the words they hear and the body signals they see are in conflict. In cases of oral/body mismatches, he found that body language made up 55% of the communicative power of a response, with intonation (pauses, sighs) making up a substantial 38%, and the actual language adding only a minor 7%. So it is not just *what* you say, but also *how* you say it that matters. Messages where the words and body language are in harmony will be the most powerful (§5).

Power Point: The points in this section form the foundation of persuasiveness, and will be built on in many of the following sections in this unit.

1. Many of the ideas in this section are discussed on this web site in more detail:

http://www.inc.com/kevin-daum/7-things-really-persuasive-people-do.html

2. The first site gives one overview of persuasive language techniques. The second gives an extensive list of examples of persuasive language. If you have kids, they will love the third one, which has amusing examples of persuasive techniques:

http://www.slideshare.net/mmcdonald2/persuasive-language-techniques

http://changingminds.org/techniques/language/persuasive/persuasive.htm

https://www.youtube.com/watch?v=zuGFiphslAk&feature=email

5

BODY LANGUAGE

Just as language conveys information, so does body language. How do I make sure my body is sending out the messages I want?

Although it is not strictly linguistic, it is widely recognized that body language sends messages to others, and is an important part of communication. In fact, it is impossible NOT to send messages via body language, whether you intend to or not. Of course, everyone knows this, at least subconsciously (e.g., you would never turn your back on someone important when you were asking them a favor). But science has revealed some interesting patterns to be aware of as you try to use language persuasively.

Body language typically comes in clusters of signals. Any single signal or posture may not be a reliable indictor of what a person is feeling or thinking. For example, crossed arms are often seen as a sign of defensiveness, but they may also be a sign the person is cold! It is therefore best to interpret all the body signals we see as a whole (from head to toe), not just any single one. We also need to consider the context and environment, because this can affect the signals: Is it cold? Is the person stressed? Is the person using signals from a different culture, where they may mean something different?

When body language matches what a person says, it increases positive feelings like trust and rapport. But when there is a mismatch, it may create mistrust and negative evaluation, and people will usually rely on the signals coming from the body (§4).

In general, moving closer to someone indicates interest and engagement, and vice versa. For example, leaning forward slightly towards the interviewer at a job interview shows positive involvement (§8), while turning your body away from the interviewer would show some degree of detachment.

Slouching indicates a person is relaxed, but in some contexts (like job interviews), it can also indicate a casual, unengaged attitude.

Fidgeting can often indicate boredom or impatience, or in some cases, deception. This can consist of things like constant readjustment of posture, tapping one's fingertips on something, or fidgeting with an object like a pen or cell phone.

The amount of space a person takes up can indicate status. Spreading oneself out (pushing away from the table, holding one's arms behind the head, crossing one's ankle over the other knee) can indicate dominance, while having a small posture (sitting tucked under the table, arms and legs held tightly against the body) can indicate feelings of inferiority.

The above point connects with the idea of personal space. Edward Hall described four key distances in the US context. *Intimate space* (from touch to 18 inches) is reserved for intimate partners, family, and close friends. *Personal space* (18 inches-4 feet) is typical for most conversations with friends and acquaintances. *Social space* (4-12 feet) is for routine social, small-group interactions like meetings or sitting around a dinner table. Finally, *Public space* is beyond this, and often relates to public speaking (§9). It is uncomfortable if someone enters space closer than their status allows, although the actual distances vary considerably from culture to culture.

As mentioned above, crossed arms are usually seen as a signal of defensiveness, defiance, disengagement, tenseness, or disbelief. This signal is amplified if combined with crossed legs. People are not so aware of their leg positioning, so it may be a good indicator of their feelings. Crossed legs can show comfort if they are extended (e.g., placing one's ankle on the opposite knee), but if tucked and closed (see 'Space' point above), can indicate anxiety or discomfort. For men, open leg postures can show confidence and a relaxed sense.

People's feet often point towards someone or something they are interested in, the direction they wish to go, or at the dominant person.

Keeping one's hands open and palms up is a sign of openness. Conversely, clenching one's fists indicates tension, stress, or anger. Hiding one's hands (in pockets, behind one's back) might show disagreement or a reluctance to talk.

Touching your face or playing with your hair excessively can make you seem dishonest and untrustworthy. Covering your mouth with your fingers or hand can also give this impression. If someone is being deceptive, blood can rush to their face, leading to warmth and itchiness, and thus rubbing or scratching. Supporting your head with your hand can make it seem that you are bored.

Eye contact generally shows engagement and attention; lack of eye contact can indicate someone is hiding something. There is some suggestion that when answering a question, if a person moves their eyes up to the left, they are recalling information from their memory. Conversely, if they look to the right, they may be either making up an answer or accessing their feelings.

Smiling is an international signal of engagement and positive feelings, as long as it is natural and not contrived.

Perhaps one of the most powerful ways to give out positive body signals is *mirroring*. Matching the positive body movements of the person you are talking to (e.g., doing the same hand motions, mirroring a smile or nod) indicates interest and convergence, and so is seen as attractive. The best handshake is usually one that matches the firmness of the person you are shaking with.

Power Point: No single body language signal is definitive, but understanding clusters of body signals can give you useful insights into what other people are thinking and feeling. But be aware that body signals can mean different things in different cultures.

1. The first website gives an extensive guide to body signals based around the eyes, mouth, head, arms, hands, legs, and feet, along with suitable caveats about their interpretation. There is also a section on body language in different cultures. The second website gives a number of pages by Joe Navarro, a former FBI Counterintelligence Agent, discussing various aspects of body language, including the difficulties in interpreting them.

http://www.businessballs.com/body-language.htm#body-language-definitions

https://www.psychologytoday.com/blog/spycatcher

. . .

2. This section talks about how other people perceive your body language. But your body language can also potentially affect the way you feel about yourself. This popular TED talk by Amy Cuddy (Harvard) shows how "power posing" can help you feel more confident.

http://www.ted.com/talks/amy_cuddy_your_body_lan
guage_shapes_who_you_are

6

HOW CAN I BE A BETTER COMMUNICATOR WITH THE PEOPLE I MANAGE?

I supervise a number of people at work. How can I get them to do things while at the same time maintaining harmony? How can the language I use make me a more effective communicator?

It is quite possible that you are in charge of a number of people at your workplace, ranging from a few bricklayers on a construction team all the way up to millions of employees in multinational companies. But regardless of the scope of your management responsibilities, it is essential to have good communication skills. Understanding the language environment of the workplace can help you be more effective.

When dealing with people, the first thing you must realize as a boss is that everyone has 1) the need to feel positive about themselves, and 2) the need not to feel imposed on. This is often referred to as "positive face" and "negative face," respectively (§90). Every company or organization also has its own culture, and every member has a sense of rights within that company culture. When giving directions to your team members, it is important to make them feel valued and that you are playing according to the rules. The language you use has a major effect on how you are perceived and whether your requests and directions are considered fair play in your context or not.

So how do you get your members to do the things you need them to do, while at the same time making them feel good about it? Much has to do with the directness of your instructions. No one likes to be commanded in a brusque manner, but what gives the feeling of abruptness? It is partially simply a matter of length. Compare the following two equivalent directions:

A: Have the report ready by Tuesday 9 a.m.

B: Could you have the report ready by 9 a.m. on Tuesday, please?

Longer phrasing tends to give the sense of a politer, softer request. But there are many other ways to mitigate the imposition of your direction (avoid negative face) and to instill a sense of partnership and cooperation in the discussion (promote positive face).

- Putting the directive in the form of a question (Even though your team member may have no realistic chance of saying no, it still seems more polite.)
- Adding words like *just, little,* and *sort of* that act as 'minimizers,' seemingly making the direction feel less of an imposition
- Saying *please,* a common courtesy most people will expect in their interactions
- Using *Let's ...* to give the feeling of collective action—even if you won't be involved yourself!

- Expressing things in terms of *Us vs. Them,* so that unpopular decisions can be seen as coming from outside the team, and not originating from you
- Using humor to relax the atmosphere after giving potentially face-threatening directives (*Whew! I'm glad I got through that last agenda point alive*)
- Being mindful of body language; and in general moving closer physically and having more eye contact to give a sense of positive engagement (§5)

Let us see what this kind of indirect, collaborative talk looks like in real life. Louise Mullany (University of Nottingham) collected the following extract from a real business meeting in a retail organization, where the boss Sarah has to give her subordinate Michelle a task at short notice, concerning the placement of signs in Michelle's department of the store. The raised letters ([A]) indicate explanatory notes that follow.

> **Sarah:** Simon says he needs plans to show where the new point of sale is to be put in relationship to the products. Have we been asked for this?[A]
> **Michelle:** Not for a plan, no, I mean we've talked about getting it with products that are new.
> **Sarah:** Yes Jo said she thought Helen had sent a memo out?[A]
> **Michelle:** No.
> **Sarah:** Well I've certainly not read it and neither had Peter (pause).[B] To say that they need plans (pause)[B] drawn up to show where the new product is located in your department so they can then just hang the point of sale there? (exhales)[B] I mean[C] how long will that take? Is that (pause)[B] not, is it, if you know a long job?[D]
> **Michelle:** Twenty minutes, half hour, to walk the shop floor. Really you don't actually mark it.

Sarah: Can you do that by this weekend?[E] Cos they really need to get it done this week. It all goes up on Monday.
Michelle: (nods and smiles)
Sarah: (exhales) Right. Sorry to land that one on you there, but you should have had that by now. Is that alright?[F]
Michelle: Yeah
Sarah: Bit of delegation there (laughs)[G]
Michelle: (smiles)

A. Sarah probably already knows this information, but asks Michelle anyway to make her feel like a collaborative partner in the discussion. The use of *we* builds solidarity with Michelle, and lets her know she is not responsible for the late issuing of the order.

B. The pauses and exhaling all show Sarah's exasperation with the lateness of the request, again building solidarity with Michelle.

C. *I mean* makes this feel less abrupt than a straight question.

D. Again, this hedged formulation is more indirect than a straight question.

E. Putting the direction in the form of a question is softer than a command. There is also justification for the directive, based on needs from outside the team (Us vs. Them).

F. Sarah apologizes for the imposition, and checks whether harmony has been maintained after her directive.

G. A bit of humor to defuse any residual tenseness from the directive.

These linguistic features are also the language strategies to be aware of when you talk to your boss!

Power Point: Every boss has to get workplace tasks achieved while maintaining harmony within the team. Using indirect collaborative language is one way to minimize the sense of imposition while promoting positive attitudes.

1. Culture varies according to country. This website looks at six ways national cultures differ, which can be important in fashioning effective communication. These include attitudes towards power inequalities in society, individualism vs. conformity, and competition/success vs. caring for others/quality of life.

https://geerthofstede.com/culture-geert-hofstede-gert-jan-hofstede/6d-model-of-national-culture

2. You can learn more about this topic by taking a short online course by Louise Mullany that runs occasionally. It is free, and takes about six hours. The above extract is taken from this course.

https://www.futurelearn.com/courses/how-to-read-your-boss

7

HOW CAN I USE LANGUAGE MORE EFFECTIVELY IN MEETINGS?

I sometimes feel imposed on in meetings, and often do not get the chance to voice my opinions. How can I better gain the floor in meetings, and hold it once I have it?

Being effective in meetings combines having something worthwhile to contribute and gaining the floor to say it. The useful information part is up to you, but knowing how language works can give you a better chance of actually being able to present your ideas. The key issue is 'gaining the floor'; that is, getting your chance to speak. Some meetings are strictly controlled by the chairperson, who calls on members of the meeting to speak and who controls their speaking time. In this 'one-person-at-a- time' environment, it may be hard to have your say regardless of how skilled you are linguistically. But most meetings are not this tightly regulated, and all members can compete for the floor. In this case, understanding the ebb and flow of language use can help.

The basic concept is that of a *turn*. Analysis of all group speech shows that people don't come in and out of a discussion at random; if they did, people would talk over each other in a big disorganized mess. Rather, there are cues that participants listen for that help them know when the speaker is finishing their turn, and when it is appropriate to take up the next turn. There are also strategies for holding onto your turn longer, and for interrupting a person who seems unwilling to give up their turn.

When is someone nearing the end of their turn?

- A speaker can explicitly state they are finished: "Anyway, that's what I think."
- A speaker can nominate a follow-up speaker: "Let's hear from Susan now."
- A speaker can direct a question to someone, which puts the responsibility on the recipient to answer. But this also means the questioner is controlling the topic, as well as having an "implied right" to speak again immediately following the answer.

If there is no explicit indication of the next speaker:

- Pauses are natural breaks that invite others to take over the turn.
- The end of a turn can be signaled by intonation; e.g., a drop in pitch or in loudness.
- When talking, speakers look down for much of the time rather than looking into the listeners' eyes. When the speaker starts making more eye contact, this signals their turn is ending and that the listener can then come in.

- The end of a turn can also be signaled by the speaker stopping the gestures they were using to accompany their speech.

How to keep your turn

The following strategies can be used to keep the floor by discouraging interruption:

- Start your turn by indicating its length: "I'd like to make four points..."
- Speed up or slow down with heavy stress.
- Avoid pauses where you can be interrupted. If you must, pause in the middle of sentences, where your listeners are expecting more to come.
- Use verbal fillers such as 'umm' to give you time to think.
- Avoid failing intonation, because this signals the end of a phrase where you could be interrupted.
- You can pre-empt an interrupter by avoiding eye contact with them.
- If someone does try to interrupt you, raise your voice above them.

How to interrupt someone to capture the floor

Conversely, here is how you can take the floor from others by interrupting:

- Pauses are a natural place to try to cut in.
- Echo a word or phrase from the speaker and use it for the first word of your turn.
- Use "agreement phrases" to start your interruption: "Yes, absolutely, that's a good point, and furthermore ..."

- Use body language and gestures (§5) to show that you want the floor: sit further forward, and signal with your hands and arms that you want to start talking.
- Raising your voice makes your interruption bid stronger.

Whether you can succeed in gaining and holding the floor will always depend on your boss and co-workers to a large extent. But understanding the cues and strategies discussed here increases your chances of managing turn-taking to your advantage.

Power Point: Turn taking is systematic. It typically happens at pauses (when there is silence), after a drop in intonation, or when the speaker indicates the end of a turn by gaze or gesture patterns. Use these natural gaps to gain the floor for yourself.

1. More on the nature of turn-taking:

https://englishonline.tki.org.nz/English-Online/Planning-for-my-students-needs/Exploring-language/The-Language-of-Conversation/Turn-Taking

2. This YouTube video by Peggy Marcy (California State University, San Bernardino) explains what native speakers do in turn-taking to manage conversations. Although aimed at English as a Second Language students and teachers, the discussion builds on many of the points in this section

https://www.youtube.com/watch?v=U_TDtmEYKko

8

HOW CAN I GIVE A POSITIVE JOB INTERVIEW?

You have already done your research into the company you are interviewing with, and you know your strengths and weaknesses. Now, how do you present that information effectively in the interview to give a positive impression?

There are many sources of advice on how to interview well. Most of them suggest that questions like the following are typically asked in interviews:

1. Tell us about yourself.
2. What are your strengths?
3. What are your weaknesses?
4. Why do you want to work for our company?
5. Why are you leaving your current job?

When preparing answers for questions like these, a few general guidelines are worth remembering.

Talk about your experience and qualifications. Questions like 1 and 2 are designed to find out about what capabilities you could bring to the company or organization. Describing your skills in a convincing way is probably the most important aspect of the interview, and you should prioritize this in the answers you give to most questions in the interview. It is always more persuasive if you can give concrete examples of your previous successes. Having your resume/CV on hand can be a useful aid.

Relate your answers directly to the position you are applying for. When discussing your skills, abilities, and experience, always emphasize how they will allow you to perform well in the new role you are applying for. Carefully analyze the job requirements of the new position, and tailor your answers to highlight how your background fulfills those specific requirements.

Give the impression you really want this job. You should have a strong answer to Question 4, as employers want to be assured that you want this particular job, rather than just any employment. Focusing your answers on the job in question (i.e., the point above) is a good start, but also emphasize how the job fits with your own development and ambitions. Show that you will fit in with the culture and work environment of the organization.

Be positive and avoid any negativity. Be enthusiastic about the job. If there are any negative aspects about the position (e.g., the salary is lower than your current income; it involves a long commute), try to put a positive spin on them (e.g., the career advancement possibilities in the new job are more important than the money; you can get some work done on the train). Question 3 about weaknesses is sometimes asked to see how you perform under pressure. Everyone has flaws, and employers want to see you are self-aware and have strategies to address your weaknesses. Just do not mention any weaknesses that are critical to the job you are applying for. Question 5 can be particularly tricky, as you never want to badmouth former/current companies, bosses, or colleagues. If you do, you risk giving the negative impression of being a complainer or an awkward team player. It is better to talk positively about your current position, but emphasize that the new position would be a fabulous opportunity for you. Basically, you want to give the impression of being a desirable, collegial colleague that your interviewers would like to work with.

Be proactive and ask about the company. It is important to show that you have done your homework about the company, and clearly understand how you would fit in. By asking insightful questions about the organization, you can also show your interest and enthusiasm. For example, you could ask about training opportunities to further improve your skills and value to the company. Or you could ask that in the event you were offered the position, what steps you could take to prepare for your start.

Delivering a strong interview is not just about the content of the answers, but also the language you choose to express these ideas. Tips on how to leave a positive impression include:

- **Use positive, active vocabulary.** Using active verbs gives the impression of a positive work history and a dynamic approach to work challenges. For example, *I accomplished X* sounds much more proactive than *I did X*. Likewise, descriptors with strong positive connotations, like *conscientious, loyal, resourceful,* and *self-motivated* are ones you want to fit into descriptions of yourself.
- **Practice beforehand so you can be fluent.** The content of what you say is important, but so is the manner in which you say it. You want to avoid waffling, rambling, and being overly hesitant (too many instances of *err, uhm, ahh*). You

will be able to guess some of the things interviewers will ask you, so practice key words, phrases, and answers in advance in order to give confident, polished responses.

- **Use STAR to give fuller, more organized answers.** In the heat of the interview, it is easy to lose track of what you have said and descend into an unstructured answer. One form of organization that many sources recommend is STAR. This stands for *Situation* (a situation you have found yourself in: e.g. influenza decimated the office staff), *Task* (you were tasked with finding a solution), *Action* (what you did to solve the problem: quickly organized temporary cover), and *Result* (the organization was able to continue without disruption). In addition, many interviewers use the STAR format to structure their interview questions.
- **Body language.** As always, body language is an important part of your presentation. Make plenty of eye contact, sit with good posture and your feet on floor, lean slightly forward towards the interviewer to show interest, do not fidget, be attentive, and try to appear as relaxed as possible. Smile when appropriate. Shake hands at the beginning and end to build rapport with the interviewer.

Power Point: Try to predict what questions you might face and think of how you will respond to them. Then practice the language that provides the most convincing and polished answers.

1. This series of web pages has wide-ranging advice on how to interview well, including some hints on both language and body language:

https://www.totaljobs.com/advice/interviews

2. This page has a list of some dynamic vocabulary you could use to give your answers some positive zing:

https://www.thoughtco.com/job-interview-questions-and-answers-1210232

9

PUBLIC SPEAKING

I'm terrified of speaking in public. What can I do to be a successful communicator?

~

Speaking in public is something that petrifies many people. This can be simply because of nerves, or because they do not know how to give a successful talk. The following suggestions can give you a start towards being more comfortable speaking in front of people.

Overcoming Nerves

Stage fright is not uncommon. It is quite normal to feel anxious before a performance, and even professionals can get nervous before stepping onto a stage or into a sporting arena. So it is all right to be nervous, but the trick is not to show it. If you do not mention your nerves to the audience and you can control your voice and body language, the audience will not know how nervous you are, and they will be able to concentrate on your message.

But it is even better to try to control nerves. The best way of doing this is with good preparation. The more familiarity and confidence you have in your material, the less nervous you will likely be about presenting it. You should focus on positive images of how you want your talk to go, as this can actually help you perform better. Also, move the focus away from yourself (and your nerves) to the audience, and what you are trying to provide to them. In my experience, most nerves occur before the presentation. Once you begin, your focus on the message takes over, and anxiety unconsciously gets pushed to the sidelines.

Before presenting, loosen your body up by moving and stretching a bit. Then take some slow, deep breaths. You might even try "power posing" (§5). Finally, smile. This actually seems to reduce stress. Then go on stage knowing the audience is rooting for you. They want a great experience, and so they will be on your side.

Content and Organization

The first step is knowing what you want to achieve with your talk. In their book *The Pin Drop Principle,* David Lewis and G. Riley Mills suggest that you should be able to state the purpose of your talk in following sentence:

> I want to _____ my audience so that my audience will _____.

These blanks could be filled in with objectives like *persuade/buy my product, warn/be more careful,* or *inform/be more knowledgeable.* Having your goal clearly in mind from the beginning will help you plan a more effective talk.

A common bit of advice is to 1) tell your audience what you will say, 2) say it, and 3) tell them what you said. This advice assumes the repetition will help your audience remember your message. This may be so, but most audiences are easily distracted and dislike having their time wasted. If they are not getting something new, they will quickly tune out. So if you do preview your upcoming points, this needs to be short. Many commentators recommend opening your presentation with something more dynamic that will catch and hold your audience's attention right from the start. This compelling opening could be a story, joke, question, fact, or the strongest point of your talk. Each listener needs to believe within the first few minutes that they will get something useful out of the talk. Catch their attention before they start looking at their phones!

It is important to not overload your audience. It is probably best to have one key idea you want to get across and then tailor your talk towards supporting that idea. The audience will also have a much better chance of remembering your key point if it is not drowned in detail. To avoid excess detail, some commentators suggest the Rule of Three: sets of three words/phrases/ideas are the optimum arrangement—enough to show a pattern yet also very concise.

Audiences tend to remember the first and last things you say (with the middle stuff being harder to remember). This puts a premium on strong introductions and conclusions that directly highlight your main point.

If you are giving a talk of any length, it is important to use signposts (e.g. *firstly, secondly, thirdly; on the other hand*) so that your audience understands how the ideas in your talk are connected.

Preparation

You have put together a convincing talk; now you need to practice delivering it. Practice giving your talk as you will give it on the day. For example, if you will be standing and using a PowerPoint presentation (§10), then practice standing up using PowerPoint. Rehearsing your talk silently can be useful, but there is no substitute for actually speaking it out loud and using your equipment and props, because it allows discovery of any potential problems (e.g. difficult to pronounce words; your clicker does not work with this projector) while there is still time to fix them.

You need to project passion about your idea(s). Emotional involvement is infectious, and your audience might get excited about it as well. This is partly indicated by your body language and partly by way you vary your voice tone. Do not read your talk. A talk that is read sounds stiff and stilted (§92). It is best to memorize the sequence of your main points, or use your PowerPoint presentation to guide you. This will allow you to project a more free-flowing, conversational tone.

Check the room, projector, and equipment beforehand to make sure everything works. This good routine can help your confidence and relieve nerves, because it minimizes unpleasant surprises.

During Your Talk

Hopefully your preparation will lead to a smooth talk. But it is also useful to think about how to handle any potential mishaps during the presentation. Some common ones include:

- Losing track of where you are in your presentation
- Technical failure like the microphone or projector dying
- Dropping your notes
- Having a sneezing or coughing fit
- PowerPoint slides unexpectedly moving forward automatically

Do not spend a lot of time apologizing. Rather, use humor to defuse the situation and move on. For example, if the microphone fails, you could say something like "I guess we forgot to pay the bills," and continue giving your presentation without a microphone if the room is small enough to permit this.

Power Point: Careful preparation and development of your material can help give you the confidence to overcome your fear of public speaking.

1. This BBC site has 23 short videos covering various hints and tips on public speaking:

http://www.bbc.co.uk/speaker/improve

2. These websites have some sensible suggestions for better public speaking. The first has a number of links for additional information:

http://www.mindtools.com/CommSkll/PublicSpeaking.htm

http://www.wikihow.com/Speak-Confidently-in-Public#Speaking_in_Public_sub

10

GIVING EFFECTIVE POWERPOINT PRESENTATIONS

I know what information I want to give in my upcoming meeting, but don't know how to communicate it successfully with a PowerPoint presentation. Are there any tips that can help me be more effective with this visual medium?

PowerPoint (PPT) is a different way of communicating, and needs to be learned like any other skill. However, it is worth mastering because research shows that information is learned better if it is presented in both oral and visual modes. From my experience, there are a number of important *Dos* and *Don'ts* in putting together a good PPT presentation:

DON'T

1. Do not put too much information on each slide. This is probably the key no-no in making PPT presentations. Think of the slides as bite-sized notes for the audience so that they can understand you better. Limit the number of points per slide. Using bullet points can be an effective way to do this.

2. Do not put up too much information that is beyond what you are currently talking about. Your audience will read each PPT slide as it comes up. To keep them in sync with you, do not let them get too far ahead by putting too many points on the slides.

3. Avoid complication and clutter. You want your slides to be easy to read, so avoid fancy fonts and templates, and anything else that can be a distraction.

4. Do not overuse animation. PPT has all kinds of movement and sounds that you can put into your presentation. While animation can be used sparingly to highlight key points, in my experience, these mainly distract (and annoy) the audience, who are trying to focus on your message.

5. Do not use notes. Referring to notes can draw your attention and eye contact away from the audience. I recommend using the PPT as your notes. You should know what you are saying about each slide, and so the slide should be a sufficient prompt. However, do bring a hard copy of your PPT in case of technical difficulties on the day.

6. Don't give a reference list at the end of the PPT. Typically these references are skipped through so quickly that they are useless, and only frustrate audience members who are actually trying to copy them down. If references are proper in your context, provide them to the audience on a handout.

DO

1. **Start with a storyline.** Develop a logical, organized flow of ideas at the very start of the process. Then design the entire presentation around this outline.

2. **Use a clicker.** Connection with the audience is crucial. Using a clicker (also called a *presentation remote*) allows you to focus on the audience and keep eye contact, rather than repeatedly looking down at the keyboard to advance the slides. It also allows you to move away from the computer.

3. **Use a legible font.** I recommend using at least 20-point font size or bigger, especially when speaking to larger audiences. You may end up speaking in a long, narrow room where people at the back can find it hard to see your slides. I sometimes use bold fonts just to make the words even easier to read.

4. **Use black letters on a light background.** This combination seems to offer the best legibility. But whatever combination you use, make sure there is a strong contrast. When using colors, be aware that many projectors seem to wash them out, and so they may appear differently than they did when you designed them on your computer screen. Red seems to be particularly problematic.

5. **Use only the top ¾ of PPT slide.** If you present in a larger, flat room, the bottom of the screen is often obscured for members of the audience sitting in the back.

6. **Use pictures to add interest.** PPT is a visual medium, so take advantage of this by using well-chosen pictures to give your presentation 'punch.' Humor is almost always appreciated, and the right picture can add interest while at the same time reinforcing the points you want to make.

7. Use graphs instead of tables of numbers. Graphs also have visual impact, and are usually better at showing trends and patterns than collections of numbers. If you must use tables, make sure they are legible and uncluttered. Audiences have difficulty deciphering large, complex tables, so reduce yours down to only the essential rows and columns necessary to make your point.

8. Have an "End" slide. Have a slide that wraps up your presentation, so the audience clearly know when you are finished. This closure slide might simply say "Thank You" or "Any Questions?", or you might have your name and contact details.

9. Have extra slides in reserve. Anticipate questions and have extra slides ready after the End slide to answer them. This is also a good place to have extra information which you did not have time to present, but which could be interesting in an extended Question and Answer discussion. This offers the possibility of using the Q & A session as extra time to make your points. And if you do not use these extra slides, no one will even know they are there.

10. Practice makes perfect. Even if you are a polished performer, you need to practice your presentation at least once to check your timing. There is nothing worse than presenters running out of time and having to skim/skip through their later slides in a hurry. This looks unprofessional, and often ruins your punchline at the end of the talk.

Power Point: These Dos and Don'ts should help you prepare more effective PowerPoint presentations.

1. This site expands on many of my suggestions, and adds more useful ideas.

http://www.lifehack.org/articles/technology/10-tips-for-more-effective-powerpoint-presentations.html

2. Here is a more radical website that shows how the visual aspects of your PPT can be ramped up to the max:

https://www.slideshare.net/damonnofar/8-tips-for-slideshare

11

HOW TO WRITE AN EFFECTIVE LETTER OF COMPLAINT

My phone bill is always wrong, and I want it fixed. How can I write an effective complaint letter to get results?

Occasionally in everyone's life, some product or service just does not live up to reasonable expectations. This is shown by the number of complaints that are filed yearly. For example, in 2019, the US government Consumer Financial Protection Bureau received about 342,500 complaints about financial services. In the UK in the same year, the government overseer for financial services (ombudsman) recorded 388,392 complaints.

These statistics show a large number of complaints, but the number of unsatisfied customers is even greater. A marketing survey reported that 96% of unsatisfied customers never complain, but nearly all of them will never come back. However, on average, they will tell between 9-15 others about their bad experience, which is far more than they would tell about a positive experience.

There is also an increasing trend for people to voice complaints on social media like Facebook and Twitter. It is no wonder that most companies prefer that you tell them if there are problems, because they then have a chance of fixing them without the bad news spreading.

There are many ways to make a complaint, but there are still times when only a formal letter of complaint will do. It officially puts your complaint on record with the company, shows them you are serious about pursuing the complaint, and helps preserve any legal rights you may have. There is a variety of advice on how to best write these letters, but the following points seem to be widely considered helpful:

Find the right person to write to. Look on the company website or ask someone at the company for the appropriate contact person who has the authority to deal with your complaint.

Be concise. Do not let your message get lost in a long letter. Complaints officers read letters all day, so make sure yours is brief and easy to understand. Be specific and stick to the point. If your situation is complex, it is still better to write a short letter and attach the details.

Be constructive. Aggression seldom helps. Make the tone of your letter firm but cooperative, and with the honest expectation of a positive reply. You are more likely to get a good result if you can build empathy with the complaints officer rather than immediately putting them on the defensive. If you are too negative and insist you will never patronize their business again, there is little incentive to help you.

Provide the necessary information. In order to make your case for the remedy you have requested (see below), make sure you give all the information that will allows the complaints officer to find your case and to convince them your complaint is justified. Never send the original evidence. Keep the originals for your records, and send copies. The evidence could include things like:

- Order numbers, invoice numbers, reference numbers, and warranties
- Receipts, serial or model numbers, and the name and location of the seller
- The names of salespeople or assistants involved
- The dates that things happened
- If this is part of an ongoing conversation, copies of previous letters, emails, and other documents
- A brief description of what happened, perhaps including photographs or videos when appropriate

Give a clear indication of what you want. Don't be vague here. Tell them what you want to happen.

Give them a reasonable chance to respond. I have seen 10 working days or 2 weeks as an often-suggested time period.

Know what your rights are. Your letter will have more authority if you know what your legal rights are. You can find out about these in a number of ways, including through the Federal Trade Commission (US), Citizens Advice (UK), or another consumer advocacy group.

Presentation matters. Make sure your letter looks professional. The spelling, grammar, and organization must be correct, and the use of more formal-sounding vocabulary never hurts (§86).

Get proof that you sent the letter. Send your letter by certified mail and request a return receipt. That gives you proof that the company got your letter and who signed for it.

To help you with writing the actual letter, there are many templates available—partially written letters into which you insert your specific details. Here is one from the Federal Trade Commission website, which includes many of the features mentioned above:

[Your Address]
[Your City, State, Zip Code]

[Date]

[Name of Contact Person]
[Title]
[Company Name]
[Street Address]
[City, State, Zip Code]

Dear **[Contact Person]**:
On **[date]**, I bought **[or had repaired]** a **[name of the product with the serial or model number or service performed]**. I made this purchase at **[location, date, and other important details of the transaction]**.

Unfortunately, your product has not performed well **[or the service was inadequate]** because **[state the problem]**.

To resolve the problem, I would appreciate your **[state the specific action you want]**. Enclosed are copies **[copies, not originals]** of my records **[receipts, guarantees, warranties, cancelled checks, contracts, model and serial numbers, and any other documents]** concerning this purchase/repair.

I look forward to your reply and a resolution to my problem. I will wait **[set a time limit]** before seeking third-party assistance. Please contact me at the above address or by phone **[home or office numbers with area codes]**.

Sincerely,
[Your Name]
[Account Number]

Power Point: Although nothing can ensure a successful result, these tips should help you write more effective letters of complaint. Good luck!

1. Here are 50 points about consumer behavior and how it affects companies.

http://60secondmarketer.com/blog/2015/01/15/50-facts-about-consumer-behavior

2. The first site is the Federal Trade Commission webpage, from which the above template comes. The second is from *Businessballs,* and gives more detailed information on the writing of complaint letters, as well as letter templates. The third site is UK-based, giving similar advice.

https://www.consumer.ftc.gov/articles/0296-sample-consumer-complaint-letter

http://www.businessballs.com/complaintsletters.htm

https://www.claims.co.uk/knowledge-base/consumer-law/writing-letter-of-complaint

12

WHY CAN'T PEOPLE JUST USE PLAIN ENGLISH?

Why do so many people and documents use English that is hard to understand? Why can't they just use plain English?

We sometimes come across language that is virtually incomprehensible. One example is the *Plain English Campaign*'s "Golden Bull" award winner for being one of the year's worst written communications in 2015. It is a blurb for the book *Thinking through Digital Media*:

> Thinking Through Digital Media *offers a means of conceptualizing digital media by looking at projects that think through digital media, migrating between documentary, experimental, narrative, animation, video game, and live performance. Hudson and Zimmermann analyze projects at the intersections of imbedded technologies, transitory micropublics, human-machine interface, and critical cartographies to forward a set of speculations about how things work together rather than what they represent.*

What does that mean? The language seems unnecessarily complex, and makes the message very difficult to understand. It is also counterproductive. If the purpose of communication is to excite potential buyers about the content of the book, it makes no sense to use language that customers cannot understand.

In response to obscure language like the above, the Plain English Campaign (PEC) was created in 1979 in the UK. Its purpose is to promote the use of clear and concise language by government agencies and other organizations. The PEC gives a number of practical guidelines for how writers (including yourself) can write easier-to-understand language. (Also check Paul Grice's ideas about successful communication: §89).

• **Keep your sentences short.** The PEC guidelines suggest a sentence length of 15-20 words on average, although that will include some shorter and some longer sentences for variety. I tell my students to not have more than two main ideas per sentence.

• **Prefer active verbs.** Generally use active sentences (*I paid the bill*) rather than passive sentences (*The bill was paid by me*). This makes your writing more straightforward and livelier.

• **Use "you" and "we."** Use *you* for the person(s) you are writing to, because it makes the communication more personal. Even when writing for a large audience, it is still possible to use the term *you*, as I have tried to do in this book. Similarly, use *we* when referring to your organization.

• **Use words that are appropriate for the reader.** For the general public, high-frequency vocabulary will be the most comprehensible (§86). For example, the PEC suggests avoiding the following words/phrases in italics and using the words/phrases in parentheses instead: *advise* (tell), *commence* (start), *in excess of* (more than), *per annum* (a year), and *prior to* (before).

• **Do not be afraid to give instructions.** Instructions (e.g., *Shut the door*) tend not to be used because they could be perceived as impolite commands. But they are often the simplest way of telling someone to do something or how to do it. For example, see how the following cooking directions are much more straightforward using the instruction style:

- Less direct: *The oven should be heated to 200°F. The fish should be placed on the lower shelf.*
- More direct: *Heat the oven to 200°F. Place the fish on the lower shelf.*

• **Avoid nominalizations.** Nominalizations are nouns formed from other word classes, usually verbs (*predict prediction*). They are not bad in themselves, but can cause comprehension difficulties when you add a long chain of modifiers to them (*the totally inaccurate and intentionally misleading prediction that ...*).

• **Use lists where appropriate.** Lists and bullet points can be an effective way of concisely presenting information, as I am doing with this list.

But it is important not to get too carried away with the idea of "plain English." First, simpler language cannot fix vague or empty thinking. Second, the key to good communication is to match the level and style of language with the intended audience. For organizations and authors wishing to convey information to the general public, there is little doubt that a simpler, more straightforward style of writing is usually best. But language also provides the tools to convey very precise meanings, and this often requires the use of more specific, technical language (§80).

Take, for example, a team of doctors discussing the best treatment for you. They will almost certainly use "medical" language so that they all understand exactly what your specific problem is and the possible treatments. Another example is lawyers speaking with each other without ambiguity in legal language about a complex legal case. In fact, knowing the technical vocabulary and ways of expressing ideas in a field is one of the essential characteristics of belonging to that field (e.g., medicine or law).

The problem is not that some language is quite technical and incomprehensible to outsiders. Rather, problems occur when the language is not appropriately adjusted to a new, intended audience. Specialists need to be 'multi-dialectal' and able to communicate effectively with both specialists and non-specialists. This entails being able to 'translate' very precise technical language into more general language that non-specialists will understand. This is actually the norm: think of doctors speaking to both patients and other doctors as a regular part of their daily life.

Power Point: Communication written in simpler language is generally more comprehensible. So when writing for a general audience, plain language is normally best. But sometimes language use needs to be very precise, such as in medical or legal contexts. In such cases, technical vocabulary allows specialists to communicate with colleagues in their field with the necessary precision and avoidance of ambiguity. As usual, good language use depends on the context, with the style of the message always adapted to suit the audience.

1. Here are writing guides from the Plain English Campaign:

http://www.plainenglish.co.uk/free-guides.html

. . .

2. This site gives 15 tips on writing plain English from the Plain Language Commission, another plain English organization.

https://www.clearest.co.uk/free-guides-on-plain-language

13

HOW DOES ADVERTISING USE LANGUAGE TO PERSUADE PEOPLE TO BUY?

The new product I just bought is not that great. How did advertisements convince me to buy it in the first place?

Advertisements are meant to show products in the best light, sometimes to the point of being misleading. Or as media education consultant Frank Baker suggests, "All commercials make products look better than they really are."

There are a number of tricks that advertisers commonly use to promote their products, and if you understand these, you will be much better equipped to resist their attractions. Of course, the pictures, images, and design are important in catching your attention, but it is language that describes the product and helps you to remember it. Here is how visual content and language combine to persuade you.

• **Association:** Ads link their product with something you already like, such as an idea, feeling, or person. An example would be the

2013 Apple Christmas advertisement where a teenager spent Christmas playing with his iPhone, in order to show his family a video of their various holiday experiences. The implication was that using an iPhone can help you build stronger family relationships. The association is usually not explicitly stated (*If you use X, you will become Y*), because it could then be legally challenged. Rather, the ad provides a suggestive context, which nudges you to make the association yourself.

• **People Power**: People of various sorts are used in advertisements. Sometimes they give a testimonial: *This product works for me*, with the implication that it will work for you too. But usually they merely give an endorsement, which essentially means they are getting paid to sell the product.

- *Beautiful people* Almost everyone would like to be associated with the qualities of beautiful people: attractiveness, radiance, and good health. They are often portrayed as rich and elegant as well. Simply buy the product and be like them.
- *Celebrities* Celebrities are interesting (or they wouldn't be famous), so people pay attention to them. The association makes the product interesting as well.
- *Experts* True experts can have useful specialized knowledge, but most people presented as experts are actually paid actors or models (notice how seldom actual names and qualifications are given in ads). However, the impression of authority that is projected can often be effective in convincing people.
- *Plain folks* Nice, typical-looking people that you can relate to are often used to sell everyday items, because then it is easy to see yourself using that product.

• **Simple Solution:** This often involves the ad underlining your fear of bad things, like body odor, and offering a simple solution to the problem: buy our deodorant.

• **Scientific (sounding) evidence / secret ingredients:** If an ad's argument sounds scientific, you may feel more confident that you are making a rational decision in buying the product. Unfortunately, the scientific evidence behind many ads often ranges from dodgy to non-existent. Special or secret ingredients give you the impression that you're getting something exclusive, although they often turn out to be nothing special or completely ineffective.

• **Bribery:** Companies sometimes give coupons, discounts, or freebies to obtain their product for the first time in order to spark habitual use.

• **Humor:** Humor captures your attention, and laughing feels good. This positive feeling might transfer to the product.

• **Bandwagon:** Ads can give the impression that everybody is buying the product, and you should too. Hurry up and buy, and do not miss out!

• **Warm and fuzzy:** Ads may use things like animals, kids, soothing music, and families playing together to create a sentimental and emotional environment in which to promote their product.

• **Intensity:** Some ads hype up the product, saying it is biggest, best, fastest, etc. Often this exaggeration is communicated by adjectives (see below).

• **Repetition:** This can involve the repetition of a message within an ad, or the repetition of the ad itself. This makes the message more memorable, but often also more annoying.

• **Playing with grammar:** Some forms of grammar can make an ad more persuasive. Imperative sentences (e.g., Nike's slogan *Just* *do it!*) can project a sense of urgency. Short sentences and phrases are easy to understand and so may be effective, especially at the beginning of a text, where slogans or headlines seek to grab the attention of the reader. Grammar can also be left incomplete in order to create vagueness. A case in point is the use of a 'better than' comparison without mentioning the thing being compared. An example is the Target slogan *Expect More. Pay Less.* (Expect more than what? Pay less than which other company?) This kind of unfinished claim gives the impression of superiority, which is in reality meaningless (§14).

- **High impact words:**

    - *Emotive, enticing vocabulary* Ads need words to conjure up positive associations with the product, which puts a premium on descriptive words (adjectives). Research by Geoffrey Leech (Lancaster University) showed that the most frequent adjectives in advertising by far were *new* and *good/better/best*. Others included *free, fresh, delicious, full, sure, clean, wonderful, special, crisp, fine, big, great, real, easy, bright, extra, safe,* and *rich.*
    - *Compound words* These can be made up and used as adjectives, and may have impact because of their novelty. The candy bar *Snickers* used several interesting compounds including *dimpatient* (My hunger is causing me to be dim and impatient) and *confoolish* (confused and foolish). The restaurant chain *Wendy's* serves a *baconator* (cross between bacon-burger and the Terminator). Some compounds have become so commonly used that they have entered mainstream vocabulary: *longer-lasting, economy-size,* and *top-quality.*

- *Glamorization* Using vocabulary to make something sound better than it is. Small portions become 'light meals,' and used vehicles are now 'previously owned.'
- *Weasel words* These words suggest something, but without being specific enough to mean anything. Geico often advertised that you "*could save 15% or more on car insurance*" (*could*—but maybe not!). Weasel words are very commonly used to make vague and unsubstantiated claims (§14). They are also used to give a product an illusion of strength: *fortified, enriched,* and *strengthened.*

Power Point: Watching out for these advertising techniques can make you a more discerning consumer.

1. This YouTube clip describes 15 techniques of persuasion used in advertising:

https://www.youtube.com/watch?v=5DAsbxr-iA0

2. Here is a site about advertisements that went too far:

https://www.businessinsider.com/false-advertising-scandals-2016-3?r=US&IR=T

14

UNDERSTANDING MISLEADING ADVERTISING CLAIMS

How can recognizing an advertising claim make me a more discerning consumer?

According to Jeffrey Schrank, a “claim” is the verbal or print part of an ad that makes some claim of superiority for the product being advertised. He explains that in many cases, products are nearly identical to their competition, so advertisers need ways of creating the illusion of superiority for these essentially equivalent products (e.g., gasoline, beer and soft drinks, soaps, and various headache and cold remedies). He goes on to identify 10 ways advertisers suggest claims about their products, without directly stating they are true. Many of these overlap with the techniques described in §13.

1. THE WEASEL CLAIM: The claim is hedged by a "weasel word" (e.g. *helps, up to, can be*) that suggests a meaning without actually being specific, effectively undoing the claim: *Honey Nut Cheerios can help lower cholesterol.* (But may not.)

2. THE UNFINISHED CLAIM: Comparisons (e.g. *bigger, better, faster*) are left incomplete, so there is nothing to compare the product to. The sports apparel company Under Armour had the slogan *Make Athletes Better* (than what? Exercising naked? Exercising in denim jeans at the gym?).

3. THE "WE'RE DIFFERENT AND UNIQUE" CLAIM: This is when the product is claimed to be different than any other product, and of course this is always true to some extent. But being somewhat different does not mean being better: *Built Ford Tough.* (Yes, but maybe *Dodge Tough* or *Toyota Tough* would be just as strong.)

4. THE "WATER IS WET" CLAIM: This type of claims gives a fact about the product, but which can also be applied to all or most competitors, and so there is no real advantage: Arby's advertises that *We have the meats.* But of course, every other fast food restaurant also has sandwiches with meat.

5. THE "SO WHAT?" CLAIM: Similar to 4, but does not necessarily apply to competitors. Nevertheless, it indicates no superiority benefit: Pop Tarts proudly advertise that they are *Baked with real fruit.* That is true, but they do not highlight that Pop Tarts only contain 2% or less of the various fruit.

6. THE VAGUE CLAIM: The claim is too vague to pin down, yet the use of emotive (but often meaningless) words can still give a positive impression: *The end of meatloaf boredom.* (But winning the lottery might end your boredom even better.)

7. THE ENDORSEMENT OR TESTIMONIAL: Someone (often a well-known person) endorses the product, and even vouches for its quality from personal experience. For example, George

Clooney certainly looks good drinking Nespresso coffee, but does he really drink it in real life?

8. THE SCIENTIFIC OR STATISTICAL CLAIM: A claim apparently backed up by impressive numbers from research, or includes an official-sounding "secret" ingredient: Before being discontinued in 2018, Certs was a popular breath mint, and was promoted as containing a sparkling drop of "Retsyn." Retsyn turned out to be a mundane combination of partially hydrogenated cottonseed, copper gluconate, and flavoring, but the slogan was effective in selling the mints. A Wonder Bread slogan claimed that "Wonder Bread helps build strong bodies in 12 ways" —but what were those ways? It appears to be a reference to 12 vitamins and minerals added to the bread to increase its nutritional value (which was not great after processing). But it was never clear, and early advertisements referred to some of the 12 ways as body parts like "muscles, bones and teeth, and blood," as well as "appetite and growth." The number 12 still sounded impressive anyway.

9. THE "COMPLIMENT THE CONSUMER" CLAIM: Flattery will get you everywhere, including softening up buyers. Coca Cola had an early ad with the slogan *Sign of Good Taste,* which featured an interesting double meaning of good soda taste and the flattering implication of good social taste as well.

10. THE RHETORICAL QUESTION: Asks a question whose answer implies the product is a good thing. Many weight loss companies ask questions like *Would you like to lose X pounds in Y weeks?* Many people would like that, but there is no direct indication that the company's product can actually deliver such results.

AD QUIZ

Can you spot the above techniques in the ads below?

_____ a. *Red Bull gives you wings.*

_____ b. *Nothing else tastes like Heinz.* (ketchup)

_____ c. *Totino's Pizza Rolls. Now crispier crust from the oven.*

Power Point: Any true superiority for a product will be enthusiastically and clearly demonstrated, but if there is any kind of hedging or vagueness, the product is probably not superior at all.

1. On this page, Jeffrey Schrank gives more detail about the 10 ways in which advertisers manipulate language to make unsubstantiated claims about their products. Some of the examples in this section come from the site:

https://docplayer.net/14585986-The-language-of-advertising-claims.html

2. Ads attempt to keep a product in your mind. This quiz sees if you can remember and match the classic slogans with the product

http://blog.hubspot.com/marketing/brand-slogan-quiz

Answers

a. 6 Red Bull does not literally grow you wings, so it is pretty vague what it actually does.

b. 3 Yes, Heinz condiments might have a slightly different taste, but are they any better than others?

c. 2 Crispier than what? Their previous version? Than a wet sponge?

15

SALESPEOPLE'S TACTICS AND LANGUAGE TRICKS

I was looking for a compact car the other day. By the end of my visit, the car salesperson had talked me into buying an expensive SUV. How did they do that?

Salespeople obviously try to get you to buy into their products or services. But to be successful, they need to make sure you are relaxed and perceive them to be on your side. They need to build rapport with you and to appear trustworthy. To achieve this, they have to know how to interpret and use body language (§5). They also can use a number of language ploys to make you more susceptible to their sales message. This section introduces nine common techniques.

1. Mirroring your body movements and language

This is a common feature of all persuasive language. People naturally like other people who are similar to them. This is one reason why *mirroring* is so effective. With body language, this entails matching the body movements of the person you are talking to (e.g., doing the same hand motions; copying a smile or nod), which indicates interest and convergence. Good salespeople mirror your body language but also mirror the language you use, including your vocabulary, grammar constructions, speech rate, and level of formality, among others.

2. Using your name as much as possible

This is an easy way for the salespeople to create a connection with you, as everybody likes to be called by their name. They will also compliment you when possible.

3. Choosing softer words

Salespeople will often choose their words carefully to make the sales process seem less intimidating. For example, on the payment pages of Internet sales sites, instead of having the button say *Buy now,* it is less intimidating to have it say *Start my order.*

4. Finding agreement before disagreeing

Salespeople do not like to disagree with you, because it creates disharmony. One way around this is for them to find some point of agreement and use this as a springboard before moving on to your objection. For example, if you do not like the style of the sofa, the salesperson can say something like "I agree with you that the style of this sofa would not be my preference either. The thing is, I believe you are looking for comfort over style, and this is the softest sofa in the store."

5. Asking permission to ask questions

Once you agree to answer the salesperson's questions, it is harder to refuse when they ask tricky or more confidential ones: "What is the most you are willing to spend?"

6. Asking questions that assume that you are buying from them

When salesmen ask questions about what you want from them (e.g., "Do you want insurance on your household items?"), this builds the feeling that you have already agreed to work with them in buying their product. Similarly, they could ask, "What type of television can I help you find today?", which makes it harder to say you are just browsing, and is the lead-in to them taking you on a tour of the various models.

7. Getting their 'Foot in the door' by getting you to say *Yes*

Salespeople first get you to say "Yes" to several trivial things, which then makes it more difficult to say "No" to subsequent questions. People do not like to say no, so it is easy for the salesman to get positive responses at the initial, inconsequential stages. But later, it is even harder for you to say "No" to the crunch question if you have already said "Yes" several times to related questions.

For example, a charity worker on the street might ask you if you care about the homeless people on the street. Unless you are completely heartless, you would obviously reply "Yes." They may then ask if you would make a small donation. You may well say yes, as it is only a few dollars. But they may then move on to a much bigger request, such as setting up a monthly donation to their charity through your bank. It is much harder to say no to this once you have already agreed to the value of their charity by saying yes to the first steps.

8. Controlling you by giving you commands

Salespeople may try to gain a subtle control over you by giving 'commands.' They start very gently with ones like "Come over here and let me show you this model" or "Come into my office and sit down so we can talk about it." Once the momentum of your obeying is in place, it becomes a bit more difficult to refuse the final "Sign right here" instruction.

9. Playing with how amounts are reported

When discussing costs, salespeople can talk about shorter-term timespans (e.g., weekly, monthly), to make them sound smaller. Conversely, they can use longer-term timespans (e.g., yearly) in order to magnify the effects of benefits or savings. This is taken to the extreme in many life-insurance ads, which say things like "Great protection for only $1.50 per day," which sounds much more affordable than the $547 annual cost. Likewise, salespeople can make figures sound smaller or larger by how they are said; for example, *Fourteen, nine, nine, nine* vs. *One thousand four hundred and ninety-nine dollars*. They might use the former style when quoting costs and the latter when discussing savings.

Power Point: These are techniques that salespeople may try with you, but you can also employ most of them yourself to make your own persuasive language more effective.

1. John Carroll explains 17 language techniques that insurance sellers use, but which probably apply to most salespeople:

http://www.insurancesplash.com/blog/17-sales-language-tricks-from-the-best-insurance-salespeople

2. An amusing cartoon about sales speak:

http://www.theguardian.com/money/cartoon/2010/sep/03/ripped-off-britons-sales-speak-explained

16

TALKING WITH YOUR DOCTOR

GETTING AND GIVING THE INFORMATION YOU NEED

I am always nervous when talking with my doctor and feel uncomfortable about asking too many questions. What can I do to better prepare for my next visit?

Some people find it tricky talking to their doctor (or other medical practitioner). In the old days, doctors often led the conversation and patients mainly listened, but nowadays a more equal partnership is usually preferred. Here is some advice on how to be an active participant in meetings with your doctor, and how to make those meetings less awkward and more productive.

- **Be prepared.** It is useful to think in advance what you what to get out of the meeting with your doctor. Write down the questions you want to ask, in order of importance. Sessions are usually scheduled to be quite short (the largest group of US family physicians reported spending 13-24 minutes per patient in a 2018 survey), and so you should have the really important questions and concerns at the top of the list. It is also useful have background information available on a list. This could include:

- Symptoms: both how your body feels and how you are feeling mentally
- Current medications, dosages, and any side effects
- Any medical changes since the last visit; e.g., changes in weight, appetite, or sleep patterns, or a visit to an emergency room
- Changes in your general life, like increased stress or a decrease in exercise

Preformatted lists are available to write this information down in an organized way. There is also a website to build a general health history journal.

• **Ask questions.** Communicating with your doctor should not be a one-way process, so do not be shy about asking questions concerning the information you need. If you do not, your doctor may believe that you understood their advice fully, when in fact you did not. Asking questions helps your doctor know if anything has been unclear. Questions also help your doctor understand what is particularly important to you. When it comes to your health, there are no 'dumb' questions. Things you might want to ask about include:

- Any terminology you do not understand (e.g., what is *glaucoma?*)
- The diagnosis (what your doctor thinks your health problem is)
- The results from tests like X-rays, blood tests, etc.

- Your medication, how to take it, and what the side effects may be
- Most medical problems have more than one treatment option. Ask about the different choices, and the benefits and risks of each.

Your health team is more than just your doctor. You can often get valuable information from nurses, physician's assistants, and pharmacists, and they may often have more time to spend with you than your doctor.

• **Review key points with your doctor and follow up.** Summarize and restate the key points of your visit so that it is clear you have understood the essential information and what you need to do. Ask for your doctor's contact information and their preferred method of communication (telephone, email, etc.). Then if you forgot to ask an important question during your visit, you will be able to contact them afterwards. It is also particularly important to let your doctor know if you begin to feel worse or if your medication is not working out.

• **Take information home with you.** It is sometimes difficult to remember everything you talked about with your doctor. To make sure you remember the important details, you can:

- Take notes during the appointment. Then check them in the waiting room directly after the visit to confirm their accuracy, and to add any additional information you did not have time to write down initially.
- Ask your doctor to write down their instructions for you.
- You might find it helpful to make a recording of the visit. Ask your doctor if it is okay to record the session. Many cell phones have a 'record' function.

- If you are distressed, having memory problems, or are otherwise incapacitated, you might want to bring a family member or friend with you to help write down the answers to your questions.
- Ask if there are any brochures or other educational materials that can help you understand your condition and medication/treatment.

• **Be honest.** Your doctor can only help you if you give accurate information about yourself, even if it is embarrassing. Doctors are used to discussing a range of sensitive personal matters. Also, be honest about the visit itself. If you felt rushed or that there was not enough time, tell your doctor. They might set up a follow-up appointment or direct you to another health practitioner who can answer your questions.

• **Get a second opinion if necessary.** For serious issues, like surgery, people often get a second opinion from another doctor. This is common practice, and doctors do not see it as questioning their abilities. They may even be able to suggest a suitable second doctor to consult.

Power Point: Talking with your doctor is a partnership. You need to have a clear idea of what you want out of a visit. You should prepare in advance and be ready to ask questions so that you get the information you need.

1. These websites give advice on how to talk to your doctor and how to prepare for an appointment, including checklists and lists you can fill out.

https://www.nia.nih.gov/health/doctor-patient-communication/talking-with-your-doctor

https://familydoctor.org/tips-for-talking-to-your-doctor

2. This website gives you access to 'My Family Health Portrait,' an Internet-based tool that makes it easy for you to compile a health history of yourself and your family.

https://phgkb.cdc.gov/FHH/html/index.html

17

UNDERSTANDING DOCTOR-PATIENT CONSULTATIONS

Doctor-patient consultations have a typical pattern. Understanding this pattern can help make the visit more productive.

Visits to your doctor are not random. You have a purpose for going to a doctor: usually to obtain treatment (or information) about a medical complaint. But your doctor also has an agenda, which revolves around giving you their expert assistance as efficiently as possible. In the UK, the average time a primary care physician spends with each patient averages around 10 minutes, with most US family physicians reporting 13-24 minutes per patient (§16). But many countries have average consultations of less than 10 minutes. In order to gather sufficient information about the patient's condition and prescribe a treatment in such a short time, doctor-patient consultations have a typical structure, which is relatively short and direct. Patrick Byrne and Barrie Long studied doctor-patient conversations and described the typical structure:

1. Greeting and relating to patient
2. Ascertaining the reasons for the patient's attendance
3. Conducting a verbal or physical examination or both
4. Considering the patient's condition (diagnosis)
5. Outlining further treatment
6. Terminating the consultation

Of course, this is a basic doctor-focused discourse structure, and it will vary in real life, especially as doctors try to better understand their patients' agendas. Regardless, doctors will often try to stick to some structure in order to provide their services in as logical and non-confusing a manner as possible. Look at the following real doctor-patient conversation and see if you can identify the steps, even though it sometimes strays from the above pattern:[2]

Doctor: Come in. Hello. How are you?
Patient: I feel shocking. You know, when I came to see you last week and you knocked those capsules off – well, every morning when I get up, and my head – Doctor, you could have amputated it. It was a terrible headache, and it was as if someone was dragging my eyeballs out. So I took more tablets, I haven't had anything since ... swollen, I've had bags under my eyes and all snuffly and watery, and at the moment, all the top of my head here feels as though there's pressure on it and I feel this stuff going down the back of my throat.
D: Are you coughing any of it out?
P: No I can't cough it out as ... when I blow my nose it's clear.
D: Is your nose blocked? Lie your head back and I'll have a look.
P: Just here and inside my throat is always very tender and

all under here ... and with both my hands tucked underneath my ribs and my head feels as if it's going to fall off.
D: Well, I'll give you a change of tablets for that and when you're over this I'll start you back on the capsules.
P: Well, all the aches and pains have gone, apart from under my ribs.
D: Well, leave it a week and come and see me again. It sounds as if it's the cold that's affecting your sinuses. Right, so a week from today.
P: Bye-bye, now.

The doctor greets the patient (Stage I), and in reply, the patient pro-actively launches into a description of their ailment, initiating the 'Purpose for Attendance' stage (II). The doctor then asks questions and examines the patient (III). Next, the doctor prescribes the treatment ("change of tablets" – (V)), followed by some more information from the patient about her condition (IV). As the last comment, the doctor makes the diagnosis ("cold" IV), and initiates the close of the session ("Right, so a week from today" – VI). It's interesting to notice how the driving force of the conversation shifts between the patient to the doctor, who then controls the flow by asking Yes/No questions ("Are you coughing any of it out?" and "Is your nose blocked?"), back to the patient ("all the aches and pains have gone, apart from under my ribs") and finally to the doctor who terminates the session once the diagnosis and treatment stages have been completed.

Another dynamic of doctor-patient consultations is the different perspectives each brings to the event. Doctors often work from a 'medical model' point of view, responding mainly to the scientific, clinical aspects of a patient's ailment, according to a time-efficient, pre-set diagnostic agenda. But patients typically come from a 'lifeworld model' perspective, where the personal and social context is important and might affect their condition. These different orientations can profoundly affect the diagnosis of the ailment. In the following extract, a patient has come to her doctor about heartburn. But her admission of heavy drinking allows her doctor to determine that this is the cause of the heartburn:[3]

P: … I've cheated and I've been drinking which I shouldn't have done.
D: Does the drinking make it worse?
P: Ho ho uh ooh Yes, especially the carbonation and the alcohol.
D: Hm hm how much do you drink?
P: (*Pause*) I don't know, enough to make me sleep at night and that's quite a bit.
D: One or two drinks a day?
P: Oh no no humph it's more like ten a night.
D: What kind of drinks?
P: Oh vodka yeah vodka and ginger ale.
D: How long have you been drinking that heavily?
P: (*Pause*) Since I've been married.
D: How long is that?
P: (*giggle*) Four years (*giggle*)

If the patient had not brought up her drinking, her doctor may not have discovered this as the underlying problem, especially since the drinking was related to issues in her marriage, rather than any purely medical reason. This illustrates that you should bring any pertinent 'life-world' information to the attention of your doctors to aid their 'medical world' diagnoses.

Power Point: Understanding typical doctor-patient discourse patterns and differing points of view can help you keep your medical conversations on track for the most constructive and efficient use of your limited consultation time.

1. This *Consumer Reports* video gives advice about how to make the most productive use of a short visit to your doctor, including five potential questions to ask about any test, procedure, or treatment.

https://www.youtube.com/watch?v=8bAccWMfyHo

2. This webpage from the National Institutes of Health has advice on preparing for your medical appointment, talking openly with your medical provider, and understanding diagnosis and treatment plans.

https://www.nih.gov/institutes-nih/nih-office-director/office-communications-public-liaison/clear-communication/talking-your-doctor

18

ASKING FOR ADVICE FROM ONLINE SUPPORT GROUPS

There are plenty of online medical support sites from which you can ask advice from other people with similar ailments. But they are not obliged to answer back. How do you ask in a way that will actually get a response?

There are many ways in which you can get medical advice. The most obvious one is from a doctor, and effective ways for communicating with them are described in §16 and §17. Nurses, pharmacists, and physiotherapists are among the many other medical practitioners from which you can receive information about the medical issues that affect you. But relatively recently, the Internet has also become a major source of medical information. There are many reputable sites that offer information and advice from specialists on a range of medical conditions. Some examples include:

✚ CANCER: National Cancer Institute
http://www.cancer.gov

✚ STROKE: National Stroke Association
http://www.stroke.org

✚ HIV/AIDS: HIVinfo
https://hivinfo.nih.gov/home-page

✚ DIABETES: DiABETES UK:
https://www.diabetes.org.uk

✚ MENTAL HEALTH: National Institute of Mental Health
https://www.nimh.nih.gov/health/topics

However, there are also a large number of sites that offer a forum for people with particular ailments to interact with each other in a variety of ways: sharing experiences and information, providing moral support, and of course a place to ask questions. These sites can be very beneficial in helping people to self-manage their conditions and also in reducing their sense of isolation. The relative anonymity of Internet sites can also be useful when discussing embarrassing topics and can encourage self-disclosure in a relatively safe environment.

But these sites tend to be informal, with people logging on and off as they please, and no one has any obligation to participate. Indeed, many people just view the sites with no interaction at all ('lurking'). This is all fine, but if you wish to seek advice, emotional support, or even just some interaction to talk about your medical problem, how do you get people to respond to you? After all, these Internet sites are not face-to-face, and it is not always easy to demonstrate you are worth responding to.

In their book *Exploring Health Communication*, Kevin Harvey (University of Nottingham) and Nelya Koteyko (University of Leicester) review research into conversations on online support groups, and conclude there are a number of things you can do to increase your chances of a response. Essentially, you need to 'legitimize' your request, so people will take it seriously. Consider the following post to an online arthritis support group:[4]

Hi. I've been reading/lurking here for a few months. [A]I've been diagnosed with AS and have been taking anti-inflammatories since May. [B]I am wondering what type of side effects others have had to these meds besides ulcers.

[A]Currently I am taking Lodine 1200 mg/day. [B]I am wondering if the swelling I've been having with my eyelids has anything to do with this drug. [B]Any thoughts? [B]Also, any other common side effects?

[E]I also want to thank everyone who's responded about depression and relationships. Reading this newsgroup has really helped me – [C]I don't feel like I'm the only one out here with this _thing_ you can't see, but can definitely feel. I'm 29 years old and I've had a hard time explaining to family and friends why I hurt, especially at a young age! [D]The threads about depression and relationships have helped me explain to my husband what I'm going through. [E]Thanks again everyone!

This extract illustrates some of the key legitimization strategies that Harvey and Koteyko identify:

- **Tell your backstory** Indicate your condition by describing your symptoms and/or mentioning the history of the disease. This is often used as an 'opener' to begin an inquiry (e.g. superscript A).
- **Make direct or indirect requests for information.** (B)
- **Make references to shared experiences.** (C)

- **Describe personal successes and elaborate on positive improvements.** (D)
- **Say thanks.** This is either for help already given or thanks in advance for potential responses. Expressing gratitude is a 'social glue' that shows that the support group is safe and sympathetic, and also gives others the license and encouragement to respond to you. (E)

Power Point: Online support groups can be a great resource from which to obtain information and emotional support from knowing you are not the only one struggling with your ailment. But before you can expect help, you must first show you belong and are worthy of other followers' time and attention. The above strategies are ways you can show yourself to be a legitimate member of the community and worthy of help in the relatively anonymous environs of Internet support groups.

Here are two websites that have support groups for a very wide range of ailments. The first is Support Groups and the second is Daily Strength.

https://www.mhanational.org/find-support-groups

http://www.dailystrength.org/support-groups

19

PERSUASION AT UNIVERSITY: WHAT MAKES LANGUAGE "ACADEMIC"?

I'd like to go to university and do well, and I know I'll be writing a lot of essays. How can I give my writing a more academic tone?

As a retired university professor, I know that one of the greatest challenges for university students is writing competent academic essays and reports. Most high school graduates can write letters, texts, and other basic written forms of communication that successfully convey a message. But this does not mean that they can necessarily write an extended composition in an appropriate and convincing manner at university level.

Academic language is a special variety of language that has its own conventions and style. To understand these, we need to first understand the purpose of academic communication. Its main functions are to advance knowledge and the exchange of information and ideas between members of particular academic communities (e.g. historians, engineers, linguists). The distribution of information/knowledge is primarily accomplished through written media; i.e. books and academic journals. The new findings or perspectives in these publications usually build on a foundation of older, established knowledge, and are based on carefully crafted arguments and detailed evidence. Academic writers use language to convey information that is precise and evidence-based, and aim to do this concisely. So what are the features that enable them to do this?

Length

University essays and reports are often 8-12 pages (double-spaced) in the US and 3,000 words in the UK. This might be longer than what you might be used to writing, but you will probably find that keeping the word length *down* to this limit is actually harder than reaching it. Writing is where students show what they have learned and demonstrate that they can apply the knowledge they are gaining about their field. Students cannot show everything, so they need to pick and choose carefully to ensure they fully address the assignment in the space allotted. Academic writing involves a lot of argumentation and citations (see below), and so there is a great deal of information to fit into a limited space. Academic language (e.g., academic vocabulary) is geared towards packing a large amount of detailed information into concise formulations.

Clear organization

Most academic writing involves constructing an argument or supporting a position about some question or topic. This requires clear organization with all your points directly connected to your argument or position. In Western academic writing, a 'linear' style is preferred, where one point leads directly and unambiguously to the next, with little room for digressions. The organization will depend on the purpose of the composition; a literary critique will have a different structure from a chemistry report. Part of learning a discipline is learning the writing organization appropriate to that discipline. For example, academic papers in my discipline (Applied Linguistics) usually have sections (e.g., Introduction, Literature review, Discussion, Conclusion), which are typically signposted with headings that make the organization of the paper explicit.

Supporting your argument

You need evidence to support your argument or position in order to make it persuasive and to give it credibility. In some cases, this may include your personal experience to a small degree, but the bulk of the evidence will almost certainly consist of references to research results and expert opinion. The most acceptable sources for these references are academic books and journals, because they typically have been peer reviewed for quality and accuracy. The Internet is becoming an increasingly important resource, but being unvetted, the quality varies widely. Information sourced from the Internet must therefore be used with caution (see Criticality below).

Citations and references

All academics build on the work of their predecessors, and they are expected to acknowledge this foundation by referring to previous work in the field that has influenced their current research or thinking. In other words, academic disciplines value a historical perspective that links new work with the older sources upon which it is based. This requires wide reading across a discipline, and this is where a large amount of a student's learning occurs. When writing, students are expected to conform to the convention of referring to sources, partly to demonstrate the breadth of the reading they have done and hopefully the knowledge they have gained from this reading.

But it is not enough to just refer to sources; students must cite them in a style appropriate to their discipline, as different fields require different referencing conventions. For example, if you want to refer to a 2007 book by linguist Steven Pinker, the science-style reference (APA convention) might look like *Pinker (2007) argues that language is innate* with the citation in an alphabetical References list at the end of the paper. Alternatively, if you want to cite commentary by Wordsworth, the literature-style (MLA convention) reference might be something like *Wordsworth stated that Romantic poetry was marked by a "spontaneous overflow of powerful feelings" (263)*, with the 263 referring to page number, and the citation linked to a Works Cited page at the end of the paper.

Criticality

The first thing to say about criticality is that it is NOT about *criticizing* something. Rather, it is the *careful evaluation* of the strengths and limitations of ideas or information. A person can be critical and conclude, for example, that a particular research study is excellent; e.g., *This research clearly shows that business ethics is important.* Or the conclusion could be more negative; e.g., *There are a number of problems with this study*. But either way, the person must have clear reasons for their evaluation, and will typically expand on these reasons in their discussion.

Academic writing is seldom just about *describing* something. Rather, it is usually about *evaluating* some idea or conclusion, often when there is no clear 'correct' answer or position. This puts a premium on the ability to critically weigh up the value of various pieces of evidence, opinions, and citations, and make a judgment.

This includes the evidence and argumentation used by the writers whose work you are critiquing, and also the evidence you gather to support your own arguments.

Indicating the degree of certainty

One of the most important aspects of criticality is the ability to indicate how certain particular assertions and conclusions are. Perhaps there are some certainties in the sciences ($E = mc^2$), but in most fields, there is still uncertainty or debate about many topics. You can indicate your evaluation of certainty (more certain ↔ less certain) through a range of phrases and hedges (*there is no doubt that X, it is highly likely that X, might/may be X, something suggests that X, we can speculate that X is*). This evaluation of the degree of certainty is a key way of having your 'voice' come out in your writing.

Vocabulary

Academic writers try to write precisely, and this includes word selection. Part of this precision involves using the *technical vocabulary* of your particular field, which indicates membership in that field (e.g. *meter* in poetry and *psychosis* in psychology) (§80, §12). High-frequency everyday words often have multiple meanings (e.g. *case* = an example of something, a container or box, a matter to be decided in a law court, etc.), while technical words usually have a single specific meaning (e.g. *tort* = a specific legal case that is dealt with in a civil court rather than a criminal court). Overall, academic style tends to use fewer **high-frequency words** if more *academic equivalents* are available (e.g. **guess** the amount–*estimate* the amount, a **strong** position—a *dominant* position). Academic style also tends not to use colloquial or idiomatic language (After the government gave up the subsidies, the economy caved in—

After the government *abandoned* the subsidies, the economy *collapsed*).

Academic vocabulary allows the packaging of considerable information in single words or short phrases. Consider the example of *mitosis*. The following extract is just the start of one description of mitosis:

> Cells divide in two steps. First, the nucleus of the cell divides and then the cytoplasm divides. Mitosis is the process in which the nucleus divides to form two identical nuclei. Each new nucleus is also identical to the original nucleus. Mitosis is described as a series of phases or steps. The steps are named prophase, metaphase, anaphase, and telophase....

Once a person understands this description, it is no longer necessary to repeat the long explanation the next time the process is mentioned, as it is all condensed into the single word *mitosis*. Without this concise packaging of information, discussion of any concept with the least amount of complexity would become extremely wordy.

Academic vocabulary is also used to summarize lists of ideas, as in the following example: *There are many problems related to obesity, including health complications, higher risk of death, lower quality of life, and self-esteem issues*. The single academic word *problems* can then be substituted for the four negative effects of obesity, eliminating the need to list them again and again. It thus helps to make the discourse more concise and less repetitive.

University education is largely about training students to become members of their chosen discipline community. As language use is a key defining feature of most communities, part of this initiation is helping them develop discipline-appropriate language. Unfortunately, this academic language does not just 'come naturally,' but must be actively learned and practiced.

Power Point: Academic communication is more clearly organized, information-dense, and critical than general language. It requires strong evidence for the arguments produced, with citations to reference that evidence. By learning the conventions of writing appropriately in one's discipline, students take a big step towards membership in that community.

1. Here are two websites describing the features of academic language in much more detail. The first is from Monash University, and the second from the University of Melbourne.

https://www.monash.edu/learnhq/resources/master-academic-english

https://students.unimelb.edu.au/academic-skills/explore-our-resources/developing-an-academic-writing-style/key-features-of-academic-style

2. There are a number of referencing conventions (e.g. Harvard, Chicago, and Vancouver). APA (American Psychological Association) is the most commonly used in the social sciences, while MLA (Modern Language Association) is used in languages and literature. Below are two websites from the Online Writing Lab at Purdue University explaining these systems, but the libraries or study support centers at many universities also have similar sites.

APA:

https://owl.purdue.edu/owl/research_and_citation/apa_style/apa_style_introduction.html

MLA:

https://owl.purdue.edu/owl/research_and_citation/mla_style/mla_formatting_and_style_guide/mla_formatting_and_style_guide.html

20

THE GRE GRADUATE SCHOOL EXAM

LANGUAGE IS THE KEY

I want to enter a Masters course, and the university requires the GRE test for admission. What should I expect on the test?

In today's competitive world, education is a powerful advantage. Figures from the US Bureau of Labor Statistics clearly show that the more education you have, the higher the salary you are likely to earn. In 2020, typical high school graduates earned $781 weekly, university graduates with a Bachelors degree earned $1,305, while Masters graduates received $1,545, and people with doctorates or professional degrees earned $1,885. Education also gives some employment security, as unemployment rates go down as you gain higher levels of education: high school (9.0%), Bachelors (5.5%), Masters (4.1%), and Doctoral/professional (2.5%).

It is no wonder that large numbers of people are pursuing post-graduate degrees. In 2020, 10.6% of the US population 25 years or older had a Masters degree, and over 1.4 million new students entered graduate school.

But to gain admission to a graduate program, universities often require a standardized test score (particularly in the US), to ensure that the students they admit have the academic skills necessary to successfully complete their courses. One of the best-known tests is the *Graduate Record Examination* (*GRE*)—467,000 people took it in 2020. It is not subject-specific, but measures the skills necessary to study a range of topics at a high level.

The GRE contains three sections. One, *Quantitative Reasoning,* measures your ability to understand numbers and graphs and to perform mathematical operations. But the other two sections focus on your ability to understand and use language effectively. The *Verbal Reasoning* section measures your ability to understand written materials and synthesize information from it. It also checks your understanding of sentence grammar and vocabulary. The *Analytical Writing* section concentrates on critical thinking and your ability to write effectively in an academic style (§19). It focuses on your ability to discuss complex ideas in a focused and coherent manner. Let us look more closely at the two language sections.

Verbal Reasoning

This section has three question types:

1. text completion
2. sentence equivalence
3. reading comprehension.

Here are some examples I created to illustrate these types. The website of the Educational Testing Service (ETS), the maker of the test, has many other examples.

1. The Prime Minister could not make up his mind: the more the situation (i)__________, the more the politician (ii)__________.

Blank (i)
(A) emasculated
(B) depreciated
(C) deteriorated

Blank (ii)
(D) prevaricated
(E) induced
(F) divulged

The second part of the sentence expands the idea in the first part that the Prime Minister could not make decisions easily. So *prevaricated* is the best choice for (ii), while *deteriorated* best describes worsening situations that require difficult decisions. Questions like this require you to understand the information in the sentences and how it fits together. It also requires you to know relatively low-frequency vocabulary (§86).

2. Choose two words which can fit into the blank:
Although the novel does contain some challenging elements, one would hardly characterize the book as __________.

A. eccentric B. stereotypical C. complex
D. trivial E. intriguing F. unfathomable

The word *although* indicates that the novel is not particularly difficult. That means that the book is not *complex* or *unfathomable*.

The reading comprehension questions require you to read a passage and then answer questions based on it. The questions are too long to reproduce here, but examples are available on the ETS site.

Analytical Writing

You will have to write two 30-minute compositions. In the first, you will read about an issue, and then state your opinion about the issue and provide support for your opinion. In the second, you will read a given argument, and then write an evaluation of how sound and convincing it is. Here is an example of the first type:

> *3. Because people can now use search engines to find almost any information on the Internet, it is less important for students to memorize facts and statistics.*
>
> *Write a response indicating the degree to which you agree or disagree with the statement. Make sure you explain your reasoning for the position you take. When developing your arguments, you should think about the ways in which the statement may or may not hold true, and explain how these considerations have influenced your position.*

As you can see from these few examples, the test puts a premium on understanding high-level language and the relationships between words, sentences, and wider discourse.

For many test takers, the most challenging part is the low frequency vocabulary. The test-preparation website *McGoosh* suggests that you need to study and understand words like *auspicious, corroborate, enervate, extant, inculpate, loquacious, mercurial, reti-*

cent, sanguine, and *soporific.* Flashcards are one way of kick-starting the learning of these words, but to really master them, you must practice using them whenever possible.

One bit of advice is in order. The GRE is not a test you can prepare for by memorizing. It requires you to use language in a critical and precise manner, and that is not something that comes quickly. I have seen suggestions that you should study from 1-6 months in advance, depending on the level you are at now and how intensively you study. Another suggestion is 50-200 hours. This will give you a chance to improve your knowledge and skills over time, so you will not forget them on the test day. In many ways, the GRE is like language proficiency tests in foreign languages (e.g. the DELF French test): short-term cramming will only have a limited effect, but sustained study can certainly improve your scores (§64).

Power Point: There are many advantages to getting a graduate degree, but first you may need to take the GRE for admission. Knowing what to expect will help you to prepare in a much more effective manner. Language ability will be a key factor in getting the score you want.

1. Here is the full graph from US Bureau of Labor Statistics showing the relationship between education level and salary / unemployment rates. The education levels range from less than high school diploma up to doctoral/professional degrees.

https://www.bls.gov/emp/chart-unemployment-earnings-education.htm

. . .

2. The GRE is developed and administered by *ETS*. The first address is their webpage providing both free and for-payment preparation materials, including the *POWERPREP* test preparation software which allows you to take two full-length computer-delivered GRE practice tests. The second website is *McGoosh,* which also has useful free preparation materials, including flash cards at the third webpage.

https://www.ets.org/gre/revised_general/prepare

http://magoosh.com/gre/gre-ebook

http://magoosh.resources.s3.amazonaws.com/Magoosh_Vocab_Flashcard_eBook.pdf

PART 3

LANGUAGE AND GENDER

COMMUNICATING WITH THE OTHER SEX

21

MEN ARE FROM MARS, WOMEN ARE FROM VENUS: ARE MEN AND WOMEN REALLY SO DIFFERENT?

Are the stereotypes that men are "strong" and women are "soft" really true?

In 1992, John Gray published the book *Men Are from Mars, Women Are from Venus*. It is one of the best-selling self-help books ever, having sold millions of copies. It claims that men and women are fundamentally different in what they think, want, need, and do. These ideas have seeped into the popular consciousness and have shaped the way people view gender and communication. For example, Gray makes the following assertions in his book, stating that the primary love needs of women and men are:

Women Need	Men Need
caring	trust
understanding	acceptance
respect	appreciation
devotion	admiration
validation	approval
reassurance	encouragement

Of course this is too simplistic, as both sexes need and desire all of these tokens of personal worth. Don't you? Gray acknowledges this, but presenting this dichotomy seemingly puts men and women in two different camps. In reality, men and women are not really so different. Contrary to Gray's cut-and-dried stereotypes, Julia Wood (University of North Carolina/Chapel Hill) argues that human behavior is much more individualistic, and she is discouraged that so many people accept Gray's stereotypical views at face value. She finds it equally disturbing that people accept that the alleged differences are natural and that we should accept and accommodate them.

It is true that there are differences between the ways men and women think and act, but these are not just intrinsic and biologically based. Rather, these differences are mainly *learned* from society and the ways it expects (and sometimes forces) men and women to act. Little Susie might want to grow up to be a firefighter, but that ambition is not actively encouraged in many societies, and some will even put unsurmountable obstacles in place. In short, it is not so much about the way men and women approach the world, it is more about how the world shapes men and women.

In order to understand these differences and how they relate to language, we should consider the words used to describe men and women. *Male* and *female* refer to biological sex, which is (usually) fixed. But words like *masculine, manly, feminine,* and *womanly* refer to the values we attach to men and women, and which usually have quite different connotations and implications (*masculine* implies strength and assertiveness; *feminine* implies softness and gentleness). These words/values belong to the concept of *gender,* which Angela Goddard (York St. John University) and Lindsey Meân (Arizona State University) define as "socially expected characteristics." They discuss an interesting idea about descriptions in their textbook *Language and Gender*:

Do you think the following words are commonly used with reference to men or women? Or can they be used with either sex?

1. dominant
2. co-operative
3. handsome
4. pretty
5. competitive
6. nurturing
7. rugged
8. submissive
9. aggressive
10. emotional
11. logical
12. hysterical

The majority of people typically attribute the odd-numbered traits to men and the even-numbered traits to women. *Handsome* and *pretty* are classic labels of male and female beauty respectively, but other than these, there is little basis in reality to assign the terms predominantly to one sex or the other. Regardless, even when the terms are used with both sexes, the connotations can be quite different. For example, a man who is 'dominant' and 'aggressive' might be seen as a strong personality, but the same traits in a woman may lead her to be seen as mean and malicious.

So unfortunately, gender stereotypes continue in our language, and you, I, and most other people continue to be party to them, either consciously or unconsciously. Goddard and Meân note with perhaps a bit of regret that "Research has consistently shown that people will willingly and easily identify characteristics which are typically male or female, but which have little to do with the actual attributes of real individuals."

This gender stereotyping can be easily seen in historical terms that originally simply meant a man or women doing something, with no value judgment (*actor, actress*). In every case, the masculine term is positive or desirable, while the feminine term has taken on subservient or unsavory meanings:

Male / Female
Governor / Governess
Master / Mistress
Bachelor / Spinster
Sir / Madame

Even a word like *tramp* has this masculine/feminine meaning duality, with male tramps being seen as not particularly despicable hobos, while female tramps are considered contemptible women of easy virtue.

Gender bias is everywhere in language whether one realizes it or not. Some efforts have been made to neutralize this with more general words like *chairperson* or *chair* taking over from *chairman*, and *actor* being used as a general term for performers, male or female (§25). But bias remains in language. If it were just a matter of word choice, it might not make much difference. But it affects opportunities, and as long as men are encouraged to be "assertive" and women "sweet," women will continue to have less prestige and lower pay than men. (The earnings of the average woman are between 70% and 95% of that of the average man in the US, depending on factors like where they live, race, education, and how the calculations are made, 2). Thus, gender differences that are assumed, but then reinforced by language, disadvantage women in real ways.

Power Point: Gender stereotypes are widespread in society, and many are deeply encoded in language. However, gender differences stem mainly from culture, and not the intrinsic nature of men and women. Understanding gender bias is important because it affects the degree of power and influence a person may have in a society, and so it is worthwhile eliminating gender bias from language use.

1. Michael Kimmel (Stony Brook University) argues that men and women are more similar than different, and that each needs to learn from the other:

https://www.youtube.com/watch?v=GQh0lt7V-U0

2. Here are two views of the gender pay gap:

https://www.aauw.org/resources/research/simple-truth

https://www.payscale.com/data/gender-pay-gap

22

GENDER DIFFERENCES IN LANGUAGE USE

Do my partner and I really communicate differently? If so, what are the differences in women's and men's language?

We have seen that men and women are quite similar in their needs and wants (§21), but people still seem more fascinated by potential differences between the genders than the more substantial similarities. Would the book *Men Are from Mars, Women Are from Venus* have sold so well if it was titled *Men and Women are both from Planet Earth*? Probably not. This focus on differences has a long history, but one of the first scholars to discuss them in more scientific terms was Robin Lakoff in 1975. In her book *Language and Woman's Place,* she argued that women were socialized into using feminine language ("speak like a lady"), but this language robbed them of the opportunities for success that the more assertive, powerful male language offered. Lakoff identified a number of features that she felt characterize women's language. For example:

- Use of "light" adjectives such as *charming* and *lovely*, which are used so commonly that they retain little meaning
- Use of hedges like *a bit* and *sort of*
- Apologizing more often (*I'm sorry, but...*)
- Use of intensifiers such as *so* and *very* (*That's so interesting*)
- Use of tag questions (The meeting ends at 4 p.m., *doesn't it*?)

These differences were identified in opposition to men's language, in a kind of "deficit" approach, where men's language was considered the norm, and women's deviations from that were considered less prestigious or forceful.

In hindsight, it became apparent that this approach had problems. One was the idea that in order to "fix" female language, all women needed to do was take on the characteristics of male language, and they would start gaining more success, prestige, and power. Of course it was never going to be that simple. Another problem with deficit-style research was that it was only ever able to identify small, rather inconsequential, differences. There were always bound to be some differences between male and female language anyway, so were they really such a big deal?

Research then began to look at language and gender in terms of "dominance," where differences in language were thought to reflect power differences in society. Some studies seemed to show that men talked more than women, interrupted them more, and controlled the topics of conversations. However, these studies often used relatively small numbers of informants, and were often set in artificial situations (e.g., describe some pictures into a tape recorder).

Later work looked at language and gender in terms of societal norms. Deborah Tannen in her bestselling book *You Just Don't Understand: Men and Women in Conversation* (1991) argued that gender and language are conditioned by society: that men and women are brought up with different ideas about themselves, their place in the world, and their expectations. This naturally affects the way they view conversation and the language they use in it. Tannen proposed that two things are key to social interactions: the relative power of participants, and how similar or likeminded they are. She argued that men are conditioned to focus more on the power aspect, while for women it is cohesiveness.

Today's view largely moves away from generalizations that apply to all men or all women. Rather it focuses more on individualism, the context of language use, and the communicative purpose of language. Although there may be some general language differences between men and women, much more language variation comes from who you are and what situation you are in. For example, female lawyers are more likely to talk like male lawyers than they are like female teachers. Male truck drivers will tend to have more in common linguistically with the female waitstaff at truck stop diners than they do with male university professors.

Context drives all language use, and all people, male or female or anything else, are sensitive to it. They are more likely to swear among close friends than strangers (§85). Everyone will speak more carefully in job interviews (§8) and business meetings than among friends in a café. One of the key contextual influencers of language use is social standing and relative power. Both men and women tend to use more tentative language when in positions of inferiority (talking to one's doctor (§16) or to a police officer giving them a traffic ticket – regardless of whether the doctor or officer is male or female). Conversely, both male and female bosses tend to use the more authoritative language of leadership.

Communicative purpose is also important. For example, Lakoff originally saw tag questions as signs of uncertainty that reflected a need for reassurance. But we now know that tag questions serve many communicative purposes, and one is to actively bring one's listener into the conversation. Thus, rather than being a sign of feminine hesitancy, they can be seen much more positively as a tool for managing discourse and giving others the chance to take the floor.

So men will often speak more differently from other men than they will from women, depending on the relative similarities or differences in occupation, education, social background, etc. Despite this, there are still a number of tendencies that do seem to hold as generalizations between the genders, although the degree of these differences is rather small.

1. Men are more information-based and focus on problem-solving (*report talk*), while women are more socially-based, focusing on building and maintaining relationships (*rapport talk*).
2. It matters who you are talking to. Men will tend to use more masculine language when speaking with other men in single gender groups than they will in mixed gender groups. The same applies to women and feminine language.
3. This adaptation is because it is typical to accommodate language to the person we are speaking with. However, this accommodation is to the *style* of the person, not their gender; e.g., if someone spoke slowly and carefully, we would adjust subtly towards that style when communicating with them, regardless of their gender.
4. Women seem to be better at listening and at providing support and positive feedback to the person they are listening to.

Power Point: The language differences between genders are small. Most of the variation in language use is driven by personal traits, and the context and purpose of language use.

1. In this extract from her book *The Myth of Mars and Venus,* Deborah Cameron explains that most of the assumed differences between male and female talk stem from myths rather than scientific facts.

http://www.theguardian.com/world/2007/oct/01/gender.books

2. Commonly assumed gender language stereotypes are parodied to good effect in this video clip:

https://www.youtube.com/watch?v=x4zu3PrsOv0

23

THE LANGUAGE OF DATING AND FLIRTING

Like most people, I get nervous and tongue-tied when I am dating. How can I communicate better, and also learn to "read the signs" so that I can be more comfortable and confident?

Dating can be nerve-wracking for even the most confident person. This applies not only to teenagers learning the ropes but also to an ever-increasing number of adult men and women, as people are getting married later and getting divorced more. (According to 2020 US census data, about half of people over 15 years old were either single or divorced/separated/widowed.) But being confident with language can certainly help, as well as being able to read body language for subtle clues about how things are going.

Body language can give a number of clues to what someone is thinking and feeling. It is discussed in general in §5, but here I will focus on how it relates to dating and flirting. Monica Moore (Webster University) observed a number of physical signals that women display to express interest in men. The following are some of the most commonly used:

- **Looking at a man** This included repeated short, darting glances, where the woman looked away within 3 seconds. They tended to occur in clusters of about three glances in a row. There were also longer gazes of 3+ seconds, where the woman looked directly at the man, even if her gaze was returned. Some women did this several times within a period of minutes.

- **Head/hair motions** Women tossed their head back, so it was momentarily tilted upwards. They also played with their hair, touching it or running their fingers through it. The head toss and hair flip often occurred together.

- **Smiling** Smiling was a very common signal. Laughing or giggling was also frequent, usually in response to someone's comment or action.

- **Gestures** Many women used rapid and exaggerated hand and arm gestures when talking. Primping (smoothing or patting one's clothes) was also common. Another gesture was playing with or caressing objects like keys, rings, drinking glasses, and cigarette packs.

- **Leaning closer** Women leaned their upper body toward the man, usually while seated. Sometimes this resulted in brushing against the man's body.

Another general signal of interest is *mirroring*; that is, mimicking the motions of the person you are interacting with. For example, if you lean forward or cross your legs, and they do so as well, that is a good indication they are engaged with you. Remember that body language comes in clusters of signals and postures. Recognizing the meaning of the whole cluster is far more reliable than trying to interpret any individual signal.

Unfortunately, it may seem that men do not always pick up on these cues very well, as it usually takes many repetitions of flirting signals before a man either notices or acts on them. Part of this is that men are generally less clued in to nonverbal signals than women. But most men are also cautious and want to make sure of a woman's intentions (e.g., by looking for repeated eye contact) before making an approach. Overall, it seems that women largely manage the flirting process, by giving signals to men to approach them (or not). The key seems to be the frequency of the positive signals, as this proved more influential than physical attractiveness in encouraging approaches from men. Average-looking women who signal often are more likely to be approached than more beautiful but low-signaling women.

There are also signs that a person is not interested. One is the simple absence of the above positive signals, and in particular the avoidance of eye contact. Moore also found that negative signals were often the opposite of the above signs. For example, rather than leaning forward with an open posture, women did things like point their body away from the man and cross their arms over their chests. Other negative signals included unenthusiastic facial expressions like frowning, and off-putting actions like picking at their teeth or nails or looking at their hair.

There has been less research showing men's flirting signals, but some include eye contact, assuming space-maximizing postures, and physically touching male friends. These last two behaviors (e.g., spreading his legs while sitting, sitting with his arms over the back of his chair, and back-slapping his buddies) imply status and social dominance within his group.

While body language can certainly provide insights into how things are going, everyone eventually has to talk during the dating process. Although it is impossible to determine scientifically what the most effective language is for dating, some of following suggestions might prove useful.

♥ **Avoid pickup lines.** They are usually unoriginal and difficult to pull off. Something simple and connected to the context you are meeting in might be a better bet, like "Lively in here tonight, isn't it?" After all, any opener is a transparent attempt to start a conversation, so what you say is probably not that important anyway.

♥ **When going on first dates, pick places and activities where talking is easy.** For example, watching movies might be fun, but they are not exactly conducive to getting to know each other, unless there is a plan for a drink or coffee before or afterwards.

♥ **Have some questions in mind if the conversation lags.** If you ask more open-ended questions (rather than simple Yes/No questions), this prompts extended replies and can help keep the conversation rolling. Talk about things you have in common. Smooth-flowing conversations often have turns of about equal length, so match the lengths of your partner. Compliments are always nice.

♥ **Be a good listener.** Show that you are interested in what your date is saying, and signal this interest with positive verbal feedback (e.g., "Yes, that's right," "Me too,") and body signals (e.g., lean towards your date, nod in understanding). And turn off your phone!

♥ **Make sure you close the conversation with a positive statement** ("I really enjoyed myself tonight"). If you felt things went well, make a tangible plan to get together again, rather than waiting to do this later. If appropriate, explain why you are stopping the conversation at this point ("I've got an early meeting tomorrow morning").

Power Point: People use body language to signal which persons they are interested in and which they are not. Once you are talking, make sure you are a good listener and signal your interest both verbally and physically.

1. This webpage gives reasonable and informative guidance on flirting, including both language and body language.

http://www.sirc.org/publik/flirt.html

2. Vanessa van Edwards, author of *Human Lie Detection and Body Language 101* talks about men's and women's body language while dating and flirting.

http://www.huffingtonpost.com/vanessa-van-edwards/how-to-read-a-mans-body-l_b_4674615.html

http://www.huffingtonpost.com/vanessa-van-edwards/female-body-language_b_3469175.html

24

HOW DOES GENDER PLAY OUT IN WORKPLACE COMMUNICATION?

Could language have something to do with the glass ceiling women often face in the workplace?

~

Women often bump up against a "glass ceiling" in their professional lives, as they struggle to get the recognition and promotions that men receive for the same quality of work. Part of this has been blamed on the style of language they use. The stereotypes are that men are more direct, assertive, and even aggressive in their communication style, while women are more indirect, conciliatory, and compliant.

Janet Holmes (Victoria University of Wellington) lists a number of widely cited features of "feminine" and "masculine" language styles:

Masculine	Feminine
direct	indirect
aggressive	conciliatory
competitive	facilitative
autonomous	collaborative
dominates talking time	talks less than men
interrupts aggressively	has difficulty getting a turn
task-oriented	person-oriented
focused on information	focused on emotions

These dichotomies were developed from research that searched for differences and dominance between men and women, as described in §22. While there is some truth in them, they have been found to be far too simplistic, as people are much too flexible and adaptable to simply conform to a single gender style in every situation. Gender does matter in the workplace, but subsequent research has found that the context has more influence. Workplaces are communities, and language use will be influenced more strongly by an individual's status in that community than by gender.

Thus, gender styles are not as black-and-white as is often believed. Both men and women use a range of language styles, which allows them to be assertive and supportive at the same time. For example, many male managers use collaborative language, while many female managers can be very direct. This is illustrated in the following two extracts from business meeting communication collected by Louise Mullany (University of Nottingham)[5]. In the first, manager Steve uses collaborative features such as rapport building (e.g., *we*; *let's*), indirectness (*perhaps*) and hedging (*you know*; *just*) to mitigate the strength of his directive to run induction days.

Steve: Do you feel that (*pause*) we need to do perhaps something like (pause) the sales department did?
Mike: Set a date to sort it out.
Steve: Cos as Sue's quite rightly pointed out, all it's all been done for us and the things etc. Why don't we just take advantage of that? (*pause*) Sue's offered her support with perhaps John? (*pause*) Err you know perhaps to run that. (*pause*) Why don't we just set a date now?
Matt: Yeah
Steve: And say right okay let's do it.
Sue: Just get everybody in.
Matt: Yeah

In the second extract, manager Carrie bluntly tells her subordinate to inform the board of problems with the local media.

Phyllis: I'm still getting a lot of er external like students (*pause*) press getting through.
Carrie: Tell the board.

Another case where language styles are blended relates to maintaining group solidarity, which is essential if the workplace is to operate smoothly. This requires effort at encouraging mutual empowerment, consensus, and good working relationships. Holmes and colleagues found that this relationship support (typically associated with a feminine style) was used just as much by men as by women.

More and more women are finding ways to blend feminine and masculine features in a hybrid language style that is effective. One example of how they do this is by using humor (§75) to soften the directness when ordering subordinates to do something.

However, this is not to say that women do not face obstacles. Just because they can be effective using language with masculine features does not mean it is always accepted. Although both men and women use a wide repertoire of language styles, it still seems to be more accepted for men to use a collaborative approach (more associated with women) than for women to use an assertive one (more associated with men). Thus, women seem to be more constrained in the language choices they have available to them.

Some of the features of masculine style in the table above are considered the characteristics of good managers, and are often taught on training programs. But when women use them, this is often negatively evaluated. And this negative evaluation is due to gender, not just the assertiveness itself. A study in which both women and men displayed exactly the same assertive behavior while they were being rated found that the women were rated as competent but less likeable than the men.

Another problem is male behavior if a female manager is not assertive enough. Research into office communication showed that men sometimes dominate even over female bosses, by holding the floor longer, interrupting more, and agreeing less with female speakers.

All of this can lead to women being caught in double bind. If they use assertive language, they are considered unfeminine and unpleasant. One example of this is a strong female manager who was considered "domineering," "abrupt," and "scary" by her female subordinates. But on the other hand, if women use a more feminine style, they are often not taken seriously. Also, using a feminine style essentially serves to maintain the status quo where men still dominate in many realms. Women may struggle to succeed unless they adopt a more forceful masculine style of communication, especially in traditionally male-dominated workplaces that require assertive behavior (e.g. politics, business, law, and the police).

Power Point: Society still holds strong stereotypes about gender language styles, even though in reality, most successful professionals use aspects of both "masculine" and "feminine" language. Women in particular may find it difficult to succeed when prejudices against them using assertive language still exist, but using only a collaborative style may result in them being seen as weak and ineffective.

1. The first web page describes the gender results of the New Zealand *Language in the Workplace Project* directed by Janet Holmes. The second site gives access to the complete project.

http://www.victoria.ac.nz/lals/centres-and-institutes/language-in-the-workplace/research/gender

http://www.victoria.ac.nz/lals/centres-and-institutes/language-in-the-workplace

2. Judith Baxter (Aston University) describes how 'alpha women' embrace masculine language to achieve success in the workplace, but how women working in lower prestige jobs still use mainly feminine language to their detriment.

http://www.theguardian.com/women-in-leadership/2013/jun/03/speech-language-determine-success-workplace

25

POLITICAL CORRECTNESS AND GENDER BIAS WORDS

I hate "political correctness" and being asked to change the way I speak. Why should I start using terms like* flight attendant *or* police officer *instead of* stewardess *and* policeman *anyway?

Political correctness is often the butt of jokes, and many people think it often goes too far. The term has negative connotations and implies a world gone mad. So why do we worry about language modification in the first place? This modification involves many aspects, including race, religion, age, and physical impairment, but let us look at gender as an example. The need for modification is based on two premises:

1. Women are disadvantaged in many aspects of life, including pay, job opportunities, societal expectations, and the traditional view that they should support and defer to their male partners. Most reasonable people are willing to concede that women in general do not have all of the opportunities that men have in general. If any

more evidence were needed, the male/female pay gap provides a pretty convincing argument (§21).

2. Language reflects the society that speaks it, but language also helps to shape it. If you take only one message away from this book, it is that language is fundamentally connected with power, and with the ability to get along in the world. Language matters. It is not neutral, and if it encodes disadvantages for any group of people, that is a negative thing, which needs to be remedied if possible.

The above argument indicates that language needs to be modified to get rid of features that discriminate against women, and to introduce features that are more neutral regarding gender. So instead of "political correctness," we could just as well use terms like "language balancing" or "language equalization" to describe the process. Doesn't that sound much more positive? This shows that labeling does matter to the way you perceive things.

Why would anybody be opposed to language balancing? One possible reason is that people get used to ways of saying things, without any intended slights or discrimination, and simply do not want to make the effort to change. This is understandable, but it still leaves the status quo in place. If a better world is worth fighting for, then surely it must be worth the small effort required to speak in a more gender-neutral manner.

Another reason is more problematic. In society, there have always been more- and less-privileged groups, and language plays a part in maintaining this distinction. Groups in power fear that any change and rebalancing will lower their influence and power, and so resist efforts by less privileged groups (e.g. women) to share in that power. This resistance sometimes takes the form of maligning language modification by characterizing it as unpleasant political correctness.

In fact, there are many good reasons to support language balancing. Perhaps the most important is that language both reflects and shapes the ways we view and interact with other people and with the world. The hope is that language balancing can eventually facilitate positive changes in society's attitudes.

Another good reason for getting rid of gender marking is simply that many traditional roles are blurring to the point of disappearance. For example, when doctors used to be almost solely men, the term "female doctor" pointed out their exceptional status. But nowadays women doctors are very common. Over 1/3 of all doctors in the US and over 40% in Canada are women. Moreover, younger doctors are increasingly female. For example, in the UK, the majority of doctors under 45 years of age are female. But the crucial point is that gender makes no difference regarding the ability of most professionals to provide good service, and so is irrelevant. For most occupations, there is simply no reason to highlight gender, and doing so raises the question of why it was referred to in the first place. Would you ever think of saying "male accountant"?

A third reason is to challenge the unspoken norms of society. In their book *Language and Gender*, Angela Goddard (York St. John University) and Lindsey Meân (Arizona State University) point out that terms like *black, homosexual, disabled,* and *elderly* all label deviations from an unspoken norm, which is white, heterosexual, able-bodied, and young/middle aged. In many cases, the norm is also male. While the acceptable terms for these variations from that norm may change over time (e.g. *black*→*Afro-American*), the people who represent the norm never get labeled at all. They are just "normal" people. This non-labeling means that this norm usually remains unstated and thus unchallenged. If we want an inclusive and fair society, it is important to not limit the norm to only one segment of the population, and to avoid using language that implicitly (or explicitly) separates any group from humanity overall. This certainly includes not distinguishing women from the rest of society based on old-fashioned ways of saying things (*lady lawyer, governess*).

In the last few decades, some progress has been made in rebalancing language. Casey Miller and Kate Swift published the *Handbook of Non-Sexist Writing* in 1981, and since then most newspapers and publishing houses have adopted guidelines that require gender-neutral language. Examples of typical guidelines include rather common-sense suggestions such as the following:

1. Avoiding the use of *he/his* when speaking in general. This can often be avoided by using plural forms:

> **X** If a person works hard, <u>he</u> will eventually get <u>his</u> reward.
> √ People who work will eventually get their reward.

2. Avoid using *man* to refer to both men and women.

> **X** <u>Man's</u> achievements over the centuries have been impressive.
> √ Human achievements over the centuries have been impressive.

3. Avoid using discriminatory job titles.

> steward/stewardess → flight attendant
> cameraman → camera operator
> fireman → firefighter
> office girl/boy → office helper

4. Avoid depicting men and women in non-parallel ways. For example:

- Describing men by achievement and women by appearance
- Referring to males as *men* but females as *girls*
- Describing women in terms of their relationship to men (the doctor's wife) but not describing men in terms of their relationship to women (the scientist's husband)

Power Point: Language affects the way we see and think about the world, and so using gender-neutral language should be a useful tool in promoting a more equal society. Language balancing has largely been achieved in the media and press, but it remains to be seen how this leads to greater equality.

1. Here is an example of guidelines for gender-fair use of language. They come from the National Council of Teachers of English (NCTE). Do the suggestions seem reasonable to you?

http://www.ncte.org/positions/statements/genderfairuseoflang

2. Here are some writing tips from the Writing Center at Hamilton College in New York on how to avoid using sexist language.

https://www.hamilton.edu/documents/Writing%20about%20Gender,%20Sexuality.pdf

26

HOW DO CHILDREN LEARN GENDER-RELATED LANGUAGE?

As my children grow up, they will start using features which are associated with masculine or feminine language. Where does this gender-related language come from? Is it innate, or is it learned through environment and experience?

The debate about what contributes to the development of human personality, behavior, and skills is long-running and complex. It has often been framed between the effects of *nature* and *nurture*. Nature is the innate physical endowment we are born with; the result of our genes. Nurture is the influence of the society and environment we are born into, and how they affect our characteristics as we grow. As with most human features, language is affected by both nature and nurture, including gender-related language.

It is clear that the brains and cognitive development of males and females differ in some ways. Male brains are typically larger than female brains, but much of this relates to the larger male body size in general and does not imply greater intelligence. There are also various regions of the brain that are more developed for one sex than the other (e.g., the frontal area of the cortex is bigger in women). Men tend to rely on their left hemisphere, which is the center of logic, analytic thought, and language. Women seem to use both left and right hemispheres in a more balanced manner than men. (The right hemisphere is the more creative, holistic side.) There are suggestions that these differences in brain development and use partially explain the generally better language skills that females enjoy.

Girls generally develop somewhat faster than boys, in the senses (e.g., vision, hearing, and smell) and memory. They also tend to be better at what might be called "social" skills, such as face recognition, responding to human voices, and recognizing emotions in others. This also helps explain why girls are typically better than boys at many aspects of language ability. Boys seem to have a clear advantage in spatial recognition and manipulation, which helps them to do well at tasks such as navigation and spatial puzzles (e.g., where you must imagine what various shapes would look like if rotated 90°). But all of these are average trends, and individual boys and girls vary widely in ability, especially boys. Furthermore, boys and girls usually catch up with each other by around puberty to become similar in level of ability for most aspects.

The above are early tendencies, but a child's environment can enhance or even change these. Children (boys or girls) that are brought up in a very interactive, communicative, empathetic environment will naturally be exposed to and practice social skills much more than children who are not, and so will become better at them. Similarly, children (girls or boys) who are encouraged to run, play physically, and explore spaces will improve their tactile and spatial abilities. Children's preferences also play a part. An 'average' girl's initially stronger social skills may encourage her to play more with dolls, and this can reinforce those skills. Likewise, outdoor activities and ball games may appeal more to 'average' boys due to their better visual-spatial skills, which of course supports further development of those skills. Happily, child development is not an either/or situation where children can only be good in one realm. Children should be given opportunities to develop a variety of skill sets. Limiting children to gender stereotypes (e.g., girls should play with dolls; boys with balls) is not very helpful in this respect.

Children appear to begin learning gender styles early in life, with kids as young as 2-3 years old already starting to exhibit distinct male/female styles of interaction. For example, Deborah Tannen (Georgetown University) found that girls typically face each other when talking, with lots of eye contact, and a supportive, inclusive communication style. Boys tend to talk sitting side-by-side, with less eye contact and verbal support. Girls tend speak in ways that emphasize group similarities, while boys often strive to outdo each other in a kind of verbal competition.

Tannen suggests that this trend of female inclusiveness and male competitiveness is due to children being socialized into different "cultures," with women expected to be gentle and supportive and men strong and assertive. Children pick up these expectations from role models and peers. Jennifer Coates (Roehampton University) argues that gender styles are picked up in a number of ways from adults, who start off by having different preconceptions of boys and girls and thus talk differently to boys and girls, which provides different language models for children to imitate. Also, adults sometimes react differently to the same linguistic strategy when used by girls or boys. For example, if girls give verbal feedback like *Yes, that's right,* adults might interpret this as just feedback to keep the speaker speaking, while if boys say this, it can be seen a positive agreement to the point being made. Furthermore, children are constantly bombarded with images (particularly from advertising, §27) that graphically illustrate society's expectations for each gender.

But children don't only learn language from adults; it can be argued that language is largely learned on the playground, from playmates. Children want to get along with their friends and be popular, and to do this, they must conform to their peers' use of language, including gender styles and language rituals.

Power Point: There are some biological differences that influence children's initial language use. However, gender styles are largely learned from the social environment, including the expectations and examples of adults and playmates.

1. This web page explains some of the early male/female biological brain differences (nature) and their outcomes. It also discusses the effects of nurture.

https://www.scientificamerican.com/article/brain-differences-in-boys-and-girls-how-much-is-inborn/

2. In this video clip, Deborah Tannen explains the different gender-specific language rituals that boys and girls have.

https://www.youtube.com/watch?v=tUxnBZxsfoU

27

HOW DOES ADVERTISING AFFECT CHILDREN'S GENDER DEVELOPMENT?

My kids watch lots of commercials that tell my son to play with Transformers and my daughter with Barbie. Does this gender stereotyping affect their development?

Children are influenced in their gender socialization by many factors, and one is how they are depicted in the media. One aspect of media that is particularly powerful is advertisements/commercials aimed at children, because these are designed to be especially attention-grabbing and appealing, and the average child sees thousands of them per year. Young children lack the critical ability to evaluate the motives behind advertising, and cannot always distinguish between programs and commercials. Thus, they are particularly susceptible to any gender-based images that they may be exposed to through commercials.

Unfortunately, children's commercials have traditionally been loaded with gender stereotypes. This mirrors advertising in American television and print targeted at adults, where men are typically portrayed as powerful, dominant, autonomous, and successful. Women on the other hand tend to be shown as softer, more passive, shy and gentle, and less capable. When shown in jobs, women tend to work in the house as a spouse or mother, while men have work outside the home.

A good illustration of stereotypes in children's advertising comes for Beverly Browne's (Oregon State University) analysis of 298 ads recorded in 1994-1995, half from the US and half from Australia. She found the following:

- The ads featured more males than females, but the ratio depended on age. Ads containing elementary school children had 56% boys and 43% girls. Those containing teenagers were much more unbalanced, with 70% boys and 29% girls. Those with adults had 62% men and 38% women.
- When the ads contained both boys and girls, the boys more often explained or demonstrated the product (61%). This was true even if the product was gender-neutral.
- Ads used mainly male narrators. This could be expected for products targeting boys, but it also held true for gender-neutral products (85% of these commercials). Female narrators were used in less than 16% of ads, mainly those targeted at girls/mothers.
- There was a clear segregation of product by gender. Boys were never shown using products designed for girls, and vice versa. When products were not gender-specific, boys were depicted using them in 70 ads, but girls in only 15 ads.
- The adult roles presented to children in the commercials were very skewed, with traditionally male roles

(professional, worker, and sports person) making up 79%, and traditionally female roles (homemaker, mother, and teacher) only 21%. Even in ads containing girls, traditional female adult roles appeared only 46% of the time.

- The boys in the commercials were rated as being more active (busy; doing a lot) than the girls.
- The boys in the ads were rated as being more aggressive than the girls. Aggression was defined as "acting against another person or thing: hitting, throwing, grabbing, loud or abusive talk, face making, and determined behavior (as in aggressively pursuing a goal)." Girls rarely displayed aggression in the ads.
- Boys were generally shown as being more effective, better able to make things work, and more often winning in competitive games than girls. Girls were more often shown caressing objects or touching them gently than boys.
- Children were seldom shown asking for or accepting help from each other or from adults.

These advertising stereotypes seem to be persistent, as Browne noted that her 1994-1995 results were similar to those from at least as far back as the 1970s. And although these stereotypes may have softened somewhat more recently, they still seem to be largely in place. For example, two studies in 2013 (analyzing 208 and 124 US children's ads respectively), and one looking at 168 UK ads from 2006-2007 both found results similar to Brown, showing boys more physically active, more aggressive, and exhibiting more independence, leadership, and risk-taking behavior. Ads targeted at girls tended to show domestic settings, more passive behavior, and cooperative activities like looking after a doll.

Gender stereotypes in advertising matter because they affect the way children form their own gender identities. The media has a substantial influence on children, as illustrated by a report on media violence by the American Academy of Pediatrics, which states that "Extensive research evidence indicates that media violence can contribute to aggressive behavior, desensitization to violence, nightmares, and fear of being harmed." This influence clearly extends to media depictions of gender stereotyping, as children as young as four-years-old have ideas of "boy's toys" and "girl's toys." Children seem to be well aware of gender stereotyping in children's advertisements from an early age. These stereotypes can reinforce views of women being less capable than men. An interesting example of this was the reluctance of some 6-year-olds to say that Superwoman was as capable as Superman (e.g., in saving people) and the belief that other people would also rate her abilities lower as well.

Stereotypical advertising is rife in advertising to older children as well. One example of this is the advertising blurbs on the boxes of toy figurines. These figurines are typically gender-oriented, with toys like *Disney Princess* targeted towards girls and toys like *Batman* targeted towards boys. Patricia Owen and Monica Padron (St. Mary's University) analyzed packaging blurbs and found that those oriented towards girls had more descriptions associated with physical appearance, fantasy, and triviality (e.g., *exotic, sparkling, fantastical*), while those oriented towards boys had more references to power, destructive action, and science and technology (e.g., *focused, awesome, crime-fighting*). They also found that the gender language was very polarized, with very few feminine-associated descriptions being used in boy-oriented blurbs, or vice-versa. This gender-oriented language is problematic, not only because it reinforces questionable gender stereotypes within society but because it can also affect children's language development. Children learn language from the language they are exposed to (§45), and if that is continually reinforcing gender-focused models, children will be hindered in developing a more well-rounded linguistic repertoire.

The negative impact of gender stereotyping in children's commercials has led several governments to restrict ads targeted at children, including Greece, Norway, Sweden, and Quebec. But elsewhere, people (both children and adults) need to be more media-savvy and aware of the stereotypes. An effective tool for demonstrating the stark differences between gendered ads are websites that show boy's ads overdubbed with the soundtracks from girl's ads, and vice-versa. Playing with such websites for only a short time drives home the blatant gender stereotyping in many children's ads. The results are amusing, but also unnerving.

Power Point: Advertising has consistently portrayed boys as active, capable, and aggressive, while portraying girls as more domestic and collaborative. These images play a role in shaping children's gender identities, and ultimately language use.

1. Anita Sarkeesian looks at children's advertising and argues that it is highly gender stereotyped, which plays a role in shaping children's aspirations and images of themselves.

https://www.youtube.com/watch?t=45&v=rZn_lJoN6PI

2. Here are two web sites that transpose girl's narratives on boy's commercials and vice versa. The first does this for Lego commer-

cials. The second lets you mix and match the audios and videos from 10 boy's and 10 girl's commercials.

http://jezebel.com/5887428/lets-swap-the-audio-for-girls-and-boys-lego-commercials-and-see-what-happens

http://www.genderremixer.com/html5

PART 4

LANGUAGE MANIPULATORS

THE MEDIA AND POLITICIANS

28

UNDERSTANDING MEDIA BIAS

I heard that we now live in a "post-truth" world. How does this affect the news I get from newspapers, radio, and TV?

In 2016, the Oxford Dictionary "Word of the Year" was *post-truth*. The dictionary defined post-truth as "relating to or denoting circumstances in which objective facts are less influential in shaping public opinion than appeals to emotion and personal belief." The term reflects the idea that many news outlets now tailor their reporting to what their audience wants to hear, rather than focusing on facts as closely as possible (§32, §37). This makes it more important than ever to be aware of media bias.

Although newspapers and the broadcast media would like us to believe that they report facts impartially, this can never be completely true. Each individual publication/channel is an organization with its own unique perspectives and restrictions. It might be constrained by its owner's viewpoints, or by the necessity of keeping its advertisers happy and on board. It might try to be inoffensive by reporting similar stories to everyone else. Perhaps it will avoid complex stories and focus on ones that are easier to explain. Almost all news outlets will concentrate on sensational stories (a $1 million bank heist) over more ordinary ones, even though the more common ones might actually be more important to the public (we are all increasingly susceptible to cybercrime). There might be an overtly conservative or liberal agenda.

Even if a news organization avoids the above biases, it is still made up of people (editors and reporters) who have their own assumptions about the world and how events in it should be reported—or not. It is simply impossible to report all of the important news stories in the nation or the world in sufficient detail to provide a comprehensive understanding of the events in question. Reporters and editors will always have to make decisions about which stories or people merit attention in the first place.

For example, Otto Santa Ana (UCLA) found that although Latinos now make up about 18% of America's population (2019 Census Bureau), only around 1 in 100 reports from a full year (2004) of ABC, CBS, NBC and CNN evening news programs (12,000 news stories) were related to Latino issues. Clearly, what is and is not reported on is a type of bias. This type of bias can be especially negative in countries with less freedom of the press, where news judged to be critical of the government is censured, or not allowed to be reported at all.

Reporters and editors also have to decide what information to provide in the limited space/time available, which is always tricky. For example, I watched the BBC television evening news on the day I was working on this section, and the average story length was 2 minutes and 16 seconds—enough for only a very limited amount of detail.

However, media bias can be most obvious in the *language* used to report the stories. The choice of **headline** can give a positive or negative initial impression (§30). Likewise, **grammar** constructions can lead to very different meanings. For example, a common British political statement is *Lessons have been learned,* used by officials when apologizing for a mistake or scandal. Because it is expressed in the passive voice, the officials avoid explicitly stating what lessons have been learned, who learned them, and exactly who made the blunder in the first place.

Perhaps the most easily manipulated linguistic aspect is **vocabulary**, which can carry connotations that go far beyond the "facts" being reported (§29). An example of this is **labeling.** For instance, the *Right to Choose* and the *Right to Life* both sound very positive, but the choice of label immediately indicates which side of the abortion debate is being taken.

Consider the following pairs of labels, which have been used to refer to the same people:

terrorist	freedom fighter
illegal aliens	undocumented workers
civilians accidentally killed or wounded in war	collateral damage
garbage man	waste collector
mentally retarded	mentally handicapped

You probably had much more positive feelings about the people described in the second column than in the first column. This shows that labeling matters, and the label a news report chooses to use will strongly slant the rest of the story.

The **metaphors** used in news reports also affect how those reports are perceived. In the mid-1990s, California voters approved Proposition 187, a controversial initiative to deny public services (e.g., health services and education) to people in the country illegally. In the run-up to the vote, the *Los Angeles Times* opposed the proposition. But in an analysis of 116 news reports, Santa Ana showed that in 58% of cases, the dominant metaphor was IMMIGRATION IS DANGEROUS WATERS. In his book *Brown Tide Rising: Metaphors of Latinos in Contemporary American Public Discourse,* Santa Ana shows how this metaphor (unintentionally) painted the immigration issue in a negative light, as can be seen in the following examples from the Times (especially when combined with strong adjectives like *relentless* and *overwhelming*):

- *awash under a brown tide*
- *the relentless flow of immigrants*
- *an overwhelming flood of asylum-seekers have put the country in an angry funk*
- *a sea of brown faces marching through downtown would only antagonize many voters*

It is noteworthy that this negative metaphor was still being widely used by journalists describing the European refugee situation in 2016; e.g., *this tidal wave of migrants could be the biggest threat to Europe since the war.*

For all the above reasons, news reporting will almost inevitably have bias of some type, even when journalists try to remain absolutely impartial. It is up to you to be aware of this bias, and the many forms it can take (see §29-32). Only then can you make the most informed decisions based on your understanding of what is reported in the media.

Power Point: News reporting will always be biased to some degree, because news organizations are made up of people (owners, editors, reporters) who make their editorial decisions about the stories and the language used to report them based on their own journalistic and personal experiences, as well as the collective ethos of the organization. You should be aware of this inevitable bias, and take it into account when interpreting and making use of the information reported.

1. This website features Otto Santa Ana talking about his book *Juan in a Hundred,* which discusses the relative lack of coverage of Latino issues in the American news media.

https://www.youtube.com/watch?v=ar9Bn2BsVOE

2. This site lists the 10 most censured countries, as described by the Committee to Protect Journalists.

https://cpj.org/reports/2019/09/10-most-censored-eritrea-north-korea-turkmenistan-journalist.php

29

COMPARING BROADSHEET VS. TABLOID NEWSPAPERS

Newspapers can be very different in their style. How is language used to give newspapers their "serious" or "sensational" tone?

There have always been various kinds of newspapers. One difference is size, with full-size broadsheets and smaller, easier-to-hold tabloids. Most serious newspapers traditionally used the broadsheet format, and so became to be known as *broadsheets,* regardless of their size. (Many broadsheets now use the more convenient tabloid format). Many broadsheets have established long-running reputations for quality, such the *New York Times* in the US and the *Times* in the UK.

But there is also a long tradition of irreverent, splashy reporting (often focusing on celebrities, sports, and scandal), which has traditionally been associated with the tabloid format (*tabloid journalism*). This kind of paper trades in sensationalism, and many of their stories should be treated with extreme skepticism. The

National Enquirer in the US and the *Sun* in the UK are often considered as examples of this kind of journalism.

So how do the broadsheet and tabloid styles of paper differ? To illustrate this, I have selected a story that was widely reported on July 27, 2016. It is the sad case of a priest in France who was murdered by two ISIS-inspired young men. Below are extracts from the reports in a UK broadsheet and tabloid. Can you tell which is which?

A.

> **PATHETIC COWARDS**
>
> ***Jihadi scum slit throat of French priest, 85, at his own altar***
>
> *Two crazed Islamic State knifemen filmed themselves trying to behead a Catholic priest on his alter after storming a church in France.*
>
> *The evil pair forced Father Jacques Hamel, 85, to kneel down before performing a "sermon" in Arabic in front of terrified nuns.*
>
> *They then slashed his throat in a frenzied attack before leaving him lying dead in a pool of blood.*
>
> *A nun who was seriously wounded by the monsters was still fighting for life last night.*
>
> *The two jihadis were shot dead by police marksmen as they emerged from the church in Saint-Etienne-du-Rouvray, near Rouen, Normandy.*

B.

> ***Priest's killing in terror attack shocks France***
>
> ***Two men took hostages in church before being shot dead by police***

> *France was plunged into profound shock for the second time in 12 days when two men cut the throat of a priest as he was celebrating mass in a Normandy church yesterday morning.*
>
> *A nun who saw the murder described how the men forced Father Jacques Hamel to his knees before killing him and filmed themselves preaching in Arabic by the alter. They also tried to cut the throat of a parishioner, leaving him for dead.*
>
> *The gruesome attack came less than two weeks after a French-Tunisian man drove at high speed into a Bastille Day crowd in the Riviera city of Nice, killing 84 people and injuring hundreds more.*

It probably was probably very clear that B is the broadsheet (the *Guardian*) and A is the tabloid (*Daily Star*). But made it so obvious? It is not actually the facts reported, as they are similar in both extracts. It is the *language* used that gives the two stories their very different tone.

We can start with the **headlines**. The *Guardian*'s provides the main gist of the story, but the *Star*'s is full of outrage and insult. The *Star* headline was also from the front page, where its capital letters made up half of the entire page.

We can also see the distinctive style in the **layout** of the stories. The average paragraph length in the *Guardian* extract is 36.7 words, but the *Star* uses much shorter paragraphs (19.8 words) of only one sentence, presumably to make it easier to read.

But the real difference is in the **vocabulary** used. The *Guardian* tends to use vocabulary without emotional overtones, with *gruesome* being the only exception in the extract. The *Star* is the opposite—it uses words intended to shock and sensationalize the events. The criminals are described as *pathetic cowards, jihadi scum, crazed,* and *evil.* The method of murder is highlighted in very graphic terms (*slit/slash throat, frenzied attack, lying dead in a pool of blood*). This compares to the *Guardian's* more neutral *cut throat.* There is also a string of words that bring up images of war (*storming a church, attack, wounded, fighting for life*). The age of the victim, *85,* is highlighted to make the murder seem even more atrocious. Even the word *"sermon"* is put in double quotes to delegitimize the murderers' motives.

These extracts are from UK newspapers, and the differences may not be quite so dramatic in the US, as UK tabloids tend towards greater sensationalism than those in the US.

But which style did you prefer? Of course, this depends on your background and preferences, but statistics can show us the overall trends of readership. In the UK, some tabloids outsell broadsheets, with the *Sun* being the most-read purchased paper with a daily circulation of 1,410,896. The tabloid *Daily Mirror*'s circulation is 508,705. In comparison, the broadsheets often sell less: the *Times* 417,298; the *Guardian* 141,160 (2019 figures). Interestingly, in the US, broadsheets dominate: *USA Today* 1,621,000; *Wall Street Journal* 1,011,000; *New York Times* 484,000; *Los Angeles Times* 418,000; and *Washington Post* 254,000 (2019 figures).

Power Point: The differences between broadsheets and tabloids largely stem from how language is used: to report information (relatively) impartially, or to stir emotions and entertain.

1. Here is website by Tony Rogers on the differences between broadsheets and tabloids. It also contains further interesting discussions about newspapers ethics, newspaper scandals in the UK, and the amount of choice available in obtaining news.

http://journalism.about.com/od/trends/fl/Whats-the-Difference-Between-Broadsheet-and-Tabloid-Newspapers.htm

2. Although designed for teachers and students, this site has a table showing many contrasts between broadsheets and tabloids, and has a quiz for you to take which shows a number of different broadsheet and tabloid newspapers.

https://webofnotes.wordpress.com/2014/04/28/broadsheet-and-tabloid-features-and-quiz/

30

HEADLINE GAMES

When I read the headline, I just had to buy the newspaper. How did the writer make the headline so interesting?

Headlines are the most noticeable feature of newspapers, with the possible exception of photographs. They serve a number of purposes. One is to inform you of the topic of the story. Another is to interest you so that you will want to read the story. But still another is commercial: to catch your attention so that you will want to buy a copy of the newspaper. Headlines may even be written so as to influence the opinion of the reader. Space is always at a premium, with only a few words and letter positions available. How do headline writers engage you with such little language?

Danuta Reah in her book *The Language of Newspapers* lists a number of techniques headline writers use to work with the concise format. One of the easiest ways to squeeze language is to

omit grammatical words. Look at the following full sentences, and then see how much shorter the actual headlines were (in italics):

- There is a new migrant surge on the way. → *New migrant surge on way*
- An eye test can be used to detect dementia. → *Eye test for dementia*
- The outdoor play time of children has halved. → *Outdoor play time halved*

Most of the information is contained in **content words** (like *test* and *dementia*), while the **grammatical words** (*there, has, the*) can often be deleted with little loss of meaning.

Another way to make language more concise is to use **noun phrases**. Instead of using descriptions like *the boy who is eating the sandwich,* the same information can be put in front of the noun in a much shorter form: *the sandwich-eating boy*. This type of noun phrase is very efficient in number of words used, and is therefore a common feature of headlines. Check the following examples:

- Police raid football hooligans in Israel. → *Israeli football hooligans raided*
- Airport meet-and-greet companies park tourists' cars on side streets → *Airport car park pirates*
- Workers risk extra taxes on their pensions. → *Pensions tax threat*

Writers often use **sound similarities** (alliteration and rhyme) to make headlines more interesting. (See §74 for more on these and other techniques used by literature and poetry authors.)

- *Billionaire baby bling: Hilton tot's gold pram* (alliteration: same initial sounds)
- *I'm not haven tax loopholes* (*having* is replaced by similar-sounding *haven*, which connects with idea of "tax haven")
- *A creed of pure greed* (this rhyming headline comments on how banks continue to be completely unethical)

Writers can make headlines catchy by making **reference to popular or well-known phrases and sayings**.

- *We did it, sunshine!* (story of a solar-powered around-the-world flight)
- *They ink it's all over* (story of removing tattoos of past lovers; plays on *think it's all over*)
- *Without a Tracy* (story of how an actress who played a soap opera character named Tracy Barlow as a child grew up and disappeared "without a trace" from the public eye)

A lot of **vocabulary** has more than one meaning (*polysemy*), and writers can exploit these multiple meanings to create attention-grabbing headlines.

- *Charles has a blast with rocket man* (Prince Charles talks with astronaut Tim Peake. So *blast* relates to both rocket launches (*blast-off*) and having a good time (*having a blast*).)
- *Robots cut it as surgeons* (robots prove effective in doing surgical procedures. *Cut it* means both 'surgical cuts' and 'be successful at something'.)
- *Arizona psychic hit by car says he never saw it coming* (literally, he never saw the car coming, but there is also the amusing suggestion that psychics should be able to foresee such situations)

Writers can also create an effect by using **loaded words**; i.e., ones with positive or negative connotations. We especially see this in tabloid newspapers (§29). The two following headlines emphasize a newspaper's distaste for a criminal (*maniac* and *monster*):

- *Hammer maniac killed girlfriend after serving 'life' for earlier murder*
- *Monster locked up again for 'extraordinary brutality'*

Conversely, see how the vocabulary in these headlines praises British rower Katherine Grainger for winning her 5th Olympic medal (*Great* and *glorious*):

- *Katherine the Great*
- *Glorious Grainger signs off with a silver medal*

Writing great headlines is an art, and understanding what goes into this creative process may even help you to enjoy them more. Knowing the principles of short, punchy writing can also help you use your own language more effectively, in everything from more widely read blogs (§31) to more effective PowerPoint presentations (§10).

~

Power Point: Newspaper writers know how to craft headlines to make them attention-grabbing and interesting with only a few words. Understanding their techniques may make reading newspapers more enjoyable, and also can provide ideas of how to make your own language punchier.

. . .

1. Here is a short webpage with a bit more explanation of loaded words (also called *emotive language*).

https://www.reference.com/education/examples-emotive-language

2. Tabloid newspapers often have the most creative headlines. This sites shows 9 classics.

https://www.mediafirst.co.uk/blog/our-all-time-favourite-news paper-headlines/

31

GOING VIRAL: BLOGS, TWEETS, AND INTERNET PAGES

What can I do to make my blogs more popular, and perhaps even go viral?

Social media has become incredibly popular. Estimates are that there were around 500 million tweets per day in 2020. Recently, other platforms have also become popular; for example, WhatsApp with around half a billion active daily users, and Snapchat with 293 million users worldwide. There are about 2.5 billion monthly active Facebook users, with the numbers steadily rising (including 269 million users in India alone). There are between 1.5 - 2 billion websites across the world (although less than 200 million are active in the sense that they get regular changes), many of them personal (all 2019 data).

With all these people putting their content out to the world, how do you get your message heard? Although there will always be some messages with massive uptake, the majority of sites only get relatively little attention. For example, less than one-quarter of tweets get a reply, and only 6% get retweeted.

Clearly, content will have a large effect on uptake—political scandals and amazing/funny photographs and videos will always be attractive to a lot of people. But there are things you can do to make your content attractive regardless of your topic. If you are successful, your messages might even *go viral*, where readers will be interested enough to reply to you or to share your message with their friends and followers on social media.

Jonah Berger and Katy Milkman (University of Pennsylvania) looked at what made online newspaper content go viral and take on a life of its own.

Content that evokes high-arousal emotions is more viral than content that evokes less strong emotional responses. This is true whether the emotional response is positive (awe) or negative (anger or anxiety).

But overall, viral content is more often positive than negative.

Content that is surprising, interesting, or practically useful is more likely to go viral.

There are many websites with advice on how to create content that will be contagious. Here are some suggestions that Neil Patel has given on his website:

- **Stop being neutral.** As Berger and Milkman found, you want to find an 'emotional hook' and get people excited, either positively or negatively.
- **Do something unexpected.** Surprising content will help you be different from everyone else and stand out.

- **Do not make advertisements.** If you are doing commercial messages, first make an interesting story, and keep the advertisement element subtle.
- **Make sequels.** If you have succeeded in gaining people's attention, analyze what went right and follow this up by providing more of the same.
- **Allow and promote sharing.** Make it easy for people to download and share your content, and put it on their social network sites.
- **Never restrict access.** Do not put up any barriers to easy access, like requiring people to register for your site or become members.
- **Connect with comments.** Be responsive to comments and show yourself to be accessible.

But beyond these techniques, using effective language is also important. First of all, headline writing is critical because it is the first impression you give your reader (§30). Advertising legend David Ogilvy famously said, "On average, five times as many people read the headline as read the body copy. When you have written your headline, you have spent eighty cents out of your dollar." Since your headline is essentially 'advertising' your message, it pays to get it right.

Linda Lai and Audun Farbrot (Norwegian Business School) found that question headlines (*Anyone need a new iPhone13?*) were more effective than statement headlines (*For sale: Silver iPhone13 512GB*) in generating readership on Twitter and a shopping website. But most effective were headlines that included the words *you* and *your* (*Is this your new iPhone13?*). Including *you* and *your* in headlines emphasize that the message is intended to be about the reader and for their benefit, which appears to capture attention.

Vocabulary that triggers emotions (awe, anger, anxiety, fear, joy, lust, surprise) is also effective in headlines. Here is a sample of words that proved successful in one website's headlines:

- *beautiful*
- *best*
- *brilliantepic*
- *fails*
- *fantastic*
- *gorgeous*
- *horrifying*
- *important*
- *lousy*
- *success*
- *ultimate*

Other words are useful because they are labels indicating the *type* of message being offered:

- *benefits*
- *checklist*
- *examples*
- *guidelines*
- *presentations*
- *reasons*
- *statistics*
- *trends*

But vocabulary is not just used in headlines; the right word choice can create interest and engagement throughout your message. John Morrow presents a list of hundreds of 'power words' that can connect with your readers' feelings in various ways. Here is just a sample:

. . .

- **Tapping into your readers' fears:** *agony, disastrous, frightening, panic, trap*
- **Perking up your readers:** *excited, jubilant, magic, triumph, victory*
- **Sex is always intriguing:** *brazen, lust, naked, naughty, sensual*
- **Create anger about injustice:** *abuse, arrogant, lies, ruthless, sick and tired*
- **Appeal to your readers' financial interests:** *bargain, discount, free, profit, savings*
- **Build your readers' trust:** *authentic, guaranteed, official, proven, no obligation*
- **Create curiosity about something forbidden:** *banned, bootleg, confidential, covert, illegal*

You can also play with the polysemy of words (§30) to create interest. For example, my heading for this unit could have been *Watch Out for Language Manipulators. Watch out* has the positive meaning of "pay attention" (*Watch out for when your favorite food is on sale*), but is more often used with the negative one of "beware" (*Watch out for pickpockets around here*). That heading would have played with both of these meanings: pay attention to the creative language use of the media and politicians, but also beware of when it is deceptive.

~

Power Point: Effective use of language, particularly vocabulary choice, can make your social media messages more engaging, and more likely to be shared.

1. On this site, Derek Halpern does a good job of summarizing Berger and Milkman's results on his *Social Triggers* website, following up with his own advice.

http://socialtriggers.com/craft-contagious-content

2. The first website gives Chris Lake's analysis of the headline vocabulary from 100 top *Econsultancy* articles. He highlights 28 words that convey emotion and 16 label words. In the second, Jon Morrow offers the full wordlists that can help you tap into a variety of your readers' emotions.

https://econsultancy.com/powerful-adjectives-verbs-headlines

https://smartblogger.com/power-words

32

POLITICS ON TALK SHOWS: FROM OPRAH WINFREY TO RUSH LIMBAUGH

It's the age of media. How do talk shows affect politics?

Politicians have long sought to use the power of broadcasting to create a favorable image. In the 1960 presidential campaign, Richard Nixon played the piano on *The Tonight Show* to show a more human side of himself. In 1992, Bill Clinton courted the young vote by playing his saxophone on the *Arsenio Hall Show*. Politicians now routinely appear on entertainment-oriented talk shows in search of a wider audience. While these shows tend to avoid taking political positions, the arrangement works for both sides. The shows often get a considerable ratings boost (generally 10%), for example, Al Gore's 2000 appearance on the *Oprah Winfrey Show* pushed the ratings up from an average 7.5 million households to 8.7 million.

The politicians also obtain many benefits. Some popular talk shows have enormous audiences, and politicians can enjoy massive exposure from talk show chats. But it is not just about raw numbers. Talk shows can put politicians in contact with hard-to-reach voters who do not follow more mainstream political programming. The softer and generally sympathetic entertainment-based approach also allows politicians to present a friendlier side than is often possible in 'harder' political programs. Talk show appearances are so effective that they have become an essential part of presidential campaigning strategies. Michael Parkin (Oberlin College) reports that between 1992 and 2012, there were more than 200 candidate interviews on daytime and late night talk shows, with nearly every presidential candidate participating.

Of course, more traditional news programming also covers politics, and usually attempts to be impartial (to varying degrees). But there are also more commercially driven broadcast talk shows, where the political content needs to be entertaining in order to maintain an audience. Richard Davis (BYU) describes ways in which these shows differ from traditional news media. They frequently personalize political news, with human interest stories being common. The content often focuses on high-interest topics like controversies, scandals, and the bizarre. Well-known personalities are sought after.

But Davis believes that the thing that sets these political talk shows apart from traditional media is their tendency to make inflammatory statements about both politicians and political groups. These provocative attacks certainly attract attention through shock value, but also provide entertainment for listeners who hold similar views.

The attacks can vary from being mild overstatements to being outright lies. Many of the techniques used are similar to propaganda techniques used by governments to discredit foreign adversaries in time of war (§36). Fair political critique is always healthy, but when attacks are knowingly based on falsehoods or deliberate manipulation of the facts, they can be considered little more than smear. Some of the techniques to look out for include the following. (See §37 for more detail on these and other smear techniques.)

- Attacking politicians personally rather than addressing their policies
- Labeling a politician with a negative label (e.g. *communist, femi-nazi*)
- Using loaded words when describing politicians (e.g. *warmonger, peacenik*)
- Telling half-truths, or bald-faced lies about someone
- Using innuendo to imply something about someone without actually saying it

There are many talk shows that use these techniques to various degrees. But for an example, it is probably fair to examine the most listened-to and influential political talk show of the last few decades (running from 1988-2021). *The Rush Limbaugh Show* had huge audience figures, being heard by millions of people (one estimate in 2019 suggested over 15.5 million weekly). Limbaugh once described himself as "the most dangerous man in America," and a CBS/Vanity Fair survey in 2009 identified him as the "most influential conservative voice in America." Davis identifies Limbaugh's show as one using a very provocative approach. So what are some examples of this approach?

Limbaugh often used loaded vocabulary to describe his targets. A favorite victim was Barack Obama, whom he called "a Chicago street thug," "a half-minority," a "Halfrican," "the little black man-child," and "essentially a primitive indigenous guy." Although political commentary should always be allowed, it is difficult to see how this kind of undignified labeling of a US Senator and President could be fair or appropriate. Equally shocking was Limbaugh's description of then Georgetown University law student Sandra Fluke as a "slut" and "prostitute."

There were also many cases of innuendo. One of his lines was "I love the women's movement. Especially when I am walking behind it," which was uttered during one of his attacks on feminism.

Then there were cases where the information was simply wrong. For example, on September 22, 2008, Limbaugh said "[Obama is] Arab. You know, he's from Africa. He's from the Arab parts of Africa." There has never been any evidence that Obama's family has an Arab background, less than 1% of the Kenyan population is Arab, and Barack Obama was born in the United States, not Kenya. Limbaugh's assertion was a clear falsehood, and few other commentators took it up. Yet it showed the power of Limbaugh's show because a substantial portion of Americans ended up believing it. An Annenberg Public Policy Center poll of 3,000 people after the 2008 elections showed that 22% incorrectly believed Obama was half Arab.

Despite (or probably because of) techniques like those above, his show remained popular with a particular demographic of listener, sometimes called *Ditto Heads*. (It is interesting that this term now has the additional negative meaning of "One who mindlessly agrees with an idea, especially those who agree because they are supporters of the person who started the idea" *Wiktionary.*)

Politics and running a country are serious business and should not be consigned merely to entertainment. People need to recognize the difference between commentary and interviews done mainly for entertainment value, and those attempting to deal with serious issues in a more thoughtful and balanced manner.

Power Point: Don't believe everything you see or hear, especially on talk shows.

1. This site has an extended talk by Michael Parkin, where he discusses information from his book *Talk Show Campaigns: Presidential Candidates on Daytime and Late Night Television.*

https://vimeo.com/140454369

2. Here is a phone interview by John Wilson, who wrote *The Most Dangerous Man in America,* a book highly critical of Rush Limbaugh and his techniques. Disregard the wonky subtitles.

https://www.youtube.com/watch?v=Av4QZt6yeE0

33

POLITICS AND LANGUAGE

Politics is complicated. What kind of language do politicians and commentators use to discuss issues, and is this language biased?

Politics. It is hard to discuss it without betraying some kind of bias or evaluation in the language you use. A politician could be labeled as liberal, conservative, or centrist, and that might seem an impartial way to describe their policies. But the terms *liberal* and *conservative* can carry very positive or negative connotations depending on the listener's viewpoint. Even *centrist* could be considered undesirable, if one feels that the politician has no strong convictions (e.g., always sitting on the fence). The way of describing the strength of their convictions on an issue can also carry emotive power. Consider the following descriptions. Do they make you feel supportive or disapproving: *extremist, radical, hawk, moderate, dove*?

So choice of language is always influential in describing politicians and their ideologies. In his book *The Language of Politics*, author

Adrian Beard shows how *metaphor, metonymy,* and *analogy* are often used in political discourse.

Metaphor

Metaphor is when a word or idea is used to establish a comparison between things that are not literally related, in order to suggest a similarity. For example, *The senator is a brick wall* does not mean that they are literally made of bricks, but the image of them stopping anything from passing through is vividly elicited. Metaphor is important because it affects the way we think and talk about the world around us. Take the metaphor ANGER=HEAT. From this, we get sayings like *blow up* for being angry, *cool down* as a request to become less angry, and *blow off steam* for the need to release stress when angry.

In §28, we saw that the use of metaphor is influential in how news reports are perceived in newspapers. The same is true in politics. Two common sources of political metaphor are sports and war, both of which have associations of physical confrontation. A small sampling of headlines from the 2016 presidential election illustrates these:

- *Trump Says He's Taking Gloves Off in Fight Against Clinton* (This refers to boxing, where taking boxing gloves off would mean fighting bare-knuckled in a much more dangerous way)
- *Home run for front runners* (Trump's primary win in New York is likened to a home run in baseball, where the batter decisively hits the ball out of the park)
- *With party conventions over, Trump and Clinton campaigns hit the ground running* (Like soldiers jumping off of helicopters, both campaigns leapt straight into the attack)

- *Clinton braces for fight on Trump's terrain* (This headline about Clinton's need to campaign more like Trump brings up images of physical battlefields)

Of course political campaigns are a contest, but the end goal of politics is to run a country successfully. This usually requires consensus-building and working together, and here is where the metaphors of sport and war can be counterproductive. If the rhetoric is always of winning (often at any cost), then anything less than total victory is seen as complete defeat, which makes it difficult to reach any kind of reasonable compromise.

Metonymy

Metonymy is replacing the name of something with something related to it, but only part of it. Examples are *Washington* for the entire US government (even though it is only the city where the government is located) and *9/11* for the whole series of terrorist attacks and aftermath (even though it was only the date).

In politics, metonymy can certainly affect perceptions. Beard gives the example of a BBC news report on the increasing tensions between the US and Iraq in the early 2000s: *The White House today threatened Saddam Hussein with military action over the UN inspectors affair.* By using *White House,* this formulation indirectly drew personal responsibility away from the President and his advisers for threating war. Also, Saddam Hussein was not popular, so using him to represent all of Iraq made the threats seem more reasonable, and took attention away from the many innocent Iraqis who might be harmed by a war. An alternative headline would have a completely different feeling: *President Bush threatened the Iraqi people with war over the UN inspectors affair.*

Likewise, *Watergate* (only an office and apartment complex) is now widely understood to represent Richard Nixon's misdeeds. It is so well-known that *-gate* has become a commonly used suffix to indicate political scandals (e.g. *Emailgate, Bridgegate, Partygate, Plebgate, Lawyergate*).

Analogy

While metaphor and metonymy make comparisons through words and phrases, *analogies* work on a larger scale. For example, when talking about the Kuwait Gulf War in 1990-1991, two contrasting analogies were used. Opponents of the war used the Vietnam War as their comparison, as the Vietnam War was widely unpopular and seen by many to have been pointless. Supporters of the war used WWII, which is typically viewed as a justified struggle necessary to stop a dangerous maniac. This also had the effect of casting Saddam Hussein as the new Hitler. It is not hard to see how the choice of analogy would lead to very different storylines.

Analogies can be used about almost any political issue. In 2012, Republicans often attacked President Obama about poor economic performance, but without acknowledging he inherited a $1 trillion deficit from the previous Republican president, George W. Bush. Obama rebutted these attacks with a restaurant analogy that everybody could understand: *It's like somebody goes to a restaurant, orders a big steak dinner, martini, all that stuff, and then, just as you're sitting down, they leave and accuse you of running up the tab!*

Power Point: In order to make politics more understandable and more interesting, politicians and commentators often make comparisons between political persons/issues and

everyday ideas. The comparisons made can lead to more positive or more negative evaluations.

1. This site gives six noteworthy examples of metaphors in presidential speeches.

http://literarydevices.net/top-6-great-metaphors-in-presidential-speeches/

2. This Wikipedia page lists a number of common political metaphors.

https://en.wikipedia.org/wiki/List_of_political_metaphors

34

POLITICIANS: SPINNING LANGUAGE

How can I know whether politicians are telling the truth or spinning language for their own purposes?

I suspect that for most people, the whole 'spin' family (e.g. *political spin, to spin a story, spin doctor*) is full of negative overtones. The whole idea of spin is not to report events or news in an unbiased manner, but rather to manipulate the information so that people understand it in a way that is favorable to the politician or political party doing the spinning. Politicians want us to believe them, but often without thinking about the real meaning of their statements. In essence, spin is a form of propaganda, and some of its techniques are deceptive in the extreme.

There are numerous spin techniques, some of which are discussed elsewhere in this book: use of labels (§28), metaphors (§28 & §33), emotional vocabulary (§29), weasel words (§13 & §14), avoiding the question (§35), and various smear techniques (§37). Some other common ones include the following:

Burying bad news

One of the most effective ways of avoiding bad news staining a politician or party is to announce it at a time when few people will notice. For instance, this could be when other important news is dominating the headlines, or on summer long weekends when no one is around.

Cherry picking

This is selecting only the bits of information that show the person or event in the best light. The reporting of unmanned drone strikes in Pakistan illustrates this tactic. Reports typically announce the number of 'militants' killed, but seldom mention (or underestimate) the number of civilians also killed. One such case was a March 17, 2011 multiple-missile attack on a civilian meeting in the town of Datta Khel in Pakistan, where people were gathered to resolve a dispute over a nearby chromite mine. US officials publicly claimed that all victims were militants, but a joint Stanford University and New York University investigation found that of the approximately 42 killed and 14 wounded, all were civilians except for four Taliban members who were also attending the meeting.

Fake denials and apologies

These are statements that are made to appear like denials and apologies, but when examined closely are actually non-denials and non-apologies. One way of achieving this is to use passive voice sentences like "Mistakes were made" (§28). This does not name the person making the mistake, and so no one takes responsibility. It also mitigates the error, because it sounds like an "honest mistake" that anyone could make, rather than a more serious error, incompetence, or dirty dealings.

A famous misleading denial was Bill Clinton's effort to deny his sexual misconduct with Monica Lewinsky: "I did not have sexual relations with that woman." Of course he did, but he was using a deceptively strict definition of 'sexual relations' to mean only sexual intercourse or *giving* oral sex, but not *receiving* it.

Presenting unproven things as facts and truths

Politicians and commentators can sound convincing by using figures and statements which they present as facts, but which in reality have little or no scientific evidence or proof behind them. If they do this knowingly and on purpose, most people may well consider this lying. For example, Donald Trump is one politician who has consistently been caught presenting unsubstantiated information presented as truth, only to have follow-up investigations show that it was false, or at least misleading.

In the 2016 U.S Presidential election, the *Washington Post* awarded its maximum dishonesty rating (4 Pinocchios – §37) to a majority of the Trump statements it checked—65% on Sept. 26, 2016. But even many of the rest received 3 Pinocchios, which means "mostly false." Some examples of these whoppers include Trump's claim that Barack Obama was not born in the US, that the real US unemployment rate was 42%, and that thousands of Muslims in New Jersey celebrated the 9/11 attacks. As President, things did not get better, with the newspaper reporting that he made 16,241 false or misleading claims in his first three years in office. Such false or misleading claims are extremely problematic, because once a claim has been made, it often gains legs, and people may continue to believe it even if it is later proven false.

Create feelings without content

Politicians are good at saying things that make you feel good without saying anything concrete which you might hold them to later. BBC presenter John Humphrys described a Labor party speech given by former British Prime Minister Tony Blair in which 163 of Blair's sentences contained no verb. When listening to the speech, Humphrys reported being excited by catchphrases like "Hope!", "Achievement!", and "The Future, not the Past!" But when he thought about it afterwards, he realized that without verbs, it was just sloganeering, without details about how these worthy goals might be achieved.

Spin works partly because, in general, people are not that well informed about politics. There are sites available to check the facts of political statements (§37), but many (most?) people are not interested in delving into the political debate to that degree. Quizzes by the Pew Research Center show that the public knows basic facts about politics, but often struggles with specific details.

For example, in late August 2016, 82% of Americans recognized Kim Jong-un as the leader of North Korea, and 78% knew that the Guantanamo Bay military prison is in Cuba. But only 52% knew the strength of the Republican majority in the US Senate, and only 33% knew that there were three female justices on the US Supreme Court. Being more knowledgeable about politics in general, and being able to spot spin techniques, are good ways to counter the effects of the widespread use of spin in politics.

Check your own political (and other) knowledge with Pew quizzes:

https://www.pewresearch.org/publications/?formats=quiz#recent-publications

~

Power Point: There are many techniques that politicians use to portray themselves in a positive light and their opponents negatively. But spin harms political debate if truth is distorted or ignored. A good defense against spin is a knowledgeable public who recognize the spin techniques.

1. David Greenberg (Rutgers University) gives his take on spin, and how it is not new or always that effective.

https://www.washingtonpost.com/opinions/five-myths-about-spin/2016/03/18/eb8153d2-ecac-11e5-a6f3-21ccdbc5f74e_story.html

2. These *Washington Post* fact-checker pages outline how former President Trump has a strong tendency to spin language in misleading ways.

https://www.washingtonpost.com/politics/2020/01/20/president-trump-made-16241-false-or-misleading-claims-his-first-three-years

https://www.washingtonpost.com/news/fact-checker/wp/2016/03/22/all-of-donald-trumps-four-pinocchio-ratings-in-one-place

35

POLITICIANS: ANSWERING QUESTIONS (OR NOT)

Why can't politicians give a straight answer to questions?

Politicians are often accused of not answering questions, and avoiding saying anything of substance in interviews. The hesitancy is real about saying anything too concrete, which could be used against them in the future, but there is more to the story than just political evasiveness. In his book *The Language of Politics,* Adrian Beard explains why short, simple, and straightforward responses may not always be appropriate. To understand why, it is important to consider a number of Beard's points about the way political interviews work.

1. Interviews are supposed to be about getting information from politicians. A simple short answer to an important question may well seem completely unsatisfactory. Imagine a politician being asked about whether the US was pursuing ways of limiting the spread of nuclear weapons, and their answer was just "Yes".

2. Expecting straightforward answers implies that the questions are also straightforward, and allow a straightforward response. This is often not the case. Political interviews have become increasingly confrontational in recent years, with interviewers often bringing their own agenda or preconceptions to the questioning. It is thus unfair to look only at the answers, without considering the questions and their biases.

Interviewers' preconceptions can come out in the form of extended questions where there are assumptions stated before getting to the question. (Note that while interviewers can interrupt answers, it is very unusual for their questions to be interrupted.) Consider the following extract from an interview with Donald Trump by ABC's George Stephanopoulos. In it, Stephanopoulos makes a number of statements about what he views as Trump's cozy relationship with Russia and Vladimir Putin:

> ***STEPHANOPOULOS:*** *Vice President Biden told me this week that Vladimir Putin wants to beat Hillary. And Madeleine Albright said that your victory would be a gift to Putin. And what they're pointing to is things like— your statements about conditioning our commitments to NATO allies, softening the GOP platform on Ukraine, even considering softening sanctions and recognizing Russian annexation of Crimea. They fear that that's gonna hurt America and advance Russia's interests.*

Politicians cannot let assumptions they disagree with remain unchallenged, or they would be seen as implicitly agreeing with those assumptions. So they must first spend time rebutting the assumptions before moving to the main question, even though this can sometimes give the feeling of evading the main question.

3. Yes/No questions may seem to like a direct route towards getting unambiguous answers. Some confrontational interviewers may use them to try to force an unambiguous answer. But for the reasons given above, it may be very difficult for politicians to give a Yes/No response without oversimplifying an issue or leaving out critical details.

4. Sometimes interviewers' "questions" actually have no questions. This can make it very hard for a politician to give a response, and can lead to them appearing less competent. For example, here is an extract from an interview by ABC newsman David Muir with Hillary Clinton in 2016. Can you find a question in his "inquiry"?

> ***MUIR:*** *So let me ask you, you have said that Donald Trump does not have the right temperament to be president. He said of you that you lack judgment. He points to your emails. The last time we sat down, you apologized. You've said it was a mistake. But Trump says, FBI investigation aside, that what Hillary Clinton is guilty of is quote, "stupidity and bad judgment." And he asks, "How can a person with this kind of judgment become the president?"*

5. Many interviews are focused on breaking political events, and so both the interviewer and politician may not be as well-prepared as they would like for a full discussion of the situation.

6. More inexperienced politicians may simply lack practice and confidence when giving interviews.

7. The time to answer questions is typically very short. This can be made even worse by the tendency to edit interview responses down to short clips (sometimes in search of the killer sound bite) that fit into tight network newscast time-frames. (The average amount of actual news time after commercials on American evening network news broadcasts is only about 22-23 minutes.) Political issues are typically quite complex, and so politicians might be rightfully cautious about making short responses that do not give an accurate indication of the reality.

Nevertheless, there are times that politicians simply wish to evade the question. Here are a few tactics for doing this.

8. Shifting the topic Also known as 'the pivot.' This involves shifting the topic from something the politician does not want to talk about to something he does. For example, in a 2004 Bush-Kerry debate, Bush moved from a question about lack of jobs to an answer about education in two or three sentences. However, Todd Rogers (Harvard) found that unless the shift is really obvious (e.g. from a question about terrorism to a health care answer), people do not seem to notice, and do not penalize the politician.

9. Using a transition device These are phrases inserted before a pivot that divert people's attention away from the original question. They often compliment the interviewer, making the pivot seem less obvious:

> *That's a good question, but what we really need to do is ...*
>
> *I'm glad you asked that because it brings up another important point ...*

10. Quoting facts and figures This can make politicians look more trustworthy, and the facts are not easily verifiable on the spot. Of course, they will inevitably pick the numbers that support their position best.

11. Pretending they did not understand the question This can be used as a stall technique by asking the interviewer to repeat or elaborate on the question. If the interview is being done remotely, the politician can pretend the line is bad.

So how can we catch politicians dodging questions? Research shows just paying better attention helps; when viewers were asked to focus on politicians' efforts to dodge, they were much more successful at detecting those dodges. Also, posting questions on the screen while politicians answered also improved detection.

Power Point: There are times when politicians wish to avoid answering questions, but sometimes it is the constraints of the interview process itself that lead to less straightforward responses.

1. This is a British website that takes a slightly tongue-in-cheek approach to political question evasion, but makes a number of valid points in a humorous way.

https://www.youtube.com/watch?v=T8QOE-IWo3I

2. Here is a National Public Radio webpage giving more details about pivots' and how people do not seem to notice them.

http://www.npr.org/2012/10/03/162103368/how-politicians-get-away-with-dodging-the-question

36

POLITICIANS: SELLING WAR

How do politicians talk us into things we do not want to do, like going to war?

Of all the things politicians can do, perhaps the most serious is taking a nation into war. Assuming all right-thinking people are opposed to war in principle, how do politicians justify going to war, and how do they whip up enthusiasm (or at least tolerance) for it? The necessity of many wars is quite murky, so to convince people to support them, politicians resort to all types of language tactics.

• **Overstated evidence** In 1998, British Prime Minister Tony Blair was trying to convince the UK to go to war with Iraq under Saddam Hussein. A key part of the evidence Blair presented was the assertion that Iraq had Weapons of Mass Destruction (WMD). Blair said he believed that intelligence "established beyond doubt" that Iraq was continuing to produce chemical and biological weapons. But British intelligence agencies were very unsure about this, with one report making it clear that as long as sanctions remained effective, Iraq could not produce a nuclear weapon. Nevertheless, Blair effectively presented the WMDs as a confirmed fact. In 2016, the Chilcot Report verified that the threats posed by Iraq's WMD were presented to the Parliament and public with a certainty that was not justified. Before going to war, it is important to pin down politicians on just how sure they are of their information.

• **Branding the adversary as evil** In order to justify attacking an adversary, it is necessary to portray them as evil in some way. Using labels and loaded vocabulary are ways of doing this (§28 & §29):

- George W. Bush called Iran, Iraq, and North Korea the *Axis of Evil*
- The widespread labeling of adversaries as *terrorists*
- References to Muammar Gaddafi as a *dictator* and to Libya as an *international pariah*
- Labeling detainees from the wars in Iraq and Afghanistan as *unlawful enemy combatants* allowed them to be held virtually indefinitely at military prisons

• **Dehumanizing the adversary** It is easier to paint adversaries as evil if they portrayed as somehow different from us. Often this involves dehumanization.

- The Nazis viewed Jews, Roma, and other groups as *unwanted elements*
- Throughout history, it has been common to come up with demeaning nicknames for the enemy once war starts: WWII: *Jerry/Kraut* = German, *Jap/Nip* = Japanese. Korean

War: *Gook* = North Korean. Vietnam War: *Charlie* = Viet Cong. Iraq War: *Ali Baba* = Iraqi insurgent or local thief/looter.

- Although not as a prelude to war, in the early 1900s, the Australian government legally dehumanized their Aboriginal peoples by explicitly excluding them from other Australian humans in terms of laws, voting rights, social security benefits, and census counting.

• **Myth of a limited war** Leaders seldom spell out beforehand just how unpredictable and all-consuming war can be. Tom Mockaitis (DePaul University) points out two important, but often forgotten, truths: "First, getting into conflicts is much easier than getting out of them."

- In mid-1914, one of the most popular sayings was that WWI would be "over by Christmas," although it lasted until November 11, 1918.
- After US military involvement since 2001, the US was supposed to withdraw troops from Afghanistan by the end of 2014. But this did not happen until 2021, in what turned out to be a very messy evacuation.

Mockaitis's second point is that "the cost in blood and treasure of virtually every major war that has ever been fought has far exceeded the optimistic estimates of the political leaders who started it." Almost all wars expand and become more involved, and there is even a term for this ever-increasing involvement: *mission creep*.

The Vietnam War is a classic example of this. On March 8, 1965, 3,500 US Marines were sent to Vietnam to provide temporary defensive protection for airbases. By December of the same year, the numbers had increased to nearly 200,000. By the time the US finally left Vietnam in 1975, around 2.7 Americans had served there.

• **Dishonesty or evasion about the costs of war** War is eye-wateringly costly in many ways. The most important cost is human lives. The US Department of Veterans Affairs gives the following figures for servicemembers killed:

- WWII (1941-1945): 291,557
- Korean War (1950-1953): 36,574
- Vietnam War (1964-1975): 58,220
- Persian Gulf War (1990-1991): 383

Wars are also expensive in terms of money. A 2010 report by the Congressional Research Center estimated the costs of recent wars (in 2011 dollars):

- Vietnam War (1965-1975) $738 billion
- Persian Gulf War (1990-1991) $102 billion
- Iraq (2003-2010) $784 billion

$ The Watson Institute at Brown University reports that most current wars have been paid for mainly by borrowing. This has increased the US budget deficit, and unless the war bills are paid immediately (basically impossible), there could be future interest payments of over $6.5 trillion by 2050s.

$ It is not only the cost of fighting the war. In 2016, the *L.A. Times* reported on the rising cost of veterans' healthcare and benefits, with the biggest increase in spending being on disability and pension pay for disabled veterans (from $33.3 billion in 2002 to $64.8 billion in 2013). Similarly, the

Watson Institute found that federal spending on veteran care doubled from 2.4% to 4.9% of the US budget between 2001 and 2020. It estimates that the costs of caring for post-9/11 war veterans will reach between $2.2 and $2.5 trillion by 2050.

- **Long-term consequences** Wars have long-lasting consequences that most politicians would rather not mention. One of the biggest scourges of past wars is landmines. The International Campaign to Ban Landmines recorded that at least 7,073 people were killed or injured by mines and other explosive remnants of war in 2020. However, the true number of casualties is almost certainly higher than this, as many are not reported. Around 60 countries are still contaminated by landmines, which are indiscriminate and remain active for decades, mainly injuring civilians, including children.

Politicians can be persuasive getting us into war, but hate to take responsibility for wars that go badly (don't they all?). A famous non-apology was Tony Blair's refusal to admit it was a mistake to take the UK into the Iraq War based on weak and faulty information about WMDs, "If I was back in the same place, with the same information, I would take the same decision because obviously that was the decision I believe was right."

Power Point: The next time you hear politicians or pundits promoting war, think about the above costs before jumping on the bandwagon.

1. This is the US Department of Veterans Affairs information sheet on war statistics, including servicemembers deployed, battle deaths, non-mortal woundings, and living veterans.

http://www.va.gov/opa/publications/factsheets/fs_americas_wars.pdf

2. Here is the full report by Stephen Daggett, which shows that the US spent over a trillion dollars for wars between 9/11 (2001) and 2010.

https://www.fas.org/sgp/crs/natsec/RS22926.pdf

37

THE ART OF SMEAR: NAMING-CALLING, LIES, AND INNUENDO

I heard a talk show commentator completely slam a politician they opposed. He claimed all sorts of scandalous things, but gave no evidence for any of it. What are some of the techniques of "smear" that I can watch out for when listening to someone like this?

We have all heard it—politicians bad-mouthing their opponents in an attempt to discredit them. Political talk show hosts promoting their agenda by painting any contradictory view as dishonest, evil, or unpatriotic. This kind of unsavory behavior can be called many things (e.g., *negative campaigning, swiftboating, character assassination*), but I will just use the term *smear* in this section.

Not surprisingly, most people dislike smear attacks. Keena Lipsitz (City University of New York) and colleagues report that the majority of Americans believe that "negative, attack-oriented campaigning is undermining and damaging our democracy" (82%), that unethical practices in campaigns occur "very" or "fairly" often

(58%), and that "in terms of ethics and values, election campaigns in this country have gotten worse in the last 20 years" (53%).

Yet they still persist, and are often perceived as effective by campaigners and pundits. John Sides (George Washington University) and colleagues found that although citizens do not necessarily like smear campaigns, they sometimes find them informative. Thus, negative campaigns do not always lead to alienation or lower voter turnout, as you might expect. In fact, Ken Goldstein (University of Wisconsin-Madison) and Paul Freedman (University of Virginia) found that negative advertisements can actually stimulate voter turnout by engaging voters, raising interest, and communicating the notion that something important is at stake in the outcome of an election.

It is unlikely that smears and misinformation will disappear anytime soon, so how do you spot them? There are a number of smear techniques to watch out for, some of which are discussed below.

- **Attacking the person rather than the policy** A classic way of drawing attention away from issues is to attack the person themselves. This is now common in many political contests, because candidates have to spend time rebutting the attacks rather than on promoting their views. A classic example of this was Donald Trump's slogan "crooked Hillary" (Clinton), even though she was never convicted of any crime.
- **Negative labeling** Attaching a damaging label on someone is a powerful way of attacking them (§28). In the US in the 1950s, Joseph McCarthy ruined the careers of many people by asserting they were communists, whether this was true or not.

- **Using loaded words** A recurring theme in this unit is the powerful effect of vocabulary, especially loaded emotive vocabulary (§29). Instead of referring to a person with descriptions such as *public servant, expert,* or *supporter of the military,* they can be described with terms like *bureaucrat, elitist,* or *warmonger* to create a much more negative impression.
- **Creating negative associations** In this technique, an attempt is made to link the person with some unrelated but negatively evaluated person, group, or idea. It is then hoped that the listener will transfer their adverse feelings onto the attacked person. In the 2012 presidential race, John McCain's campaign showed Barack Obama along with pictures of celebrities Britney Spears and Paris Hilton. By doing this, it tried to portray Obama as only a lightweight celebrity himself and not serious presidential material. In 2020, Donald Trump often called Joe Biden "sleepy Joe" in an attempt to associate Biden with a feeling of diminished mental ability.
- **Half-truths** A smear can be more effective if it contains some grain of truth, often selectively extracted from a bigger picture. This can then be exaggerated and exploited as if it were the whole truth. In the 2016 Brexit vote of whether the UK should leave the European Union, a claim was made by the Leave campaign that Britain was sending £350 million per day to the EU. While basically true, this (intentionally) failed to report that the UK received much of this back from the EU in rebates, subsidies, and grants, and so the net output was nowhere near the £350 million figure. This is also called *cherry-picking* (§34).
- **Pure Lies** Simple—just make something up about your opponent. In the 2016 presidential campaign, Donald Trump asserted that Barack Obama literally "founded ISIS.

I would say the co-founder would be crooked Hillary Clinton." While it could be argued that Obama's and Clinton's foreign policy and military decisions helped create a space in which ISIS could operate and expand, Trump's claim of literal founding was so wild that the Politifact web site rated it as *Pants on Fire*.

- **Innuendo** This is an indirect remark or reference that implies (rather than states directly) something negative. A classic example of this is Lyndon Johnson's 1964 "Daisy" television commercial, which showed a young girl counting as she picked petals off of a daisy flower. This led into a rocket-launch countdown and a nuclear explosion. Although never mentioned by name, or explicitly stated with language, the implication was that a win by Johnson's opponent, Barry Goldwater, might lead to nuclear war and the death of many such girls.
- **Intentional vagueness** When making assertions, one tactic is to remain vague, so that one cannot be pinned down about facts. A very common case of this is asserting something based on some unknown authority; for example, *People say that ...* or *Scientists have found that ...* (What people? What scientists? What is the evidence? Are there even any scientists involved?)
- **Quotes taken out of context** Extracted sections of quotes without their context can be extremely misleading. Businessman and 2012 presidential hopeful Mitt Romney was criticized for his quote "I like being able to fire people," which sounds exceedingly insensitive. But the full context shows he was talking about health care and the desirability of being able to fire one's healthcare providers if they prove unsatisfactory and to choose a competing health insurance company. In this context, the quote seems entirely more reasonable.

- **Repetition** The simple repetition of a falsehood can eventually give it the appearance of truth.
- **Black and white approach** Limiting options to two extremes can cut out any nuanced central ground. The slogan *America: Love It or Leave It* is a good example, discounting any possibility that a person can love the US but also see problems that need to be addressed.

Power Point: Smear techniques rely on putting forth false or partial information that is presented as fact. They also incorporate negative labeling and associations to promote damaging impressions.

1. Smear techniques have much in common with propaganda techniques, as one of the main purposes of propaganda is to discredit people, movements, and governments seen as undesirable. This Wikipedia entry lists a number of propaganda techniques.

https://en.wikipedia.org/wiki/Propaganda_techniques

2. Here are three fact-checking websites. The first is the Pulitzer-prize winning website *Politifact* run by the Poynter Institute for Media Studies, which rates political statements on a *Truth-O-Meter* scale (TRUE, MOSTLY TRUE, HALF TRUE, MOSTLY FALSE, FALSE). There is also a PANTS ON FIRE rating for statements that are not accurate and make a ridiculous claim. This comes from the rhyme *Liar, Liar, Pants on Fire. Your nose is as long as a telephone wire*. The second is run by the Annenberg Public Policy Center at the University of Pennsylvania. The third is run by the

Washington Post, and uses 4 'Pinocchios' to indicate serious 'long-nose' whoppers.

http://www.politifact.com

http://www.factcheck.org

https://www.washingtonpost.com/news/fact-checker

PART 5

THE LANGUAGE OF TEXTING, COMPUTERS, AND THE INTERNET

38

WRITTEN LANGUAGE: THE EXPLOSION OF TEXTING

Young people text a lot nowadays. Is this a problem?

Technology has always affected language use from the earliest days. Around 3,000 BCE, humankind learned to store language on clay tablets in a wedge-shaped written script called *cuneiform*. In medieval times, applying ink to parchment made written text much more versatile. Later, the printing press made written language available to a much wider audience. The telegraph made long-distance communication possible through a language system called Morse Code (e.g. · · · / — — — / · · · = SOS). The telephone allowed voice communications at a distance. Each of these inventions influenced language and the way it was transmitted to wider and wider audiences.

However, few of these innovations could rival Short Message Service messages (i.e. *texting*) for the speed in which it became a dominant mode of communication. The first text message was sent to a phone in 1992, but for several years texting was mainly confined to businesses. Eventually phone companies figured out how to charge for the service and made it available to the wider public.

It was taken up slowly at first, with only 35 messages per month for the average user in 2000. But after that, use mushroomed, especially among younger users. In 2010, the Pew Research Center reported that half of teenagers sent 50 or more texts per day and one-third sent more than 100 a day. By 2013, the average figure for smartphone users had risen to 67 per day, though by 2019, it had dropped to a still substantial 39 per day.

It seems likely that text messaging will continue to be popular, but texts are increasingly being sent over the internet through instant messaging apps rather than over phone networks. For example, WhatsApp reported handing more than 100 billion messages every day in 2020.

While young people are the most active texters, adults also text extensively. While it is hard to find good information about current usage, the graph below is still indicative. It shows the relative amounts of texting by US smartphone users of various ages in 2013. The number of texts per month decreases with age, but even people over 55 still used texts over 16 times per day on average. Overall, people tend to use their smartphones more for texting than calling. For everyday chat via phones, there has been a shift from oral to written communication. Clearly, texting is a widespread phenomenon that is not restricted to teenagers, with the term *texting* making it into dictionaries.

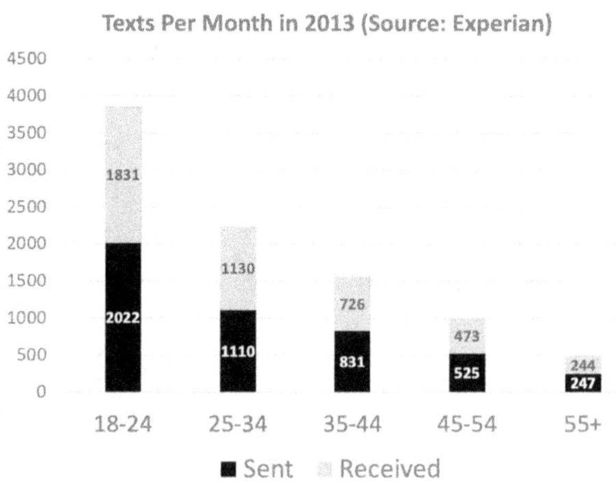

Why is texting so popular? It obviously fills a communicative need, and has many advantages. The one that really got texting going was that it is generally cheaper than a voice call. For some simple communications ("meet me at 5pm"), it is quicker and easier than calling. Also, you can send and answer texts when you like without worrying about your friend's schedule. It can be less annoying in public places than talking on the phone. Texts can also work better in areas of inconsistent network coverage.

People text about anything and everything, and the frequency of texting suggests that texting is bringing people closer together, or at least in more frequent contact.

The increased writing involved in composing numerous texts might even lead to some learning advantages. Beverly Plester (Coventry University) and colleagues found that frequent use of textual abbreviations and other alterations ('textisms') corresponded with better reading ability for 10-12 year-old school students in the UK.

So are there any downsides to texting? Linguistic purists might think that texting is degrading language, but this prejudice has no basis in fact (§39). However, there are some real problems. All cell phone use while driving is dangerous, and that seems particularly true of texting. Below are some scary statistics, but they are from around 2010, and hopefully people have learned about the dangers of distractions while driving since then:

- 40% of American teenagers said they had been in a car where the driver put people in danger because they used a cell phone.
- The crash risk of texting while driving was 23 times worse than driving while not being distracted.
- 11% of drivers aged 18 to 20 surviving an automobile accident later admitted they were sending or receiving texts when they crashed.

Loss of sleep is another problem. People text at all times of the day, including night time. Over half of 18-24-year-olds polled said they sent or received texts every hour up until midnight. In another study, 20-25% of teenagers were woken up from sleep by texts. This constant texting disrupts sleep patterns, and the blue light from phone screens also seems to interfere with the ability to fall asleep by interrupting the release of melatonin.

Texting is also becoming more common during school hours. A survey by Mary Madden (Pew Research Center) found that of teenagers who take their phones to school, 48% had them turned on during school every day, 31% sent or received a text during class every day, and 4% even made or received a call during class every day. Even in schools that prohibit all phones, 58% of students admitted to having sent or received a text in class at some point.

This can be distracting in class, but for some teenagers, texting has become an addiction. Kelly Landman (Delaware County Community College) and co-researchers gave a questionnaire about texting use to 356 8th grade and high school juniors, and found that more girls than boys were compulsive texters. Surprisingly, compulsive texting did not seem to affect boys' academic achievement. However, compulsive texting did lower girls' reported grades, their perceptions of their own competence, and their attitudes towards school.

Power Point: Texting can be a convenient means of communication, and is currently the most common use of cell phones. However, it can be problematic if misused, potentially leading to loss of sleep, and distraction while driving or at school. It can also become compulsive, especially for teenage girls.

1. Here are some 2022 statistics about texting on the website SlickText. They are interesting, but are likely to quickly become out-of-date with such a fast-changing technology.

https://www.slicktext.com/blog/2018/11/44-mind-blowing-sms-marketing-and-texting-statistics

2. This *New York Times* piece by Roni Caryn Rabin discusses teenage compulsive texting in more detail.

https://well.blogs.nytimes.com/2015/10/12/compulsive-texting-takes-toll-on-teenagers

39

IS TEXTING RUINING OUR LANGUAGE?

Texting looks messy and not at all like "proper" writing. Is it killing our ability to write?

Many people worry that technology is negatively affecting our language. With email and social media, fewer people write and mail letters nowadays. People sit alone at their computers for hours on end and do not have face-to-face conversations with anyone. But one of the things that worries and irritates some people most is texting on mobile phones. The writing looks different to someone not used to it, and this causes some people to think that it is destroying our ability to write in the traditional sense of the word.

But is this true? In an informative and amusing 2013 TED talk, John McWhorter (a linguist from Columbia University) argues this is an overreaction. Spoken and written language have their own distinctive styles and ways of expression (§92), and people generally have no problem keeping the two types of language separate. For example, you would not have a nice chat with your best friend in the style of an encyclopedia entry. Conversely, you would not write a wedding invitation in the same manner you would chat with your friend at a barbecue.

Just as people can keep spoken and written styles separate in their minds, McWhorter explains that they can also keep different writing styles separate. This should be obvious; all of us know that the written style we use for grocery lists differs from personal letters, which differs from the essays we submit to university courses. In fact, the ability to switch comfortably between these written styles is a good thing and a mark of proficiency with language. McWhorter argues that texting is simply one more style (or "dialect") of writing, which is useful for many people to know.

Before we criticize texting, it is worth taking a closer look at it. First, it exists for a purpose. Mobile (cell) phones and cheap texting rates are everywhere, and people want to use them to communicate via texts. However, the text format has space limitations, and phones do not have full-sized, easy-to-use keyboards. This created the need for a shortened written format to use on portable electronic devices (§40). Second, texts are used much more like quick spoken utterances than full-blown written passages. This is not surprising, as spoken language has historically been the primary means of communication. Spoken language has been around for perhaps 100,000 years, while written language is a relative newcomer, with the earliest writing dated to around 3,000 B.C. Thus, McWhorter finds it unsurprising that texting is essentially speaking in a written form (he calls it "fingered speech").

Thus, it is wrong to think that texting is simply a corrupted form of more formal writing, and that all its changes are for the worse. McWhorter argues that it is a lively, innovative, and very dynamic form of language. Its users are creating new forms of expression as the need arises. For example, in face-to-face speaking, there are visual and verbal clues that a person uses to change the topic (e.g., saying something like "Hmmm, makes you think"). But texting did not have such clues, so this need was filled with the word *slash* (*OK meet at 8 slash your dress yesterday was fab*). It is also creating new expressions: *lol* used to be an acronym for "laughing out loud" but now is a more general term indicating empathy or accommodation (*lol I hate that too*).

McWhorter is not the only one who sees texting as an interesting new form of language. In his book *Txtng: The gr8 db8* (Great Debate), David Crystal makes a number of additional positive points about texting:

- People worry that texting is ruining children's language. For example, there was a hoax news story that a student submitted a school essay in texting language. This is an urban myth. Students have little problem keeping texting and other writing styles separate in their heads, and use these in their appropriate contexts. So students do not use a texting style in their schoolwork or examinations, and their teachers would not let them in any case.
- Texting does not lead to bad spelling, because you need to know how to spell before you can text.
- Language learning is driven by massive exposure to language and engagement with it (§55). Texting improves literacy by giving users more exposure to, and practice with, reading and writing. This can be especially useful for school-age children.

Overall, Crystal shows that texting is not causing people to write poorly in non-texting situations. Rather, they are simply using a new form of writing that it is appropriate and optimized for a new age of electronic communication devices.

Power Point: There is no reason to fear that texting is destroying people's ability to write. They are simply learning a new dialect of writing, while retaining their ability to write appropriately in all of the other writing styles they used previously.

1. Here is the TED website with John McWhorter's talk.

https://www.ted.com/talks/john_mcwhort
er_txtng_is_killing_language_jk

2. The first website is *Bad Linguistics,* written by Pauline Foster from St. Mary's University. Here she comments on a short interview in which Jean Gross (then UK Government Communications Champion) was suggesting that texting may be bad for children's language development. The second website is a related BBC news page which reports that texting helps students to spell.

https://badlinguistics.wordpress.com/2010/02/10/is-texting-bad-for-childrens-language-develop/#more-11463284

http://news.bbc.co.uk/1/hi/education/8468351.stm

40

IS TEXTING REAL LANGUAGE?

Some people say texting is so unlike regular written language that they can't understand it. But is that still the case?

We will see in Section §92 that spoken language differs from written language. It is not surprising that there are also different styles of written language. For example, it is pretty obvious that the language of the gossipy message you put on a postcard will be very different than the language you use to make a formal letter of complaint (§11).

Some people dislike texting, but why? How is text language different from other more traditional forms of writing? In 2008, David Crystal took a close look at text language in his book *Txtng: The gr8 db8* (Great Debate), and described 6 distinctive features. Most of these stemmed from the constraints of using small phone screens and number pads.

1. **The use of symbols, numbers, and letters to represent words**

Perhaps the most noticeable feature of texting is the way the messages are shortened and condensed from "full writing." This was originally done partly because only 160 characters were allowed. Also, the generation of cell phones before smartphones required users to spell out letters on the 0-9 number keyboard. This was tedious, and so all manner of shortcuts were devised. These included:

<u>Using single letters to represent words:</u>

b = be
n = and
r = are
u = you
w = with
xoxo = hugs and kisses

<u>Using numbers to represent words:</u>

2 = to
4 = for
8 = ate

<u>Using numbers to represent parts of words:</u>

2nite = tonight
b4 = before
4ever = forever
d8 = date
wan2 = want to

Sometimes a meaning or part of a word was represented by a symbol. Everyone knows the 'smiley.' It was first drawn as :-) but soon morphed into many clever variations (§100):

;-) = wink
:p = smiley with tongue hanging out
*<):o) = clown
%*} = too much alcohol

2. **Using Initials to Represent Words**

This involves cutting words down to their initial letter. This technique is commonly used in the wider world with well-known examples like *radar* (radio detection and ranging), *scuba* (self-contained underwater breathing apparatus), and *FAQ* (frequently asked questions). Some of the examples from texting include the following:

BRB = Be right back
PRW = Parents are watching
WYWH = Wish you were here

3. **Omitted letters**

This is the same idea as using initials (i.e., deleting letters), but less drastic. The number of letters deleted ranged from a single one to many:

txt = text
hv = have
wknd = weekend
bf = boyfriend

4. **Nonstandard spelling**

Another way to save space is to use shorter nonstandard spellings. Some of these have been around for a long time. Crystal reports that several are 75 or more years old:

cos = cause (1828)
wot = what (1829)
luv = love (1898)
thanx = thanks (1936)
ya = you (1941).

Gonna, wanna, sorta, and *dunno* are also old.

5. **Shortenings**

This is a kind of abbreviation where parts of words are deleted. Again, this is a very common practice in language overall, and not unique to texting. Common examples are *exam*(ination), (tele)*phone*, *Mon*(day), *etc*(etera) and *Jan*(uary).

6. **Genuine novelties**

In Crystal's last category, he lists forms that he believes were original to texting. They were mainly longer strings that may combine several of the above shortening techniques: *hldmecls* = hold me close, *ttyl8r* = talk to you later, and *ijc2sailuvu* = I just called to say I love you. Many are these seem to have stemmed from texters' desire to play with the texting language, and might have only been understood by friends familiar with the texter's abbreviations.

Nowadays, smartphones have full keyboards and larger screens, so shortenings like Crystal describes have largely disappeared. Also, software usually changes smileys into better-drawn symbols . Symbols like this are called *emoticons/emojis,* and were initially meant to express emotions or actions. But now they represent anything from airplanes (✈) to umbrellas (🌂) to dinosaurs (🦕).

There are even very short (often humorous) video clips (.gif files) that are inserted into texts to indicate your feelings or attitudes. Thus, texting language is becoming multi-modal, combining linguistic, graphic, and video elements.

It is interesting how language has adapted to the technology of the times. In the early days of texting, people found ways to condense texting language to take account of technology's limitations. Now that those limitations have largely disappeared, language has again adapted, and texts typically consist of fully spelled out words. This is especially true since the predictive text and autocorrection features commonly found on computers and smart phones will suggest fully spelled words. Plus, texting language now has a rich vein of additional meaningful output, like emojis. Language is always changing to meet the needs of its users, and no doubt it will change again in the future to take account of future technology.

Power Point: Early texts did have a number of distinctive features that allowed the message to be expressed in fewer characters. But most of those forms of text abbreviation are widely used in language in general. Texting on modern smartphones no longer requires these shortenings, and the majority of text language today is not so different from other forms of written communication.

1. Here are three pieces by David Crystal. The first is an interview about various English language issues, including texting. The second is a blog discussing the reaction to his *Txtng: The gr8 db8* book. The third is a British Council YouTube video where he discusses the effects of technology on language

https://www.davidcrystal.com/Files/BooksAndArticles/-3955.pdf

http://david-crystal.blogspot.co.uk/2008/08/on-txtng-reaction s.html

https://www.youtube.com/watch?v=qVqcoB798Is

2. Here is one of many sites that offer an amazing variety of emoticons. This one focuses emoticons for Facebook

http://www.symbols-n-emoticons.com

41

SPELLCHECKERS AND YOUR SPELLING

How well can you spell? Are spellcheckers making us all worse spellers?

Spellcheckers have been around as long as mainstream word processors, and are now a standard part of the writing process for many people. Spellcheckers work by comparing the words in a text to an internal dictionary of correctly spelled words and identifying mismatches. These mismatches are flagged for the writer to consider, often with a list of possible replacements. Many spellcheckers now also check grammar.

Spellcheckers are getting better, but they still have problems. One of their main difficulties is distinguishing between words with the same sound but different spellings:

1. I ran this text threw the spellchecker. (through)

They also cannot always catch when word boundaries are wrong. In my writing I often miss-hit the space bar and type in something like:

2. *We need to keep their limitation sin mind* (*limitations in* – an actual error I originally made below).

Newer spellcheckers are beginning to take a word's context into account to improve their accuracy, but they still have some way to go.

Most people would see spellcheckers as a useful tool, but critics believe that over-reliance on them leads to a deterioration in spelling ability. That would be a problem because spellcheckers make mistakes. They do not catch contextual errors like *threw* and *through* above, and they highlight some correct words and sentences as being wrong. We need to know language well enough to not only check for errors ourselves, but also to check the spellcheckers.

One study shows that we are giving spellcheckers too much credit and lazily accepting their judgments without thought. Dennis Galletta (University of Pittsburgh) and colleagues studied 65 university students, split into one higher and one lower group based on SAT and GMAT scores. The students were asked to edit a business letter with a number of errors. Some students had use of a spell/grammar checker and some did not. There were three types of errors: A) errors the spellcheckers caught, B) errors the spellchecker did not catch, and C) correct language that the spellchecker nevertheless indicated as an error.

The researchers found that without the spellchecker, the stronger students found most of the Type A errors by themselves, while the weaker students did less well. But with the spellchecker, both groups fixed virtually all the errors. So far, so good. The stronger students were also much better at catching Type B errors without the spellchecker than the weaker students, but with the spellchecker on, became just as bad as the weaker students. It seems they became overconfident in the spellchecker's ability and did not hunt for errors that the spellchecker missed. Both the stronger and weaker groups changed correct Type C language and thus introduced errors based on the spellchecker's false indications.

Overall, the results show an overreliance on spellcheckers, sometimes making our language worse. While spellcheckers are useful for indicating potential errors, we need to keep their limitations in mind and use them for guidance, rather than as gospel. In the end, we need to retain and practice our language proficiency, as it will always be more sophisticated than a spellchecker.

Roy Peter Clark (Poynter Institute) recommends ways of doing this, particularly for children:

- Writing by hand in a spiral notebook
- Printing out documents to edit manually
- Asking your child to identity cases where the computer missed a mistake in her paper or gave bad Type C advice. Frame this as a challenge/game: "Are you smarter than the computer?"

More adult ways of improving spelling include:

- Playing word games like Scrabble, Boggle, and Wordle
- Referring to a dictionary if you know the first letters of the word
- Reading a lot, which helps by giving wide exposure to the written forms of many words

How good is your spelling? See if you know 12 of the most misspelled words in English:

1. separate / seperate / separete / seperete
2. definately / definatly / definitely / definitly
3. embaras / embarass / embarras / embarrass
4. ocurrence / occurence / occurrence / occurance
5. rhythem / rhythm / rythym / rythem
6. grateful / gratefull / greatful / greatfull
7. calendar / calender / calandar / calander
8. concencus / concensus / consencus / consensus
9. I like (its / it's) style.
10. The news will (effect / affect) him badly.
11. I drink (alot / a lot) of whisky.
12. Better to be silent (than / then) obnoxious.

Power Point: Spellcheckers are a useful tool, but need to be used as a supplement to proofreading, not as an unquestioned final authority. Over-reliance on spellcheckers can actually lead to poorer language accuracy.

1. Here are two spelling quizzes. The first is for kids. The second is from the British *Guardian* newspaper, and is a real challenge for adults:

https://www.funbrain.com/games/spellaroo

http://www.theguardian.com/books/quiz/2009/feb/09/spelling-society-quiz-test

. . .

2. An amusing poem written with numerous mistakes that spellcheckers probably will not catch.

http://grammar.about.com/od/spelling/a/spellcheck.htm

Answers:

1. separate
2. definitely
3. embarrass
4. occurrence
5. rhythm
6. grateful
7. calendar
8. consensus
9. I like **its** style.
10. The news will **affect** him badly.
11. I drink **a lot** of whisky.
12. Better to be silent **than** obnoxious.

42

COMPUTER GAMING: ARE THERE ANY LANGUAGE BENEFITS?

My kids play computer games all the time. Are there any language benefits?

Computer games (also called video games) are now everywhere, and many children play them a lot. In 2016, the World Health Organization reported on the percentage of children who played video games for two hours or more on weekdays. The average for 39 European countries (plus Israel and Canada) for 11 year-olds was 46% (boys) and 28% (girls). For 13 year-olds, it rose to 56% and 35% respectively. For 15 year-olds, it dipped slightly to 54% and 30%. In 2019, 3-4 year-old children in the UK spent 4.7 hours per week on average gaming, 5-7 year-olds=6.3 hours, 8-11 year-olds=9.5 hours, and 12-15 year-olds=11.6 hours (Statista).

Clearly, computer games are good fun, and although parents may worry that their children are wasting their time, it is useful to know that gaming also has a number of benefits. Some are physical, including improved hand-eye coordination and practice in focusing your eyes. And while gaming is sedentary, sports games may interest children in practicing those sports in real life. If you are recovering from an injury, games can provide a distraction from the pain. If you are totally immersed in a game, this can even cause your brain to change the way it perceives pain, lowering its intensity.

Many games offer social benefits, as members of gaming communities have to provide leadership, negotiate relationships with other players, and solve problems together. Gaming can also spark an interest in the topics involved in games; for example, history, culture, or math.

Games have many mental benefits as well. Many require you to hold a lot of information in memory at once, keep track of many items at the same time, make very rapid decisions, and move quickly. These requirements essentially give your brain the type of exercise that can sharpen perception, memory, attention, and decision-making (some of the basic building blocks of intelligence). Gaming can be particularly beneficial for older players (50+) in keeping their brains functioning well.

Games can also be effective for learning. James Paul Gee (University of Wisconsin-Madison) argues that games are not mindless entertainment, but can be useful learning experiences. He identifies 36 principles of learning that are built into well-designed computer games (e.g., players get lots of practice in a context where that practice is not boring), and believes such games can be fruitful learning environments.

But what about language? In his book *Computer Games and Language Learning,* Mark Peterson (Kyoto University) reviews the research on this topic, looking at several different game types. His review shows that games can be an effective way to learn language.

Although the research focused on ESL learners, there is no reason to believe that games would not be equally effective with children playing in their mother tongue. Peterson comes to the following positive conclusions:

- Commercial simulation games (e.g. the *Sim* series), role-playing games (e.g. *Ever Quest* and *World of Warcraft*), multi-user virtual environment games (e.g. *Quest Atlantic* and *Erie Isle*) and other games are useful language learning tools.
- Learners generally had positive motivation and attitudes about learning through games.
- Depending on the type of game, gains were seen in vocabulary, reading comprehension, listening, pronunciation, awareness of writing for an audience, and willingness to communicate.
- Playing led to social interaction and language output.
- The provision of supplementary materials and problem-solving tasks supported collaboration and language use by learners.

But there were also some negative findings. Games can be challenging for lower-level students as well as inexperienced gamers, though teacher assistance can help these learners. Also, the participation and engagement with the games unsurprisingly depended on whether the games matched the interests of the learners. Overall, games can be an effective way to learn language, but for maximum effectiveness, games seem to benefit from the supplementary help, advice, and materials that a teacher, parent, or other more advanced user can provide (e.g., lists of the vocabulary/phrases that appear in the game; explanations about culture).

A large number of software programs and Internet learning sites have been specifically designed to teach language (§62). The best combine the excitement and competition of games with a principled approach to language development. You might not imagine that children would take language tests for fun, but they are doing so in great numbers because they are embedded in a competitive game format, and the bragging rights to the highest scores seem to be highly prized.

Power Point: Computer games can offer a number of benefits, and one of these is language learning. Research shows that if computer games are the right level for the learner and matches their interests, gains in language proficiency are facilitated. This is combined with generally positive attitudes towards the learning and increased social interaction in collaborative games.

1. These two websites outline a range of benefits from playing computer games.

https://www.parents.com/kids/development/benefits-of-video-games

https://www.mentalfloss.com/article/65008/15-surprising-benefits-playing-video-games

2. This FluentU webpage explains how learning language through gaming can be effective. It also has descriptions of a number of language games.

http://www.fluentu.com/blog/best-way-to-learn-a-new-foreign-language-online/

PART 6

HOW YOUNG CHILDREN LEARN THEIR MOTHER TONGUE

IS MY CHILD LEARNING NORMALLY?

43

HOW SHOULD I EXPECT MY CHILD'S LANGUAGE TO DEVELOP?

It is a joy for any parent as their child begins to speak. But when should children begin to talk, and what stages do they go through?

Every young child achieves a number of milestones that mark their growth and development. These include smiling, laughing, crawling, and walking. Likewise, children's language develops through a number of milestones and stages. Having a good understanding of these stages can give parents reassurance that their child is developing normally.

I have examined a number of child language development guides, but found that each one differs slightly in their descriptions and timings. I have collated a number of them into the following general summary that you can use to gauge your child's progress. But please note that every child is obviously different, so the timings of the stages are only approximate.

0-3 months

- Responds to your voice

4-6 Months

- Responds to their name and the word *no*
- Responds to different voice tones (e.g., angry and friendly)
- Experiments with the sounds they can make (babbling)
- Can make 'urgent' noises to get your attention

7-12 Months

- Listens when spoken to
- Recognizes the names of familiar objects (*Daddy, ball, eyes*)
- Begins to understand simple requests (*Give it to Granny*), instructions, and questions (*More juice?*)
- Produces first single words (*mama, dada*)

1-2 Years

- Understands simple commands (*Push the ball, Please give me the toy*) and questions (*Where's the bunny?*)
- Likes listening to simple stories (often the same one many times!)
- Begins to use words in 2-word combinations by 24 months (*baby crying*)
- Has a vocabulary of around 5-20 words by about 18 months and 50 or more by 24 months (perhaps even as many as 150+), mostly nouns (*baby, ball*)
- Begins to use words like *I, me, you, my*, and *mine*

2-3 Years

- Understands two-step commands (*Get your socks and put them in the basket*)
- Understands opposite concepts like *hot/cold, stop/go, big/little, nice/yucky*
- Understands most simple questions concerning things they are familiar with
- Vocabulary is exploding; you won't be able to count all the words
- Verbs are becoming much more prominent
- Uses phrases of 3 words or more (*Me go too, Mummy get in car*)
- Grammar is beginning to emerge, including pronouns (*I, you, me*), some plurals and past tenses—even if not on the right words (*mouses, runned*), and prepositions (*in, on, under*)
- Most of what is said should be intelligible

3-4 Years

- Can understand simple *Who?, What?, Where?,* and *Why?* questions
- Uses longer sentences with 4 or more words
- Can talk about things that happened at different times and places (i.e., not just about the 'here and now')
- Starting to use adjectives (*big, red, funny*) and some adverbs
- Practices language with much repetition of words and phrases (even syllables and sounds)
- Speech is mainly fluent and clear; non-family-members can usually understand it

4-5 Years

- Can understand nearly all of the speech directed to them
- Uses many adjectives and adverbs

- Can construct long sentences with multiple parts (*I want to have a horse of my own like Evan, and Daddy says when he wins the lottery, he'll buy me one*)
- Speech is now mainly grammatically correct
- Can tell long stories and remain on topic
- Can communicate easily with familiar adults and with other children

Power Point: Although there will be some variation, the above description will give you a general idea of what to expect during your child's language development.

1. A website that describes the developmental stages of child language development up to age 8.

http://childdevelopmentinfo.com/child-development/language_development

2. This very informative website gives Dr. Caroline Bowen's summary of child language development up to age 5. Many of the language examples in this section are taken from this description, and information from the site has been incorporated into several of the following sections

http://www.speech-language-therapy.com/index.php?option=com_content&view=article&id=34

44

HOW DO I KNOW IF MY CHILD'S LANGUAGE IS NOT DEVELOPING NORMALLY?

My child is not achieving the expected language progress for their age. Are they just a late talker, or should I be worried and seek professional advice?

Descriptions of language development, such as given in the previous section (§43), are useful guidelines to gauge the language development of your child. Of course, these guidelines can only be a rough indication, as inevitably there are individual differences in when children achieve developmental milestones. As a parent, you are obviously thrilled if your child meets, or even exceeds, the normal expectations. But when is it time to become concerned if your child consistently fails to meet the normal developmental pattern? Most speech-language pathologists seem to agree on the following advice.

1. Trust your own judgment

You are the person who is constantly with your child and are best placed to sense if there are any potential problems with their development. Follow your instincts, and if you are concerned that there may be some language delay, it is worth getting the advice of a doctor or a speech-language pathologist. Do not be put off by well-meaning friends and relatives saying that "everything will work out." It may turn out that there really is no problem, but the reassurance of hearing this from a trained professional should calm any worries you might have. If something does turn up, then early diagnosis is the best way to get your child back on track without losing too much development time. Also, it is comforting to know that speech-language pathologists have techniques to diagnose even the youngest infants, so do not wait until you think your child is 'old enough' to be assessed. It is never too early.

2. Do not expect perfection

Your child is just that: an infant, toddler, or a pre-schooler. They will inevitably make mistakes with their words, sentences, and pronunciation. They will also sometimes misunderstand what they hear. This is normal and to be expected. Your child is learning a complex language system, and mistakes are part of the learning process. Also, do not assume your child will follow developmental guidelines very precisely. Think of the timings as general indications, not fixed deadlines for performance.

3. Progress should be steady

Children vary in how they learn language, so do not compare one child against another. It is more important to watch that your child is making steady progress from one milestone to another, rather than their speed.

. . .

4. Your infant should respond to sound

All infants respond to sound, and if yours does not, it is a cause for concern. If your infant pays attention to the visual things around him, but not sounds, then this may be a sign of hearing loss. If your infant does not start making sounds and babbling, this may also indicate hearing problems. Your child has to hear language in order to learn it, so if they show signs of delay, then it is important to have their hearing checked to confirm this is not the underlying problem.

5. Your child should be interested in communicating

It is normal for children to be communicative and sociable, even if they are sometimes shy. If your child does not seem interested in communicating with other people, or only just repeats back to you what you have said in a word-for-word manner, then this might indicate that their communicative skills are not developing as they should, or may even indicate autism (§66).

6. Your child should not be hoarse or stutter

Your child's voice should not be hoarse, unless they have an infection like a cold. Although every child will sometimes get tripped up when they speak (adults do this too!), persistent stuttering (more than 6 months) is not normal, and should be checked. You can help by being a language model: using slow, even speech patterns, and patiently listening to your child without interrupting them.

7. Your child is not learning enough vocabulary

One of the easiest ways to observe your child's development is by the new words they understand and speak. One rule-of-thumb is that children should have a spoken vocabulary of at least 50 words by their second birthday (not necessarily pronounced perfectly). If your child has less than this, they might be a 'late talker' and professional advice should be sought. By 18 months, they should know at least 6 words.

In addition to this general advice, there are several more age-specific "warning signs" lists to consult. Just remember that the timings in these lists should be seen as only approximate. Still, it is important to identify and address any communication problems your child might have. If left untreated, they can lead to further problems later on, including learning problems (particularly with reading and spelling), social problems (relating to other people), and general dysfunctional behavior.

Power Point: Warning signs can provide guidelines for problems to be aware of concerning your child's language development. But you as a parent are the best person to judge if there may be a potential problem. If you are concerned, that is the time to seek professional advice.

1. Another page on Dr. Caroline Bowen's website which outlines what is and is not normal in child language development

http://www.speech-language-therapy.com/index.php?option=com_content&view=article&id=35

2. A website that describes the developmental warning signs up to age 4.

http://www.babycenter.com/0_warning-signs-of-a-toddlers-language-delay_12293.bc

45

WHAT CAN I DO AS A PARENT TO FACILITATE MY CHILD'S LANGUAGE LEARNING?

I want my child to grow up having good language skills. How can I help them to acquire language in the best way possible?

Besides checking for potential development problems (§44), what can you do to help your child as they learn language? Children will learn their mother tongue if they are exposed to it, and have plenty of meaningful input. Most advice for parents is pretty simple, and mainly revolves around being involved and engaged parents who provide this necessary input.

Communicate With Your Child

From the very start in infancy, talk and sing to your child, and encourage their attempts at making sounds and gestures. Encourage other people to do the same.

Find Ways of Using Language with Your Child

Be creative and use as much language as possible with your child in everyday situations. Examples could include pointing to and naming animals at the zoo or in a picture book, describing what you are doing as you clean the house, pointing out things on the street as you take a walk, and commenting on sounds like birds singing or airplanes flying by.

Ask Questions

One way of engaging your child in language is by asking questions that naturally encourage a response. Ask about what they are doing or feeling, which helps make language real for them. Pay attention to their answers, and reply back. This shows that their attempts at using language (even if it is hard to understand in the early stages) are having a positive effect and are worth attempting. If it is too early for them to respond to questions, then answer the questions yourself, or comment on what they are doing.

Be Meaningful

Try to communicate with your child in ways that they have a chance of understanding. Keep your language simple, and do not overcomplicate things. In the early stages, focus on the 'here and now,' so your child can relate your language to something they can see or hear in their immediate environment.

Model Good Language Use

Your child mainly has you for their language model, so do not use "baby talk." Use natural language, so they can come to understand the sounds and rhythms of their mother tongue. Repeating what you say gives them the recycled input necessary to understand and learn new words and sentences.

Give Your Child Time to Respond

Your child needs more thinking time than adults, so be patient and attentive while you are waiting for them to formulate a response.

Read to Your Child

One of the best things you can do to help your child's language acquisition is simply to read to them (oral story-telling is good too). This initially helps the development of their oral language, and has massive benefits in supporting their literacy later on.

Begin reading early, perhaps as soon as 6 months. There are a vast number of children's books available, so it should be easy to find ones that appeal to them (and quite often yourself!). Find books where your child can be as involved as possible, either with some kind of gesture, sound, or imitation. Early books could include tactile ones, which incorporate parts that can be touched (such as having rabbit fur embedded on a page telling a story about bunnies). Later books might encourage them to make the sounds of the animals on the page. Some books have pictures that are good for them to point at once you name them, and later on to name themself.

Children like books that have repetition and are predictable, so they can soon begin to guess what is coming next. Many children's books also have rhyming text, which can help them get to grips with the sound system of the language. This is one reason why books like the *Cat in the Hat* series by Dr. Seuss continue to be so popular. In time, this early exposure will help them to begin reading in their own right (§49).

Make Language Fun

Perhaps more than anything else, associate language use with fun. Using language enthusiastically for games (*peekaboo, touch your nose*), reading time, and other enjoyable activities should have the effect of making your child an eager participant in their own language development.

Extra Time Together Might Be Necessary if Your Child is a "Late Talker"

Some children, even with an adequate amount of exposure, develop language more slowly than other children. If your baby has not started speaking their first words by about 18 months, it might be time to spend a little extra one-on-one time with them. This might include spending at least half an hour a day just playing and interacting with them with no distractions. Often, this extra language exposure is enough to prime the pump and get them back on the path to more typical language progress. Advice from a speech-language pathologist can often be helpful in setting up the most beneficial way of using this time, including what activities to use.

Power Point: Be an involved parent who regularly talks to and reads to your child, and they will learn language.

1. This website suggests 9 ways of supporting your child's language development

https://www.parents.com/baby/development/talking/9-ways-to-help-your-childs-language-development

2. This site suggests a number of sensible ways in which you can encourage your child's language development.

http://www.nct.org.uk/parenting/how-can-parents-encourage-language-development

46

HOW CAN I RAISE MY CHILD BILINGUALLY?

I speak English, and my partner is from Spain. We speak English together for everyday purposes. But we want our child to be bilingual, so what is the best way to achieve this?

In §45, I said that children will learn their *mother tongue* if they are exposed to it and have plenty of meaningful input. But you could just as well insert "any language" in this statement, because any language that children begin learning in their early years will essentially become additional mother tongues. This may seem unrealistic in predominantly monolingual countries like the US and the UK, but it is in fact quite normal in many parts of the word, such as Quebec, Belgium, and South Africa. All children need is sufficient meaningful interaction. How much? There is some evidence that children need to be engaged with a language for about 30% of their waking hours in order to learn and use it actively. Given a 12-hour day, this means about 3.5 hours per day or 25 hours per week.

So the key is to maximize the interaction in each language by whatever means; for example, by talking and reading to them and singing songs together. This might entail more than two languages —children can become multilingual if they get enough input.

Providing for this amount of language interaction can be a daunting prospect, and often requires a **family plan**. There are two main approaches, although these need to be adjusted according to each family's circumstances.

1. One Person, One Language (OPOL) In this approach, each parent (and other care providers) speaks only one language to the child; e.g., mother = Language A and father = Language B. The rationale for this is that children need consistency and predictability, and having each person consistently use a particular language is less confusing than if they switch languages. If it is difficult to generate enough input for a language, other speakers of that language can be brought on board, such as relatives, or a nanny or an au pair. One of the best sources of input is other children who speak that language, so organizing a playgroup is an excellent solution. In fact, it is quite useful for your child to see other people using the language, to counteract the idea that it is only Daddy or Mommy language. If you have more than one child, the task becomes easier if the older child already speaks more than one language.

2. Minority Language at Home (ML@H) Here everyone speaks the minority language at home. The assumption is that the child will receive plenty of input outside the home in the dominant community language (e.g., English in most of the US), such as in the neighborhood parks and daycare. This is partly because much language acquisition occurs as children play and interact with each other. The approach has the advantage of the primary caregivers all speaking the same language, which gives the maximum exposure to the less-accessible minority/ heritage language (e.g., Spanish in many parts of the US).

Knowing more than one language offers many advantages (§58), so it is definitely worthwhile raising your children bilingually if possible. But there are some issues to be aware of as well. Your child will be learning two languages and double the vocabulary of monolingual children. They will naturally take a little longer to absorb and work through this additional information. There may also be some initial mixing of languages, but this will soon sort itself out as they learn more vocabulary. These issues mean your child may be a little slower in reaching some developmental milestones (§43). But do not worry, they will eventually catch up with monolingual children (by around age 5), and then be proficient in two languages.

Overall, there is no evidence that learning a second language when children are young will adversely affect their first language in the long run (§59). Their brains have 50% more brain cell interconnections than they will eventually have as adults (some say 100% more), so children have plenty of physical "brainpower" to handle multilingual acquisition.

Whichever bilingual/multilingual approach you choose for your children, you will need patience and dedication. Language acquisition is a long-term process, and it will take several years before the full fruits of your efforts begin to emerge. Also, do not forget to praise your child a lot during the process.

And one last point: ration the television (§50). Unsurprisingly it has been found that parents and caretakers speak to and interact with children less when the TV is on and audible. If you do watch TV with your children, use it as a springboard to start interaction (*What's that boy on the TV doing?*).

Power Point: Young children can easily learn two or more mother tongues simultaneously. All they need is enough meaningful input and interaction.

1. The Bilingual Monkeys website gives a range of ideas on raising bilingual kids, based on the experience of raising English/Japanese children in Japan. This particular page shows how the parents managed over 25 hours of English exposure per week.

http://bilingualmonkeys.com/how-many-hours-per-week-is-your-child-exposed-to-the-minority-language/

2. Here are two sites discussing child bilingual learning. The first is the initial page of a 6-page series by Christina Bosemark that deals with raising your children bilingually. The second is an article by Fred Genesee (McGill University) debunking several myths about child bilingualism.

http://www.omniglot.com/language/articles/bilingualkids1.htm

https://www.researchgate.net/publication/254440434_Early_childhood_bilingualism_Perils_and_possibilities

47

WHAT HAPPENS WHEN CHILDREN ARE NOT EXPOSED TO LANGUAGE?

THE CASE OF GENIE

Can a child learn language if she is deprived of it for the first 13 years of her life?

In §43, I discussed how all non-disabled children learn their mother tongue and become fluent speakers. But this depends on a key requirement: that children are exposed to enough language when they are young. This section shows the awful outcome when this simple condition is not met.

Of course, almost all families are communicative and parents talk to their children, although this varies quite a lot in terms of the extent and type of parent talk. The only way children would not be exposed to language is if they were locked away in isolation. Unfortunately, this did happen to a young girl in the 1960s, given the pseudonym *Genie*. Attempts to teach her language once she was released from her locked room illustrate the devastating consequences of a lack of language input while one is young.

Genie lived with her father, mother, and older brother in Los Angles. Her father believed that she was severely mentally disabled, and decided to lock Genie in her room before she had reached age 2. She was usually tied down to a potty chair or her bed, so all she could move was her hands and feet. Her father made sure she had very little contact with her mother or brother, and he would growl at her like a dog. He beat her if she made any sound, so she learned to remain silent as a defense mechanism. She was made to survive on an extremely meager diet. Overall, she was forced to live a life with very little interaction or stimulation of any kind.

This continued until Genie was 13½ years old. Her mother managed to escape from Genie's father, and was attempting to apply for disability benefits for being blind. It was then that social workers noticed Genie with her, and immediately realized something was wrong. They assumed the child was only 6 or 7 years old, but when they found out she was over 13, they called the police. Genie's parents were arrested and Genie sent to Children's Hospital Los Angeles.

When she was rescued, Genie was malnourished, underweight, uncoordinated, and had virtually no language. A doctor examining her described her as the most severe case of child abuse he ever encountered. Genie's deprivation left her with many social, mental, and physical problems, and there was a concentrated effort to help her with these. But there was also considerable academic interest in her on account of her language deprivation, as she offered a unique chance to discover whether humans have a *critical period* for learning language (§57).

A critical period is a time window, after which it is difficult/impossible to learn something. Scientists hypothesized that this might also apply in language learning, so that if a language was not learned early in life (by around puberty), it might not be learned at all. If Genie could learn language after she had been deprived of it in her formative years, it would disprove the critical period hypothesis. Conversely, if it was impossible for her to learn, it would suggest that a critical period exists.

A number of researchers studied Genie over the next few years. They found she had strong nonverbal communication abilities, although language came very slowly and unevenly to her. But she eventually learned the names of most things in her daily life, though she could recognize much more vocabulary than she could produce. In contrast, Genie had much more difficulty learning grammar. She spoke mainly in short utterances, and with a lot of imitation and repetition. Also, her ability to hold a conversation remained very limited. Overall, the researchers studying Genie concluded that although she had gained some basic language competence, it was far below what could be expected from normal children, and it appeared that she was unable to fully learn a language.

On the surface, this appears to support the idea that children must learn their mother tongue when they are young, or the window of opportunity passes. Genie never did learn language to any truly functional level, even though she received a great deal of attention and language input in the years after her rescue.

However, the picture may not be so clear-cut. Genie was undoubtedly traumatized emotionally, and it is unclear whether she was in fact mentally disabled to some degree. She was also shuffled between a number of caretaker environments over the years, which was certainly disruptive. It is impossible to know to what degree her lack of language progress was already due to one of these factors in addition to the delayed language input. It is unknown how far she could have progressed if her caretaker environment had been more stable. But there seems little doubt that the lack of early language input caused problems for Genie in her later attempts to learn language.

In the end, Genie's sad case illustrates the point that children need language input to prosper in their language development, which reinforces the recommendations in many sections of this book that parents should take the time to talk and read to their children as much as possible (e.g. §45 & §50).

Power Point: Genie was cut off from exposure to language until she was over 13 years old, and never recovered from this deprivation. Her sad case illustrates the importance of language input when children are young and developing their language abilities.

1. Here is a TLC documentary on Genie.

https://www.youtube.com/watch?v=VjZolHCrC8E

2. Here is more on Genie, including some discussion of the ethical issues involved in the tension between rehabilitating Genie vs. studying her for linguistic purposes.

https://www.verywell.com/genie-the-story-of-the-wild-child-2795241

http://abcnews.go.com/Health/story?id=4804490

PART 7

LEARNING TO READ AND WRITE (LITERACY)

HOW CAN MY CHILD BEST LEARN?

48

LEARNING TO READ: WHAT IS IMPORTANT?

What does my child need to know in order to learn to read?

Reading is one of the most important things anyone will ever learn to do. It enables many of the things that make life worthwhile (reading books and birthday cards) and also many other essential survival tasks (completing income tax forms).

But for children, reading is especially crucial because it largely determines their academic success at school and career opportunities. A National Endowment for the Arts (NEA) report on reading in the US shows that the more children read for pleasure, the better their scores on reading and writing tests (§50). Another report confirms a strong relationship between reading and mathematics scores. Reading proficiency is also strongly related to income level and access to higher-level professions. Weak readers are much more likely to be unemployed. Clearly, it is important for your children to learn to read well. But before you can help them learn this key skill, it is first necessary to understand how reading works.

Reading experts once thought that readers' background knowledge was the key to successful reading. It was thought that readers only needed to sample a limited number of words from the text they were reading, because their background knowledge would already supply most of the necessary information. Thus, readers would skip over many words in a text. It was only when readers ran into new information that they would need to read more carefully and read all the words. This was known as *top-down* reading, where readers started with their existing knowledge, and then used reading to fill in gaps in that knowledge.

A very different view of reading was the *bottom up* perspective, where meaning is mainly built up from the words in text, rather than relying on previous background knowledge. This would be like building a brick wall from the bottom up, brick-by-brick. We now have equipment that makes it possible to track the eye movements of readers and see which letters and words that readers' eyes focus on while reading. Research with this eye-tracking equipment shows that the readers actually focus on most of the words in a text (over 80% of the *content words* [e.g. *cat, grasp, handsome*] and 40% of the *grammatical words* [e.g. *the, at, on*]). Also, they almost never skip over more than two words. The eye movements are also very fast, with each focus lasting only 1/5 to 1/4 of a second (200-250 milliseconds).

Reading is now understood to be an *interactive* process, where both bottom-up and top-down processes are in play. Fluent readers read most words in a text in a quick and automatic manner, which frees their mental resources to focus on comprehension. Poorer readers tend to have poor word recognition skills, so use more resources on word recognition. They rely more on top-down knowledge to compensate for their relatively poor word recognition skills.

From this very brief account, we can see that reading is more than just understanding individual words on a page. Catherine Snow (Harvard University) and colleagues list several things that are necessary for children to learn to read:

1. Have a working understanding of how sounds are represented alphabetically

This knowledge is essential for reading, and consists of at least two things. First, children need to develop the ability to recognize and categorize the sounds of the language, which is called *phonemic awareness*. An example would be understanding that the word *cat* is made up of three sounds: c/a/t. Then they need to learn which letters match onto those sounds (e.g., the final sound in *cat* is represented by the letter *t*). The *Phonics* teaching approach focuses on these aspects (§51).

2. Sufficient practice in reading to achieve fluency with different kinds of texts

The NEA report showed that more pleasure reading related to better language skills, so children need to be encouraged to read as much as possible. The reading should be spread across a range of reading material, which will give children exposure to a variety of language and text types (e.g. children's books, recipes, signs). This will help them understand the way stories and readings are structured. For example, fairy tales often begin with *Once upon a time*. There is a hero or heroine who will have some kind of problem or trial, but will usually overcome it and live happily ever after. The *Whole Language* teaching approach emphasizes this kind of 'learning in context' (§51).

3. Sufficient background knowledge and vocabulary to render written texts meaningful and interesting

Readers generate ideas about what is happening in a text based on what they know about the world and what happens in it. Thus, children need knowledge of the world, culture, and social conventions to understand books. So in early reading, choose texts that match your children's experience. As they become more proficient, they can use reading to learn about the world. Children also need to know most of the words in a text to be able to comprehend it, so a growing vocabulary is an essential prerequisite for fluent reading (§52).

4. Control over procedures for monitoring comprehension and repairing misunderstandings

Everyone misunderstands a text sometimes. Children need to learn to be engaged readers who check if they are understanding correctly. If not, they need they need some strategies for getting back on track. Examples of such strategies include re-reading the passage causing problems, looking up unknown words in a dictionary, and guessing unknown words from the surrounding textual context.

5. Continued interest and motivation to read for a variety of purposes

Reading needs to be enjoyable, and reading instruction needs to be positive and engaging so children are not turned off from it before they even get going. There are numerous ways parents can motivate their children to read, including reading to them (not only at bedtime), having children read to a pet (pets are non-judgmental!), or checking children's understanding with book-based games. One example of a comprehension game is "Two Facts and a Fib." In it, you pick two facts from the book you are reading and make up a third not in the book. The game is for the children to pick out the fib.

Power Point: In order to learn to read, children need to 1) know how the sounds and writing system of their language works, 2) be exposed to a lot of reading across a variety of text types, and 3) be immersed in an environment where reading is fun, motivating, and meaning-based.

1. This section's account of reading is inevitably very basic. This *Reading Rockets* site by Catherine Snow, Susan Burns and Peg Griffin offers a much more detailed discussion about reading and preventing reading difficulties in young children.

https://www.readingrockets.org/article/preventing-reading-difficulties-young-children-executive-summary

2. Reading involves many facets. The first website discusses phonemic awareness. The experienced kindergarten teacher Jeannie Partin offers some suggestions on how to teach it in a fun way. The second website gives useful tips on how parents can encourage their children's love of reading.

http://www.earlychildhoodteacher.org/blog/5-quick-easy-and-fun-phonemic-awareness-activities/

https://www.beanstalkcharity.org.uk/Listing/Category/grow-a-love-of-reading?

49

WHAT ARE THE STAGES OF LEARNING TO READ?

What are the stages my children go through when learning to read, and what can I do to help them at each stage?

Learning to read is an extended process that will take many years before your children are reading at a proficient adult level. As you might expect, there are a number of stages in this long-term process, and educational scholars have described these stages in various ways. Below I present the description proposed by Maryanne Wolf (Tufts University) in her interestingly titled book on reading *Proust and the Squid*. There are also suggestions about what you can do at each stage to help develop your children's reading ability.

Emerging pre-reader (typically between 6 months to 6 years old)

This is the stage where your children are getting ready to read. They learn about the language, the sounds in it, and start speaking (§43). Along with this, they learn about the world and society and how things work. They learn that reading is something that people do. Hopefully, they have the experience of you reading books to them, and begin to realize that stories and other meaningful language is somehow connected with books. They can probably go through a familiar book and tell its story, but at this point, it is mainly based on memory and pictures rather than actual reading. They might be able to read very basic words, like their names.

The main thing you can do for your children is to simply expose them to as much language as possible at this stage (§45). Talk to them as infants and toddlers, and begin reading to them early. When reading, direct their attention to words in the story, so they will start thinking about letters and words, and begin to make the link between the story words and their written forms.

Novice reader (typically between 6 to 7 years old)

At this stage, your children develop their understanding that the sounds of the language and the letters on the page are systematically related. That is, they learn their ABCs. To do this, they must first better develop their understanding of the sound system, and be able to hear and categorize all the sounds in the language (*phonemic awareness*—§48). Once they can decode the individual letters, they must learn to sound them out as they appear in words, and to recognize the word and its meaning from that sounding out. Your children will eventually start to recognize some words more automatically without having to sound them out.

You can help your children's phonemic awareness by doing anything that focuses on parts of words and how they fit together. Playing with nursery rhymes is useful, as it helps children understand that some words have a similar (rhyming) sound structure. Language games like clapping to the rhythm helps them segment words into their syllables. Other games involve 'building' words from their parts (*s* + *at* = *sat*). Activities like these help children understand how sounds are blended together to make words, which then helps them decode those words when they see them in reading. Having your child read aloud reinforces the relationship between oral and written language. Most importantly, there should be lots of reading practice.

Decoding reader (typically between 7 - 9 years old)

In this stage, children are decoding more efficiently and are beginning to read more fluently. Part of this involves reading words by larger segments (*ham* + *burg* + *er*) rather than letter by letter. Children will start recognizing common prefixes (*pre-*, *un-*) and suffixes (*-ed*, *-s*). Increasing numbers of words will be recognized as wholes without any conscious segmenting at all (also known as *sight vocabulary*). All of this increasing knowledge about language allows your children to use more of their cognitive resources to focus on meaning. Indeed, one hallmark of this stage is the transition from focusing on decoding written word forms to focusing on the meaning of the text.

Give your children practice working with word parts: prefixes, stems, and suffixes. They must also learn to read a lot more vocabulary, at least 3,000 words. This mainly comes from regular reading, but your focus on vocabulary can also be helpful in reaching this goal. Playing word games like Hangman, I Spy, Bingo, and Unscrambling Words are one fun way of doing this. Encouraging rereading can be useful, so that your children can focus more on comprehension in the second and subsequent passes. They also need to know when to reread in order to repair a misunderstanding, when their initial interpretation of the text does not make sense. Do not forget to give your child lots of encouragement, so that they will continue moving on to more challenging texts and keep progressing to higher levels.

Fluent, comprehending reader (typically between 9 - 15 years old)

The two key reading aspects developed during this extended stage are fluent reading speed, which then allows your children to comprehend the deeper meaning of the texts they are reading. Decoding readers understand the meanings of the words they read, but at the Fluent Comprehending stage, children learn to understand meaning beyond the word level, like the flow of a narrative, author point of view, irony, and metaphor. Reading at this stage becomes more strategic, as children begin to apply their prior knowledge, make predictions about what will happen, draw inferences, and read between the lines. Your children will also begin to learn from their reading, as they tackle textbooks on school topics like history and science.

You want to help your children read more independently at this stage. Encouraging them to read texts with layers of meaning (e.g., fantasy like *Harry Potter* or *Lord of the Rings*) allows them to venture beyond concrete meaning and relate to the hopes and fears of their heroes and heroines. Encourage them to ask themselves critical questions to see if they are really understanding what they are reading: *Can I summarize the content? What are the key issues? What didn't I understand? What happens next?* Encourage your children to read for pleasure.

Expert reader (typically from 16 years and older)

Reading is now a life skill for information-gathering and pleasure.

Power Point: Learning to read progresses through various stages that require distinct kinds of support from parents and teachers.

1. This page gives more information on the stages of reading, and connects to a larger site with lots of information on reading and writing.

http://www.theliteracybug.com/stages

2. These sites give two different views of reading development. The first summarizes an alternative description of the stages of reading by Jeanne Chall (Harvard). The second illustrates how Oxford University Press divides its early readers into various levels.

https://newlearningonline.com/literacies/chapter-15/chall-on-stages-of-reading-development

https://cdn.oxfordowl.co.uk/2019/07/19/13/52/18/160/OxfordLevelsAndBookBands.png

50

HOW CAN I ENCOURAGE MY CHILD TO READ FOR PLEASURE?

The schools will help teach my children HOW to read, but how can I ensure they actually READ? I want them to read because they enjoy it and so will keep reading. So how can I promote reading for pleasure?

When children are taught how to read, there seems to be an assumption that they will take this information and just carry on and read of their own accord. While this may be true in many cases, the fact is that children now live in a world full of entertainment and distractions (e.g. smartphones), and they may choose these over reading books. One answer to this problem is develop the idea that reading is enjoyable in its own right, so that it can compete against life's many diversions. Here are some suggestions about how to promote your child's *reading for pleasure*.

1. Set aside times for reading

Perhaps the most important factor in developing the reading habit in your children is making time for it. Find one or more times in the day where you can sit down with your child and read. Even 10 minutes a day can have substantial benefits. But ringfence this time, as consistency is also very important. Children who were read to at least 3 times per week were almost twice as likely to score in the top 25% in reading compared to children who were read to less frequently. A common time to schedule reading is in the evening, where bedtime stories are an ever-popular hit with young children. But take books along with you so you can grab some extra reading time whenever the chance presents itself: car trips, in the park, waiting for the doctor. Interesting your child in reading is a long-term commitment, so you will need to set aside dedicated reading time through early childhood and early school years. Unfortunately, many parents stop reading with their children from the age of 7.

2. Limit screen time

Reading for pleasure takes time, and one of the problems is that there are simply too many things competing for your child's time and attention. In recent years, one of the most serious is technology with screens: television, computers, tablets, smartphones, and other recreational screen media. This technology is now readily available to children. A 2019 *Common Sense* report indicated that 19% of 8-year-olds, 53% of 11 year-olds, and 83% of 15-year-olds owned a smartphone. This is not a problem in itself, but the amount of time that children and teenagers devote to these devices is astounding. The report showed that children aged 8–12 watched screens for 4.7 hours a day on average, and teens 7.4 hours. This behavior is essentially addicting and children find it difficult to self-regulate their usage.

Using screens for communication or playing games provides instant gratification, and releases the chemical dopamine, which is connected with the feeling of reward. Unfortunately, excessive screen time leads to several problems in relation to reading. The first is the most obvious: it burns up potential reading time. But reading from a screen is also a different type of reading: typically very short (e.g., texts or internet pages), which does not provide the extended, thoughtful reading that children also need to improve their reading skills. The instant gratification also makes it more difficult to interest children in activities that take longer to develop and bear fruit, such as reading. The result is predictable: children who spent more than 2 hours per day in front of screens were 67% more likely to have attention problems than their peers.

The solution is to regulate screen time, setting up rules early in childhood when it is still feasible: e.g., no screens in the bedroom, make screen time a privilege and not a right, and set a watershed time after which all screens are shut off. Do this for yourself too.

3. Make reading pleasurable

Reading should always be an enjoyable experience for your children and never a chore. There are several things you can do to make sure this is the case. In the beginning, read to them. Most children love this, and the happy time spent together becomes positively connected with the idea of reading. Always be enthusiastic about reading, and never use withdrawal of reading as a punishment.

Be a good reading model: if you and older siblings read regularly, this demonstrates reading as a desirable activity, and also models time away from screens. Find books and other texts that your children find interesting, and one of the best ways of doing this is to let them pick what they want to read or have read to them. Even if their picks become repetitive (and they probably will be as all children have favorites they want to hear again and again), never show boredom. You can add some variety by letting them pick one book and you another. You do not have to always read the whole book, and if they are getting restless, stop and pick the story up again later.

Once they begin reading for themselves, many children like book series, where they can become involved with recurring leading characters, and become familiar with the writing style.

Power Point: Parents can make reading enjoyable by making it a regular time for happy interaction with their children. But make sure this time is not hijacked by addictive screen devices.

1. Many of the ideas and information in this section were drawn from the book *Help Your Child Love Reading* by Alison David. On this website, she encourages parents to read to their children.

https://www.teachearlyyears.com/learning-and-development/view/reading-to-children-is-powerful-simple-and-yet-so-misunderstood

2. These sites show a series of four short reports by Egmont children's press on promoting children's reading for pleasure. Chapter 3 has interesting information on how reading time often goes down as screen time goes up as children grow older.

https://www.storyhouseegmont.co.uk/wp-content/uploads/2014/06/Egmont-Reading-Street-ch1.pdf

https://www.storyhouseegmont.co.uk/wp-content/uploads/2014/06/Egmont-Reading-Street-ch2.pdf

https://www.storyhouseegmont.co.uk/wp-content/uploads/2014/06/Egmont-Reading-Street-ch3.pdf

https://www.storyhouseegmont.co.uk/wp-content/uploads/2014/06/Egmont-Reading-Street-ch4.pdf

51

TALKING TO YOUR CHILD'S TEACHER ABOUT READING

I want my children to learn to read well, but I don't know much about reading instruction. What do I need to know before I talk to their reading teachers?

Everyone wants their children to grow up being good readers. The question is how to best facilitate this essential goal. Happily, there has been a great deal of research into reading, and reading scientists are now able to offer a fairly comprehensive model of what is involved in skilled reading.

Unsurprisingly, reading turns out to be a multifaceted process involving a variety of types of knowledge and skills that interact with each other in complex ways. This complexity has created challenges for identifying effective approaches to reading instruction that are able to address all of the aspects of skilled reading.

Up to now, the two main approaches to reading instruction have been the *Whole Language* approach and the *Phonics* approach, and each has emphasized different aspects of reading. The Whole Language approach is meaning-based and prioritizes comprehension. The Phonics approach emphasizes the link between speech and writing and focuses on teaching children how to map the sounds of the language onto the letters of the alphabet; e.g., learning that the letter *s* corresponds with the first sound in the word *soda*.

Unfortunately, these two approaches are based on incompatible underlying assumptions. The Whole Language approach assumes that comprehension can be achieved without the need to explicitly teach children about sound-symbol correspondences. The Phonics approach assumes that awareness of sound-symbol correspondences is a key foundational reading skill on which comprehension is built.

This incompatibility means that people involved in reading instruction have fallen into two different camps and these camps tend not to talk to each other. The extent of their disagreement is so great that it has been referred to as the "Reading Wars." One result of is that approaches to reading instruction and discussions around them have become very emotive for many people involved, including teachers. For parents wishing to discuss this potentially controversial issue with their children's teachers, it is useful to better understand what is necessary for learning how to read, and what each approach offers in this regard.

Reading is a skill that must be taught

This point may seem almost too obvious, but I think it is important to emphasize this. As we saw in Sections §43 and §45, all children (except those with brain-related disabilities) naturally learn to speak their first language from the spoken language in their environment. Learning to speak seems to be hardwired into the human brain. This is not surprising because humankind has been speaking for perhaps hundreds of thousands of years. (Estimates vary widely, from 50,000 years ago to 2 million years ago.) This has given plenty of time for humans to evolve the ability to learn oral language more-or-less automatically.

Since reading appears to be the next developmental step in language learning, it is easy to see why many people might think that reading can also be picked up naturally without instruction. However, this is not the case. Written language is a relatively recent development, having appeared only about 5,000 years ago.

This means humans have not yet developed the ability to learn to read simply from being surrounded by the written word in their environment. Writing is essentially a code to represent the sounds of speech, and children need explicit instruction to learn how to break this code and create connections between sounds and letters.

Aspects of Reading

Models of reading show us that reading requires the integration of a range of knowledge and processes. In this brief introduction, we will look at just four aspects important for successful reading: comprehension, vocabulary, phonemic awareness, and fluency. I have chosen these because research reviewed for the 2000 US National Reading Panel report shows that they can be effectively taught.

Comprehension is the goal of reading, but it takes knowledge about language to achieve it.

Research shows strong links between successful comprehension and *vocabulary* knowledge. Depending on their home environment, children normally begin school with an oral vocabulary of between 3,000 and 5,000 word families (§81).

In order to make use of that oral vocabulary knowledge in reading, children need to develop knowledge of the sound system of the language or *phonemic awareness.* This includes knowing the relationship between sounds and letters; e.g., the f sound can be realized in print in different ways (*fish, phone,* and *cough*), knowing that some words rhyme (*book* and *look*), and knowing how many syllables are in a word (§48). *Fluency* contributes to comprehension because as students move from deliberate decoding of words they already know to automatic recognition of them, they are better able to hold more elements of a text in memory. This makes it possible to build comprehension beyond the single word level to sentences, paragraphs, and whole stories.

Reading scientists such as Mark Seidenberg, Matt Borkenhagen (University of Wisconsin-Madison), and Devin Kearns (University of Connecticut) point out that the interrelatedness of these aspects creates a virtuous circle for young readers as improvement in one aspect supports the development of the others. For example, knowing more vocabulary allows word patterns to become more obvious, which supports the extension of phonemic awareness (i.e., knowing *book, look* and *cook* can help children recognize *hook* more easily), which supports fluency development, which in turn leads to increased comprehension, which eventually makes it possible to learn new vocabulary from reading. This means that instruction also needs to be inter-related rather than focusing on individual aspects of reading in isolation. Learning to read is a process with several developmental stages (§49), and it is important that children receive appropriate instruction at each stage of the learning journey.

The need to learn the sound-symbol correspondences of a language

Children come to school already knowing how to speak and comprehend daily oral language (e.g., telling stories, understanding basic instructions). Learning to read requires children to take what they already know about oral language and comprehension and apply it in a new way to printed language. So an early key to reading is helping them to map words they already know orally onto written symbols.

Children who have had a lot of exposure to written text by regularly being read to may already have begun to notice some of the relationships between sounds and letters. However, the vast majority of children benefit from direct instruction in the initial stages of learning to read to develop phonemic awareness.

This type of instruction is called *Phonics,* and its aim is to show children how words can be broken down into distinct segments of sound, e.g. *cat* = /k-A-t/ and how knowing these sound/letter combinations can help them to sound out and recognize other words they come across in reading; e.g. *pat* = /p-A-t/ and *mat* = /m-A-t/.

There are some people who do not like Phonics. They see Phonics instruction as boring and demotivating because they think it turns reading instruction into dreary rote learning. But this misses the point. Phonics instruction *enables* children to read, which in turn makes all of the other reading activities taking place in a well-integrated reading classroom more interesting and enjoyable. Once some sound-symbol correspondences have been learned, children have access to the words on a page, which increases the written input they can understand. As they engage with more written input, they then begin to learn other sound symbol correspondences without every correspondence needing to be explicitly taught (e.g., the *hook* example above).

Learning to read is a process with several developmental stages, and the establishment of phonemic awareness is an essential early stage. Just as practicing scales is necessary before a musician can play a concert, phonics instruction is a prerequisite to skilled reading—but only one part of the total constellation of knowledge required. It might be best to see Phonics instruction as a way to jumpstart the journey of learning to read (and spell).

Understanding meaning

While knowledge of sound-symbol correspondences is important, it is a means to an end, and that end is comprehension. After all, children can learn to decode words without knowing what the words mean. Reading instruction needs to help children to contextualize words once decoded, by fitting them meaningfully into larger chunks of language.

It can do this in a number of ways. One is by focusing on the meanings of written words embedded in stories. Another is choosing texts on topics that children already know a lot about. Background knowledge supports both the decoding of words and the linking of ideas in texts to the wider world. Teachers can maximize meaningful engagement with reading by offering interesting books. This interest can in turn, boost the amount of reading children do. Teachers should also focus on expanding children's oral vocabulary, as this will increase the amount of written text a child can understand. They should also not be afraid to explicitly help children with their attempts to build meaning. Discovery learning, whereby children work to discover key concepts about reading on their own, has its place, but for struggling readers, this can often become an exercise in frustration, which may result in them being turned off reading.

Many of these useful meaning-based principles are highlighted by the Whole Language (and later *Balanced Literacy*) approaches, but they still require phonemic awareness as a co-requisite, which comes from early Phonics training.

Increasing fluency

Fluency is essentially about building automaticity (§49). When children first learn some sound-letter correspondences, they decode words slowly and methodically, letter by letter. All of their attention is taken up at the word level. With regular practice, the decoding becomes faster and more automatic, freeing up attention to recognize larger and larger units of text (syllables, whole words, phrases). Reading instruction can facilitate this transition with exercises showing whole words and phrases under time pressure, so that children begin recognizing them by their shapes rather than individual letters.

Increasing fluency is important because it supports comprehension. Children must read something like 100-150 words per minute (WPM) in order to begin to understand how the meanings of the various words fit together to develop the meaning of the overall story. Anything less than this means that too much attention is still being given to decoding and reading at a word-by-word level.

Fluency frees up attention and makes it possible for children to draw on background knowledge, pay attention to the structure of the text, and respond creatively to ideas in the text. Proficient adolescent and adult readers of English generally read in the order of 200-300 WPM, and so usually have no problems in building a coherent model of the message in a text.

"Learning to read" versus "Reading to learn"

Children typically begin learning to read in Year 1 at school. But as children move on to later grades (around Year 4), there is an increasing shift to learning new information about science, math, history, and so on.

Textbooks play a key role in this instruction. In order to learn from textbooks, children must already be successful readers. This means that children must learn to read independently in a timespan of only around three years (compared to 5-6 years for speaking). Otherwise, they risk missing out on a large amount of content knowledge.

The National Assessment of Educational Progress (NAEP) has been testing literacy (and other subject areas) of American students since 1992. Unfortunately, around one-third of 4th grade students only meet the requirements of the NAEP Basic level (and not Proficient or Advanced levels), while another third fail to even reach the Basic level. These results have been consistent since 1992. The requirements for the Basic level include skills like locating relevant information, making simple inferences, and interpreting the meaning of a word as it is used in the text. This level is well below that required to "Read to Learn." The situation is not much better at the 8th grade, with around one quarter failing to reach the Basic level (e.g., identifying statements of the main idea of a text or its author's purpose, stating judgments with some support). These failures highlight the need for reading instruction in the Learning to Read phase, which effectively addresses all of the important aspects of the reading process.

Power Point: Children need to be taught to read. This instruction needs to include substantial phonics instruction in the early stages. Reading is a complex process, and reading instruction needs to facilitate many aspects of reading (comprehension, vocabulary, and fluency, among others) to help children develop into efficient and flexible readers.

1. Here are four sites discussing the reading process in more depth. In the first YouTube video, Mark Seidenberg argues that learning the sound-symbol correspondences of a language is essential for children to learn to read. In the second YouTube video, David Kilpatrick (State University of New York-Cortland) discusses what is important to remember words once they are decoded through sound-symbol correspondences. In the third video, educational reporter Emily Hanford talks about models of reading, the Reading Wars, and critiques the Balanced Literacy approach. The final website presents Hanford's American Public Media report "Hard Words: Why aren't kids being taught to read?"

https://www.youtube.com/watch?v=eg0891-8dKQ

https://www.youtube.com/watch?v=54J5llogLuc

https://www.youtube.com/watch?v=1HGS9EG0HgU

https://www.apmreports.org/episode/2018/09/10/hard-words-why-american-kids-arent-being-taught-to-read

2. This is the NAEP report showing how nearly 294,000 US students were performing in reading at Grades 4 and 8 in 2019.

https://www.nationsreportcard.gov/highlights/reading/2019

52

HOW MUCH VOCABULARY DOES IT TAKE TO READ?

Reading is largely about knowing the words on the page. How many words does my child need to know to read well?

The amount of vocabulary required for reading depends on the type of reading. You are probably familiar with children's books like *Cat in the Hat* where the vocabulary is very limited and often repeated. Your children can enjoy this kind of reading with a relatively limited number of words. However, once they grow older and start reading textbooks, newspapers, magazines, and internet sites, they will obviously need to have a much wider vocabulary.

To determine how many words are necessary to read these types of texts, we must first consider what percentage of the words in a text must be known in order to understand it. Knowing 100% is the ideal case, but obviously you can understand large amounts of text even if some words are unknown. The question is what percentage of unknown words you can cope with. Can you understand a text if 1% of the words are unknown? 5%? 10%? 25%?

Researchers have given texts with various percentages of unknown words to readers to see how well they can comprehend the ideas in those texts. Here is the chance to try it for yourself. Below is the introductory paragraph of the Wikipedia entry *Origins of Language*[6], slightly edited and shortened to 120 words. I deleted 12 (10%) of the least frequent words (the ones most likely to be unknown) and replaced them with blanks. Can you still understand the gist? Can you catch all of the details? Can you guess the unknown words?

> The origin of human language has been the topic of discussion for centuries. In ______ of this, there is no ______ on the ______ origin or age of human language. One problem makes the topic difficult to study: the lack of direct evidence. Consequently, scholars wishing to study the origins of language must draw ______ from other kinds of evidence such as the ______ record, ______ evidence, ______ language ______, studies of language ______, and comparisons between human language and systems of communication existing among other animals (particularly other ______). Many argue that the origins of language probably relate closely to the origins of modern human behavior, but there is little agreement about the ______ and ______ of this connection.

Even though 10% unknown does not sound like a lot, I think you will agree that reading is very difficult in this condition. You probably could understand the overall gist, but much of the detail is missing, and it becomes difficult to guess the unknown words when so many of the surrounding words are also unknown. Also, annoyingly, unknown words often tend to occur close together, compounding the difficulties of comprehension. If nothing else, nobody would want to read long passages with 10% unknown; it is just plain hard work.

Now try the same passage with 5% unknown (6 words):

> The origin of human language has been the topic of discussion for centuries. In _____ of this, there is no _____ on the ultimate origin or age of human language. One problem makes the topic difficult to study: the lack of direct evidence. Consequently, scholars wishing to study the origins of language must draw _____ from other kinds of evidence such as the _____ record, archaeological evidence, contemporary language diversity, studies of language acquisition, and comparisons between human language and systems of communication existing among other animals (particularly other _____). Many argue that the origins of language probably relate closely to the origins of modern human behavior, but there is little agreement about the facts and _____ of this connection.

You almost certainly found this much easier, but probably still would not want to read for long periods with this many holes in the text (1 unknown word in 20). Let us try it one last time with only around 2% unknown (3 words). Insert *spite, consensus,* and *primates* in the 1st, 2nd, and 5th blanks respectively. Most people find this level of unknown vocabulary manageable, and so most reading specialists recommend knowing 98% of the vocabulary in a text or more. Applying this percentage to a large number of texts in language *corpora* (language databases) (§77), we can calculate that it takes about 8,000-9,000 word families (§81) to have the lexical resources to read well across a variety of texts. If you were happy to read knowing only 95% of the words in a text, then the vocabulary size requirement drops to between 3,000-5,000 families.

Of course, reading is more than just knowing vocabulary, but the research is pretty clear that the more vocabulary you know (at least up to a 10,000 word family threshold), the better you will be able to understand the texts you read.

These vocabulary size requirements are usually not a problem for adult native speakers, who typically have vocabulary sizes above 10,000 word families (§81). But native children will take years to reach this level. They come into their school years knowing something like 5,000 word families, but these are mainly known only in their spoken form. Children first have to learn the written forms of these 'known' word families, and then push on to learn new word families, largely through reading. For ESL learners, the vocabulary size requirements are a major hurdle, and are one of the most challenging aspects of learning English to a high level.

Note that these figures are for reading in English and may differ for other languages, but the overall message that a large vocabulary is necessary for effective reading should apply to all languages.

Power Point: 10,000 word families should make it possible to read without vocabulary knowledge being a problem. If your child is more tolerant of unknown words, then they should be able to begin accessing adult texts with between 3,000-5,000 word families, once they can recognize the word families in their written forms.

1. This Reading Rockets website discusses vocabulary learning for young children at home and in the classroom.

http://www.readingrockets.org/teaching/reading101/vocabulary

2. David Moore (Arizona State University) provides a scholarly, yet accessible, account of 'Why Vocabulary Instruction Matters'. He mentions the commercial product 'Edge', but this does not detract from the informative discussion.

http://ngl.cengage.com/assets/downloads/edge_pro0000000030/am_moore_why_vocab_instr_mtrs.pdf

Missing words: *spite, consensus, ultimate, inferences, fossil, archaeological, contemporary, diversity, acquisition, primates, facts, implications*

53

HOW CAN I ENCOURAGE MY CHILD TO WRITE?

My teenager has learned to write, but needs some inspiration. How can I get them interested in writing?

Many young people dislike writing their school assignments. They feel they are writing just because they have to, on topics they are not really interested in. Writing instruction is certainly necessary, because writing (like reading) is not just learned automatically from daily spoken communication. It needs to be taught. But writing is also supposed to be enjoyable, just like reading.

One way of promoting writing for pleasure is to encourage young writers to do creative writing on topics that interest them. In order to do this, they need to understand how good writing does and does not happen.

First of all, no one is born a good writer. It is a skill that needs to be developed by practice. Second, not even the best writers can produce finished results on their first try. Good writers write draft versions of their story and then regularly revise and polish those versions until they are happy with them. For example, this section probably went through at least 10 different stages of idea development, reorganization, and revision. Third, a story often develops as it is being written, rather than being completely mapped out before the writing even starts. This makes writing much more a process of discovery than a mechanical recording of ideas. Good writing is like a puzzle: What are the main ideas? What order should they be presented in? What is the overall storyline tying everything together? Typically, these elements take time to develop and knit together in a satisfying way.

So how does someone learn to write a story? There is plenty of advice in numerous self-help books and on the internet. One good example is the wikiHOW web page. Like other websites, it gives a number of tips on the writing process. In essence, writing involves a number of steps:

1. **Generate ideas.** Read a lot, especially in the genre of writing you want to do (e.g. romance, crime, historical fiction). Brainstorm ideas. Research your topic area so your writing will be more realistic (e.g. knowing how space travel actually works will lead to better science fiction writing).
2. **Organize the ideas.** Figure out the overall storyline. Create an outline or make a graph to visualize how the story develops and how the different characters and plot elements interact.
3. **Start writing and fill in the details as you go.** Just start writing. Remember that the first draft is only your starting point. Do not worry about mistakes, bad spelling, or punctuation. The point is to get something down on the page, which you can then work with. If you have writers

block, set a timer and just write for a few minutes. The result may not be great, but there will probably be something that you can build on. Do not worry if the ideas are disconnected to begin with.

4. **Revise and polish the manuscript.** Constantly go back and improve what you have written. Focus on different aspects in different revisions. One approach is to get your ideas down in the first drafts (what you want to say), then revise the organization and details in later drafts (effective presentation of storyline), and finally polish the text (get the spelling, grammar, and punctuation right).
5. **Be flexible and don't stress.** The hints here and elsewhere are only guidelines. Creative writing is a very personal experience, and everyone will have their own approach. Try different things and find the techniques that work the best for you. Writing should be fun and it is important to discover the best ways to shape your interesting ideas into a story that other people will enjoy.

Knowing *how* to write is one thing, but *wanting* to do it is another. To make the process of writing attractive and rewarding, a writer needs readers. In the best case, the readers will give constructive feedback on your writing. Luckily, there are now many exciting and creative outlets for young (and not so young) people to hone their writing skills and create stories for each other as part of supportive writing and reading communities.

A very good example of this is the internet site Wattpad. It has a large amount of reading in genres ranging from adventure to horror to teen fiction, and everything in between. One nice thing about Wattpad is that the stories are written by ordinary people for one another's enjoyment. Another is that the site is interactive, with readers commenting on stories and authors responding.

This makes it an excellent site from a language point of view. First, it is good place to find interesting stories, which should encourage the kind of extensive reading that improves reading proficiency. This is especially true for younger readers because many of the authors are also young, and so writing from a similar point of view. These younger authors writing for pleasure are also great role models for budding writers. The site is supportive of new writers and has lots of tips on both how to get started writing, and how to best promote the work you have written. The tips range from finding initial inspiration, to composing the story, to promoting your creation on social media. There is also a series of short YouTube videos from existing authors showing how to get started.

Power Point: Writing is a lot more exciting if you are writing about your personal interests for readers you care about. Sites like Wattpad make it possible to write for a community that will value your efforts and will be supportive as you develop your skills.

1. Here is the wikiHOW site that gives useful advice on writing.

http://www.wikihow.com/Write

2. The first site gives tips on how to start writing on Wattpad. The second site is the first of a series of 30 YouTube videos giving writing tips from Wattpad authors.

https://a.wattpad.com/image/WritingOnWattpad101.pdf

https://www.youtube.com/watch?v=9mG3Cf5BDA8

54

TEEN TALK: THE DOOM OF LANGUAGE OR ITS FUTURE?

Teenagers talk differently than adults. Are they using language poorly, or are they simply creating new ways of expressing ideas?

There are occasional criticisms in the media that teenagers are ruining language by the way they speak, and also the way they write. You may even agree with some of these criticisms. But are they fair? Are teenagers driving language to the dogs?

Sali Tagliamonte (University of Toronto) has been studying teen talk for over 20 years, and she does not think so: "When I hear people disparage youth and their language, I am always defensive. Teenagers are the innovators and the movers and shakers of language change and they are the hope for the future. Let's hear what they have to say."

So how is teenage communication changing language? In her book *Teen Talk*, Tagliamonte describes a number of developments, and I will summarize some of her points here. She has collected millions of words of spontaneous teen talk, and so I will focus on oral language.

• ***like*** The traditional meaning of *like* is to indicate a comparison; i.e., A is **like** B: *Life is **like** a camera—Just focus on what is important.* But Tagliamonte documents a completely different use of *like* in teenage talk: introducing what someone is thinking or saying. This 'quoting' function has traditionally been carried out by the words *say, think,* or *go*: *He says he has no plans to run for governor*; *And she goes What's the big deal?* But starting in the early 1970s, teenagers started using *like* as a quote indicator, and now it has largely displaced the previous words for this function.

> *I was like, "I better stop being an idiot." It's like, "This is really weird."*
>
> *I'm like, "Oh no!"*

• ***and stuff*** Traditional grammar says that we express our ideas in a sentence and then end with a period. But in spoken language, people often end their sentences with some kind of embellishment like *right?* (*I was like six or seven, right?*) or *you know* (*There are rules here, you know*). Some of the most common sentence-enders are used to extend the idea(s) in the sentence to a larger set of things: *and things* (*She loves cats, dogs, and things*) or *something like that* (*I want fish, like a nice piece of salmon or something like that*). One of these 'extenders' is becoming extremely widespread among young people (*and stuff*), and now often means simply a vague generalization: *We're going to visit Europe and stuff.*

• ***weird*** There are many words in English to describe strangeness: *odd, unusual, creepy, bizarre,* etc., with *strange* formerly being the most typical. But *weird* is now replacing virtually all of them, with teenagers using it about 85% of the time.

• ***stuff*** English has always had words to refer to a collection of things that you do not want to describe in any detail. The most common generic word used to be *things* (*I've got things to do*), and still is among people over about 40 years of age. But *stuff* is gaining with younger speakers, and now is used about as much as *things*: *You can go out on the streets by yourself and go buy stuff*. With this trend, *stuff* looks like it will eventually become the dominant unspecific term.

• ***whatever*** Some uses of *whatever* are unremarkable and familiar to everyone: *She could eat whatever she wanted.* But teenagers are increasingly using *whatever* as a stand-alone expression that shows a lack of interest: *Okay, never mind. Whatever.* In some ways *whatever* acts like a spoken shrug of the shoulders.

Using the Google Books Ngram Viewer, we can see some of these changes over time, as they appeared in books since 1800. The four words and phrases I analyzed in the Ngram below have been in use for a long time (from before 1900), but the graph shows an obvious rise in the last few decades. But notice that the graph lines begin to rise around 1990-2000, before today's teenagers were even born!

This highlights one of Tagliamonte's main points: much of what is thought of as "teen talk" is actually a collection of language features that have been developing over time. She explains that much language change happens over generations. For example, your parents may have predominately used *things* to refer to an undescribed collection of items. You started using *things* that way, but as you grew up, you might have ended up using *things* and *stuff* more or less equally. Your children started with that 50/50 mix, but then the language input in their world encouraged them to use *stuff* much more often.

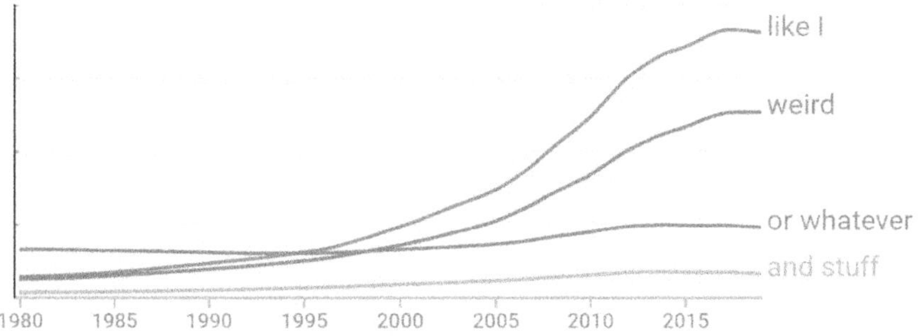

And so it goes on. It is unfair to blame teenagers for ruining language. They are simply this generation's stage of language evolution—the same way we were for earlier stages when we were younger. Young people are adapting language for their purposes and keeping it alive and fresh. I think Tagliamonte is right: teenagers and their language are the hope for the future.

Power Point: Language has always changed (§76), and teenager talk is just the current stage of this evolution. Teens are simply developing new ways of expressing ideas that have always been important across generations.

1. Here is a 20-minute YouTube video in which Sali Tagliamonte discusses various aspects of language change. The first eight minutes focuses on the language change in Teen Talk.

https://www.youtube.com/watch?v=tapgQNcKuFo&t=1008s

2. Google Books Ngram Viewer. This site produces graphs like the one above. You can type in any combination of words, and see their patterns of usage over more than 200 years (1800-2019 as I write this). It is very addictive.

https://books.google.com/ngrams

PART 8

THE BEST WAYS TO LEARN A SECOND LANGUAGE

55

WHAT ARE SOME IMPORTANT PRINCIPLES FOR LEARNING A SECOND LANGUAGE?

I'd like to learn a second language as efficiently as possible. Are there any principles to guide me in more effective learning?

There are many principles that have been proposed to guide effective second language teaching and learning. I have chosen four key ones that I think will help you to either tailor your own learning or to better select an appropriate language school or language learning app for your needs.

1. Maximize your exposure to the second language.

In many of the previous sections discussing children's acquisition of their mother tongue (both oral and written), we found that maximizing exposure to language promotes good language learning (§45-§50). This is also the most important requirement for learning a second language. Children receive many hours per day of language exposure over a number of years. Most second language learning contexts offer much more limited opportunities for language input, so it is important to create as much exposure as you can.

Of course, how to do this will depend on your situation. If you are living in a country where the second language is spoken, then the opportunities for interaction are everywhere, but you will first need to learn some beginning language to get conversations started. You could do this by just immersing yourself in the second language environment and trying to figure it out. But it is much more efficient to start with some explicit study. What you learn in a classroom will help you understand some of the language in the everyday world much more quickly. One way to make a quick start is to learn some useful phrases, such as are found in tourist phrasebooks. For example, learning to count in the second language and the names of some everyday items, along with translations of phrases like *How much is ___?* will allow you to begin doing some basic shopping. Learning phrases for greetings (*Hello*) and being polite (*please*) will show that you are trying to fit into the second language world, and make people more inclined to talk to you. After that, simply interacting with the locals is a great way to learn. I learned much of my second language (Japanese) by actively talking to taxi drivers.

Most of us, however, will be learning in our home country and will need some form of instruction. Many will use language apps like Duolingo or Rosetta Stone, and I discuss these in Section §62. The other main option is a language school or course. Find one which emphasizes using the target language (e.g. Italian) as much as possible in the classroom, rather than relying on mostly grammatical explanations in your mother tongue. But even the best language classrooms will not be able to supply enough exposure to the second language. You will need to find ways to get additional practice with your second language outside the classroom. Everything helps, and the more the better, for example watching TV or movies or playing computer games (§42).

But probably the best way is to read as much as possible in your second language. There is now an unprecedented amount of material available in many different languages on the Internet. If you are at an intermediate level or above, then reading newspapers and magazines is a useful and enjoyable activity. But if you are a beginner, you will not yet have enough language to access these texts. Some languages have *graded readers* (short books written especially for second language learners, in which the vocabulary and grammar have been simplified). The easiest versions of these readers can be read by basic beginners. There are many graded readers for English second language learners, but they are written for other languages as well, including French, Spanish, German, and Chinese. Reading children's books in the second language is another option for accessible reading materials.

2. Focus on meaning.

Language is about communication, so focus on how to express meaning in the second language. As most meaning is expressed by vocabulary, it makes sense to emphasize vocabulary learning at the beginning. Language apps can be particularly useful for this, because they can offer you many repetitions of new words in a systematic way, often in some kind of context. Many are set up to repeat words that you have seen, but not yet mastered, more often. As you gradually learn them, the app reduces the repeat exposures, and switches its emphasis to other words you do not know as well.

But for a truly quick start to vocabulary learning, simply memorizing words can be very effective. *Flash cards* (also known as *word cards*) are one good way of doing this. In the old days, they were typically index cards with a new word written on one side, and its mother tongue definition or picture on the other side. Research shows that people can learn more than 30 words per hour on average with this kind of decontextualized study. Today flash cards have been computerized, with websites like *Anki* (https://apps.ankiweb.net) presenting virtual flash cards, and offering the same kind of adaptive recycling mentioned above. Low-tech approaches can also work well. Before I went to Japan, I learned a lot of basic vocabulary by simply pasting Japanese labels on items around my household.

Once you have a stockpile of words, then you can begin to consider how they are put together in meaningful sequences (i.e. grammar). One way to bolster your understanding of grammar is to memorize phrases and sayings. You will know the meaning of these phrases and so can then start to analyze how the individual words are sequenced to create this meaning. As mentioned above, phrases are also an effective way of becoming communicative more quickly. For example, memorizing the French phrase *Je voudrais le <u>steak</u> s'il vous plait* [I would like the steak please.] is a good way to jumpstart your ability to order food while in France. By learning to substitute the 'food slot' with other dishes (*moules*=mussels, *potage*=soup), you can quickly learn to order a range of foods in a restaurant.

3. Focus on *doing* as well as *knowing*.

Although there will many facts about your second language which you will need to learn (e.g. that verbs come at the end of the sentence in Japanese), do not let your language study be mainly about memorizing grammar rules. This *knowledge* is important, but it is better to focus on being able to *use* the language when listening, speaking, reading, and writing. There are too many second language students around the world who are good at explaining their second language on tests, but are not able to use it in real life. Also, when you are practicing using the language, do not be too hard on yourself about the errors you will inevitably make, because they are a natural part of the learning process. You will make faster progress by challenging yourself and making some errors than by playing it safe and only using the second language in ways you are already comfortable with.

4. Learning a second language takes time and effort, so find ways of keeping yourself motivated over the long run.

Despite some advertising claims, there is no quick way of becoming proficient in a second language. Language learning should be enjoyable, but the timescale is going to be measured in years, not months. For success, it is crucial to keep yourself engaged with your second language over this extended period of study. Thus, maintaining motivation is an essential aspect of learning second languages. Motivation is highly personal, and you will need to find what works for you. For some people, internal motivation is important, e.g. learning a language simply because you enjoy it, or because it makes you feel more confident. For other people, external motivation may be more influential, e.g. learning a language to travel in a foreign country, or to get a better job. Many people find that working with others with the same language learning goals can be motivating. Whether in a school or informal learning group, the social aspects can help you keep going when progress seems slow. Others can also reassure you that you are not the only one having difficulties learning particularly tricky aspects of the language.

Power Point: Anyone can learn a second language. The keys are willingness to stick with it, to fully engage with the language, and to focus on meaningful communication.

1. This page on the website gives practical phrases in over 300 different languages and dialects. Other pages give translations for numbers, colors, time expressions, idioms, and several others:

http://omniglot.com/language/phrases/index.htm

2. This website gives tips on how to keep your motivation going while learning a second language:

http://www.omniglot.com/language/articles/stayingmotivated.htm

56

DO I NEED TO HAVE A SPECIAL LANGUAGE APTITUDE TO LEARN A SECOND LANGUAGE?

My friend and I are studying Spanish as a second language. She just seems to pick it up, while I struggle. Do some people really have a knack for learning languages while others do not?

It is a common belief that some people just have an ear for languages and are able to pick them up much more easily than even really smart people. It is easy to find stories on the internet about people who know 10 languages, and some who know many more. For example, the polyglot Alexander Arguelles claims to have a working knowledge of around 36 languages. So do these people have an exceptional knack for learning languages, regardless of intelligence?

Most language researchers agree that something like *language aptitude* exists, partially overlapping with intelligence and mother tongue language ability, but still distinct in its own right. But they have difficulties in describing exactly what it is, because it does not seem to be just a single ability. Rather it appears to be made up of several interconnected components. One of the best-known descriptions of these components was developed by John Carroll in 1965, and is still in use today. His four components of aptitude include:

- **Phonemic coding ability** (he ability to code foreign sounds in a way that they can be remembered later) This ability is essentially the phonemic awareness and knowledge of a language's sound-symbol relationships discussed in Sections §48, §49, and §51.
- **Grammatical sensitivity** (the ability to recognize the grammatical functions of words in sentences) This entails understanding how word parts (e.g., prefixes, suffixes) and word order lead to meaning.
- **Inductive language-learning ability** (the ability to identify patterns of correspondence and relationships involving form and meaning) This involves the ability to recognize the patterns of a language in the language input received (§97). This is usually done unconsciously, and so is more about benefitting from exposure than learning by explicit study.
- **Rote-learning ability** (the ability to form and remember connections between aspects of language) This is the ability to acquire language knowledge by direct study, and is particularly applicable to vocabulary learning, e.g. connecting a word's spelling and meaning together with flashcards (55). It is strongly linked to memory.

People can have higher or lower levels of these various abilities. Those with high levels of all four components will have the highest overall language aptitude. Others may have high levels of some, but not all, components, while still others may be relatively weak in all areas. But the way in which the various components affect language learning partially depends on the language learning context.

There are two general ways of learning language. The first is in a *naturalistic* manner; i.e., learning language from input without explicit instruction, as children do with their mother tongue. The second is through *intentional study*, usually with explicit instruction from a teacher (often classroom study) or language-learning app. The various components of language aptitude seem to affect learning more or less strongly depending on whether you learn language in a naturalistic or an intentional way.

The key thing for learning almost any language (whether mother tongue or second language) is the amount of exposure you get to that language (§55). In cases where you are immersed in the language (e.g., by being in its home country, like Peru when learning Peruvian Spanish), the continual exposure makes naturalistic learning possible. There are plenty of chances to make the links between the language forms and something meaningful (e.g., *cuy* = a tasty Peruvian guinea pig dish).

But to take advantage of all this exposure, you need some ability to discern the differences between the various sounds of the language so that you can make out the individual words in the continuous speech stream you hear. You also need some ability to understand how those words fit together to make meaning. So although all components are helpful, in naturalistic environments there can be a premium on phonemic coding ability, grammatical sensitivity, and inductive language-learning ability.

In instructed learning environments, there is usually more language analysis, although this depends on the type of class. In more formal classes or apps (which focus on practicing grammar rules, memorizing vocabulary in isolation, and rote drills and repetition), the ability to analyze language and understand grammatical explanations will obviously help your learning. There is also typically a lot of memorization in this type of environment. This makes high levels of rote learning ability particularly beneficial.

But if your language class or app is built around a "communicative" approach, which emphasizes using and practicing language in meaningful communication situations rather than explicit language explanations, then the same aptitude components as for naturalistic learning will be more influential.

If you do not have particularly high levels of language aptitude, will you be able to learn a second language regardless? Happily, the answer is **Yes**! As mentioned above, the amount of exposure and language input are keys to learning. Anything that increases this exposure and input (whether naturalistic or instructed) should facilitate learning. People with high levels of aptitude will benefit the most from this input, but everyone will obtain some benefit. The key is sticking with it, and continuing to benefit from the language input over time. This makes learners' *motivation* to continue learning and *willingness to work hard* over the extended period of time it takes to learn a second language crucial. Indeed, Alexander Arguelles suggests that high motivation, a proactive approach, and hard work were the secrets of his success.

While language aptitude (along with high intelligence) will help you learn a second language more quickly, they are not requirements. They will eventually be outweighed by personal motivation and persistence. This is good news because these are traits, unlike aptitude and intelligence, which can be strengthened and nourished, both by teachers and by learners themselves.

Below is a small sample of a test my colleagues and I sometimes use to get a quick measure of language aptitude[7]. The box contains words and phrases from an imaginary language, along with their English translation. Based on these, try to work out which of the four translations is correct for the two example questions. With time, anyone can work them out, but was it easy or hard for you?

- **kau:** dog
- **so:** watch
- **meu**: cat
- **ciu:** mouse

- **kau meud bo:** The dog is chasing the cat.
- **kau meud bi:** The dog was chasing the cat.

1. The dog is watching the cat.

   a. kau meud so
   b. kau meud si
   c. meu kaud so
   d. meu kaud si

2. The cat was watching the mouse.

   a. meud ciu so
   b. meu ciud so
   c. meud ciu si
   d. meu ciud si

Power Point: Good language aptitude assists language learning, and being smart never hurts. But in the end, factors that we have some control over (our motivation and willingness to work) will do the most to improve our chances of success.

1. Here is a piece by Alexander Arguelles. He reports that learning languages takes time and commitment, but that the rewards are many.

https://www.theguardian.com/lifeandstyle/2012/mar/16/i-speak-50-languages-experience

2. The Modern Language Aptitude Test (MLAT) is one the most-used tests for language aptitude, although it has its critics. It is based around the four language aptitude components discussed in this section. If you want to see some sample test questions, follow this link.

http://lltf.net/mlat-sample-items/

~

Answers: 1. a 2. d

57

IS THERE AN AGE AFTER WHICH IT IS VERY DIFFICULT TO LEARN A SECOND LANGUAGE?

I've heard that children learn second languages easily. I want to learn French as a second language, but I'm an adult. Does this mean that I have missed the boat and will never be able to learn French well?

This question does not matter for children learning their mother tongue, as all non-disabled children learn their mother tongue and become fluent speakers. Indeed, this learning begins even before birth, as the embryo in the womb hears and becomes accustomed to the sounds of the language as their mother speaks it. Even deaf children will learn sign language as their mother tongue if exposed to it when they are young (§87). The only real requirement seems to be that children are exposed to enough language when they are young (§47).

The story is much more variable with second languages. If learned when a child is young, then second (or third, fourth...) languages are essentially additional mother tongues, and the child will very predictably move on to being bilingual, trilingual, and so on. But the study of second languages often begins during adolescence or adulthood, and then it can be much more difficult, less predictable, and much less successful. The reason for this less successful later learning is one of the most interesting yet controversial questions in language development.

One possible explanation is the idea of a *critical period*. In the natural world, there are cases where learning needs to be within a certain advantageous time window, or the opportunity disappears. A well-known example of this is of newly hatched birds. The scientist Konrad Lorenz found that incubator-hatched baby geese accepted the first moving thing they saw as their mother, even if it was a human. This imprinting seemed to be irreversible once in place, but needed to be completed within a short critical period of only about 36 hours. Scientists thought the same principle might apply in language learning, and if a language was not learned by around puberty, it would no longer be possible to attain the proficiency level of a native speaker (§97).

As so often happens in the study of language learning, the effects of age and a critical period proved to be more complex than this. First, there are many people who have learned their second language after puberty and have achieved native-like proficiency. It is certainly not the norm, but it is possible, and so the critical period is not an absolute deadline. Overall, it is estimated that perhaps 5%-10% of late learners in naturalistic learning environments have reached nativeness.

Second, various aspects of language are affected differently by age. In terms of pronunciation, it does seem very difficult to achieve native-like pronunciation after quite a young age, perhaps as young as year 6. It is still possible, of course, and actors routinely learn new accents for their roles. Nevertheless, the majority of learners will carry a mother tongue accent if they do not learn their second language early.

Knowledge of grammar and morphology also show critical period effects, but they are much less strong and occur later, perhaps between puberty to late teens. While learning before this period can result in surer intuitions of language structure, grammar and morphology can certainly be learned later than this. The best adult learners may be virtually indistinguishable from early learners in everyday language use.

Learning vocabulary does not seem to be dependent on age, and all people in all languages can learn new words throughout their lifetimes. There is no research that shows a critical period hurdle, and so learning vocabulary is dependent on memory and the motivation to study.

Another explanation of the difficulty of later learning is simply the amount of input learners get. Children learning their mother tongue get a massive amount of meaningful language input. People learning later often do it in classroom environments, where the input is typically very limited. Even using language learning apps, few people would study for more than one hour or two hours a day. It is difficult to know for sure, but it might be that if late second language learners received as much language exposure as children, most of the age-related learning problems would disappear (though probably not for pronunciation).

Power Point: It is possible to achieve high language proficiency when beginning as a teenager or adult, depending on your motivation and your ability to maximize the amount of

language exposure you get. You will probably end up with a foreign accent, but as long as you are comprehensible, this is fine. In today's multilingual global society, this is now the norm.

1. This New World Encyclopedia entry gives more information on imprinting, ranging from the Lorenz geese example to the use of hang gliders to reintroduce threatened species of raptors into the wild.

http://www.newworldencyclopedia.org/entry/Imprinting_(psychology)

2. Here is a more detailed discussion of why it is better to strive for comprehensibleness in pronunciation, rather than trying to sound exactly like a native speaker.

https://ideas.time.com/2012/04/04/how-to-speak-like-a-native

58

SHOULD MY CHILDREN LEARN A SECOND LANGUAGE?

There are so many subjects to study at school. Will my children really benefit from the time and effort put into learning a second language?

The simple answer to this is YES, because learning a second language will benefit your children in many different ways throughout their lifetime. In addition to the obvious benefits and pleasure of being able to communicate in more than one language, your children will profit from several other tangible advantages:

1. Better academic achievement in other school subjects

Contrary to some beliefs, learning a second language as a child does not hinder any abilities in their mother tongue—in fact, quite the opposite. Children who study a second language seem to do *better* at other subjects (especially mathematics) than children who do not (§59). This is because learning a second language is an exercise in cognitive problem solving, which leads to increased critical thinking skills, creativity, flexibility of thought, and the ability to multi-task. An example of this is that young children who are bilingual develop the concept of "object permanence" at an earlier age. That is, they learn that objects remain the same, even though they are called a different name in another language. So a triangle is still a triangle and has three angles and three sides, even though it is named *triangle* in English and *kolmio* in Finnish.

It seems that learning a second language is as much a cognitive problem-solving activity as it is a linguistic one, and it is definitely good for the brain. It is interesting that children who study a second language (and so have fewer hours in school to study mathematics) still do better on math tests than children who have more mathematical instruction during the school day because they are not studying a second language. So the mental problem-solving involved in learning a second language seems to be directly transferable to mathematical skill development. Thus, studying a second language is certainly not time wasted for anyone, and can provide students with the intellectual and developmental challenges they want and need.

2. Advantages for university admission

There is also a strong relationship between learning a second language and university admissions test scores, with SAT scores going up for every year of language study. That is, every additional year spent studying a second language helps. Furthermore, while university admission officers mainly base their judgments on transcripts and test scores, they are also looking for a diverse group of successful students with the right stuff. Knowing a second language is one of the things that helps to give this impression. This gains in importance the more prestigious and competitive the university is. Although it is impossible to look into the future to know what university your children may eventually want to enter (or even if they want to go), having a second language will be one thing in their favor at admissions time, and will open up more options for them.

3. More options in employment

In 2010, US Secretary of Education Arne Duncan highlighted that only 18% of Americans reported speaking a language in addition to English. In 2018, it was estimated that this percentage rose to a still-low 22%.

In contrast, over half of Europeans could speak a second language. Furthermore, increasing numbers of people in all parts of the world are, or are becoming, multilingual.

Where monolingual English speakers used to have an advantage, because they knew the world language (§2), this advantage is fast disappearing. Now an enormous number of people worldwide know English as a second language, plus they also have their mother tongue, and quite often a third or fourth language as well. This means that the time when English monolinguals could successfully compete for jobs based on their English alone are over. In order to regain competitiveness in today's global world, Duncan emphasized that "Americans need to read, speak and understand other languages."

You might be thinking that second languages are useful for diplomats, intelligence officers, and airline crew, but not for the majority of jobs. But modern transportation and technology have led to ever-increasing contact between people who speak different languages. This means that there are now a surprising number of jobs that require second language skills. These include obvious careers like Hospitality (e.g. hotel workers), Customer Service (sales clerk), and International Business (salespeople), but also many that you might not have thought of. As the world becomes more multilingual, people in the following fields are increasingly likely to deal with people speaking other languages: health care, law enforcement, social services, and communications.

4. Avoiding dementia in old age

Everybody gets older, and with average life expectancies increasing (around 80-85 years for the US and European Union in 2020), most of us will reach a time when our minds start slowing down. For many of us, this will end in dementia, with its memory loss and difficulties with thinking, problem-solving, and language. It would be great if we could do something to slow this process down. Well, there is—learning a second language (§70 & 71) (and perhaps eating dark chocolate!). It has been found that regularly using two languages in your daily life can delay the symptoms of dementia by 4-5 years!

Power Point: The mental exercise one goes through in learning a second language helps sharpen the brain for learning other subjects and for delaying dementia in old age. Second languages also help in obtaining university admission and good employment.

1. For much more on the many benefits of learning a second language:

https://www.actfl.org/research/research-findings

2. For more information on how second languages delay dementia:

http://www.bbc.co.uk/news/uk-scotland-edinburgh-east-fife-24836837

59

LEARNING A SECOND LANGUAGE WILL HELP YOUR CHILDREN IN MANY WAYS

I am thinking of having my young children learn a second language, but will it hinder their first language development?

There are a number of very good reasons why you should want your children to be bilingual (§58, 1 & 2). Bilinguals have been shown to be better at multi-tasking, critical thinking, and problem-solving. They have wider options for university admission and in career choice. These advantages continue throughout life, as in the later years, bilinguals have greater resistance to loss of language due to dementia and Alzheimer's disease.

So learning a second language is certainly a good idea. This is uncontroversial when it is learned as teenager or an adult, but raises concerns for children still learning their first language. There is a myth that learning a second language while still a young child will somehow interfere with the development of the mother tongue. Happily, this myth is completely unfounded, and there is plenty of evidence that it does *not* hinder the mother tongue. In fact, it actually *helps* the development of the child's first language. Let us look at the various ways second languages can enhance mother tongue development.

Two important functions of the brain are 1) to organize the vast amount of knowledge it has stored and 2) to manage a constant inflow of sensory information. The better the brain can regulate this mass of information, the more effective it can be. This ability to regulate multiple strands of information is called *executive control.*

Like any skill, the more the brain practices executive control, the better it becomes at it. Balancing two or more languages seems to be one of the best kinds of practice there is for improving executive control. Enhanced executive control leads to a number of advantages, not all connected with language. For example, it has been found that bilingual children typically do better with mathematics. It seems that the enhanced executive control helps children to better handle numerical information and understand the underlying mathematical principles.

Beyond better executive control in general, learning a second language strengthens the first language. It does this by increasing children's ability to work with both sounds and symbols.

Children get a lot of exposure to the sounds of their mother tongue and soon learn to discriminate between these sounds. But when they are exposed to the sounds of a second language, they have to deal with new sounds as well as old sounds in new second-language words. This leads to better overall *phonological awareness* and increased attention to the sounds of their mother tongue. Better phonological skills support the development of literacy skills in children, as they are better able to match the sounds of a language (e.g., the *a* sound in *cat*) with their written equivalents (the letter *a*). Importantly, it is general phonological knowledge, rather than just knowing the sounds of one's mother tongue, that facilitates learning to read.

Of course, one excellent way of teaching children a second language is to speak that language in the home (§46). But the best proof that learning a second language while young actually improves first language performance comes from the standardized test scores of students who have studied a second language in school.

Comparisons have been made between the scores of monolingual children and those who studied a second language. The results are clear: children who have studied a second language tend to have better scores across the board, with a particularly strong advantage in literacy and mathematics.

For example, Grade 5 students who had studied a second language did better on the language section of the Iowa Test of Basic Skills (ITBS), and the English language arts, mathematics, science, and social studies sections of the Louisiana Educational Assessment Program for the 21st Century (LEAP21) test. Furthermore, the longer children study a second language, the higher the scores on standardized tests. Grade 10 children had higher scores in English and math on the Massachusetts Comprehensive Assessment Test (MCAS) if they studied second languages for 2-3 years, but those with 7 years of study had even better scores.

If we look at just mathematics scores, we find even more evidence for the value of second language education. Grade 3 students in Georgia who received four years of second language instruction (30 minutes a day; 5 days a week) did better on the mathematics section of the ITBS than students with no second language training but with more math instruction during this time.

~

Power Point: Rather than impairing a child's first language, studying a second language actually improves 1) the child's skills in their first language, and 2) many other school subjects as well. This facilitation has been consistently shown by scores on a variety of standardized tests.

1. An interview with cognitive psychologist Ellen Bialystok, outlining several reasons why bilingualism is advantageous:

http://www.nytimes.com/2011/05/31/science/31conversation.html?

2. An easy-to-understand listing of some of the benefits of learning a second language:

https://www.languageconnectsfoundation.org/connect-with-language/the-benefits-of-learning-languages

60

AT WHAT AGE SHOULD SECOND LANGUAGE TEACHING START IN SCHOOLS?

Some schools are beginning second language instruction earlier and earlier. Does this head start always lead to better second language learning?

It may seem intuitive that starting to learn a second language earlier in school is better than waiting until later. But it is not always true that earlier equals better. It depends on many things, including how children learn, and how the second language is taught. Children develop more than just "school knowledge" at a young age, and formal schooling may not be the best way to develop their overall skills while this young.

In England, where children start school at age 4, around 130 early childhood education experts argued that formal education should not start until age 7. Instead, they believe that earlier schooling should be informal and should consist of play-based learning. This is because play is important for children's development: it stimulates healthy growth of the brain, the ability to learn in general, and social development. In essence, play-based learning prepares children for later formal schooling, where success is largely dependent on their emotional and social maturity.

So what may be more important than the *age* children start schooling is what *kind* of schooling they get. Focused play-based learning organized by teachers who understand young learning patterns will probably be beneficial. But formal instruction in (and often the testing of) numbers, reading, and writing (the three Rs) at too early an age may well be counterproductive.

How does this relate to learning second languages? Should schools start language lessons in early grades or not? To answer these questions, let us take a closer look at how children learn as they grow older.

Young children have undeveloped cognitive abilities, and so have difficulties taking on board grammatical explanations and other types of language analysis. They are much better at learning skills like speaking and listening, where emphasis is on *doing* rather than *memorizing knowledge*. Similar to the play-based ideas above, early learners need schooling where language is meaningful, fun, and embedded in interesting, engaging activities. With this kind of coaching, young learners can benefit from early language instruction. Conversely, more formal, rule-based instruction is unlikely to be effective.

But there also needs to be enough classroom time to make the training worthwhile. While there is no magic number of how many hours per week is enough, a single hour a week is almost certainly not sufficient. Children need consistent exposure to the second language to learn it in a naturalistic way (§56) and to make enough progress so that they feel successful. Language programs need to be realistic about the number of hours necessary to learn a second language, and drip-feeding students with very limited classroom time will not produce advanced second language speakers, even if they start early. More likely, it will only frustrate them and put them off languages altogether.

Older children are more cognitively mature and have better-developed analytical skills than younger children. They are better at learning grammar and morphology (the more rule-based aspects of language). They can analyze language as a subject, which allows the learning of language through analysis, in addition to meaning-based exposure. Older learners also have more knowledge of their mother tongue to support the learning of their second language. All this means that older learners are better able to benefit from language instruction that teaches about rules, although even with older children, maximizing language input and interaction in classrooms is crucial.

Older children generally learn faster in formal schooling than younger children, and so can catch up to children who start languages earlier but learn at a slower rate. Some Canadian research suggests that it take more than 1,000 classroom hours for early starters to retain their head start advantage. Given that many schools only offer minimal hours per week in second languages, most children will likely fall short of this total. In these cases, older children who start learning languages later may well overtake early starters, in spite of the early starters' head start.

Overall, teaching needs to be designed with an understanding of these kinds of younger/older differences, and can only be taught efficiently if teachers are trained in children's developing educational characteristics and needs. The teachers also need training in the art of language instruction. Just because a person speaks a second language does not mean they can teach it effectively!

Against this background, it must be said that there is a trend internationally to begin second language instruction earlier in school systems. For example, in Austria, Italy, Luxembourg, and Spain, children start learning their initial second language at age 6, and so many of the issues of starting young discussed earlier in this section apply. In the US, fewer than one-third of elementary schools even offer second languages, and most students who study a second language do not start before they are 14. In these cases, students are more cognitively mature and should be able to benefit from whatever type of class that is offered.

If you are in the position to choose your children's school, here are some important questions to ask about their second language provision:

1. How many hours per week will my child get in the second language—not only this year, but in the coming years?
2. What kind of teaching approach does the school use: playful, communicatively situated activities, or more formal learning of rules and language drills? Is this appropriate for the age of your child?
3. Do the teachers have any qualifications/background in second language teaching, as opposed to just being able to speak the language?

Power Point: Teaching second languages earlier in school only makes sense if 1) there is plenty of language input, 2) the teaching is based on meaningful, interesting communication activities and not just drills, and 3) the teachers are well trained in the educational needs of early language learners.

1. On this BBC webpage, Sophie Hardach discusses learning languages when people are either younger or older:

https://www.bbc.com/future/article/20181024-the-best-age-to-learn-a-foreign-language

2. If you really want to give your children a good start to learning second languages, then it pays to begin at home. This site explains that even one hour per day of play-based social interaction in a second language can help young children begin to learn that language without negatively affecting their mother tongue development:

https://theirworld.org/news/babies-can-learn-second-language-in-one-hour-per-day/

61

THE PROBLEMS OF IMMERSING CHILDREN WITH ENGLISH AS A SECOND LANGUAGE IN ENGLISH-ONLY SCHOOL SYSTEMS

Monolingual children learn English in English-only school systems, so why shouldn't this also work for children with English as a Second Language?

The substantial number of English as a Second Language (ESL) students challenges school systems. (These students are also often referred to as English Language Learners, or ELLs). Virtually everybody would agree that children should learn the primary language of the country they are living in. The question is, what is the best way to achieve this?

There are various approaches, and several use instruction in the child's first language as a way of supporting academic achievement while the second language is being mastered. However, in the United States, there is a trend towards an English-only approach, where children are placed into schooling exclusively in English whether they can understand the teacher or not. This has partly been driven by the No Child Left Behind (NCLB) and Race to the Top policies (RTT), which stress high-stakes testing of English proficiency but give little/no credit for knowledge of other languages.

So how has this sink or swim approach worked out? Not especially well, it seems. There is very little evidence that English-only policies and NCLB/RTT policies have led to gains in the English language proficiency of ESL children. To understand why not, we need to understand how language learning takes place.

Language is too big and complex to just speak of knowing a language or not. In school terms, it is useful to distinguish between general language used for everyday purposes (*Where did you buy your new bicycle? I like her red shoes*) and academic language used to understand and discuss school subjects (*A thermometer is an instrument used to measure temperature*).

General language is about things children already know about (bicycles, shoes) and so they only have to match new English words to known concepts. This makes it easier to learn, and children generally pick it up from the environment, largely from playing and interacting with other children. It is also learned mainly in the spoken mode. English-only instruction may help with learning this kind of language, but children are probably going to learn this on the playground anyway with time.

Academic language is different. It is largely written, and involves learning new concepts (the nature of heat) and the words that go with them (*thermometer*). Thus, academic language is learned together with the ideas it is attached to. Success at learning academic language also requires quite a lot of general language to be in place, because it will always be part of any academic explanation. (Try to explain how thermometers work without using basic words like *hot, cold, heat, up, down,* and *glass*). It also requires literacy, because as children move through school, an increasing amount of information comes from textbooks. So it is extremely difficult for children to learn academic language and ideas without a solid foundation of general language plus literacy, because a child will simply not understand the explanations, written or spoken.

It is estimated children know about 5,000 word families in their mother tongue by the time they are 5 years old, although this can vary considerably due to socio-economic background. (A *word family* contains similar forms of a word that have the same meaning: *play, played, playing, player, playful.*) This amount of vocabulary allows teachers to explain their subjects. But ESL children often come into school with little or no English, and fall behind academically until they have learned enough to understand the teacher's explanations. Often, they never catch up with their native-speaking classmates.

So what can be done to overcome this problem? One solution that has been shown to work is bilingual education. The idea is to teach grade level content in children's first language for the first few years while they learn enough English to be able to benefit from English-medium classrooms. In this way, once the children do transition to fully English language classrooms, they will not have a gap in their academic knowledge. They will also have two functioning languages, with all of the advantages that this brings (§59).

There are also a large number of other benefits:

- Children can understand instruction in their first language, and this is far more motivating than being lost in a class where they cannot understand the teacher.
- Research shows that children who can read in their first language find it much easier to learn to read in a second

language. So it makes sense to teach literacy in the mother tongue first, which leads to a faster transition to English literacy.

- Many children come from families where their parents do not speak high levels of English. English-only education serves to completely cut these parents out of their children's education. This frustrates both children and parents, and leads to the children becoming disaffected with their parents, who cannot help them with school work.
- Bilingual education protects the heritage (first) languages of the children. The government recognizes the need for US citizens to be multilingual in an increasingly global world, both for security and economic reasons (§58), so second languages are a national asset. Also, a number of heritage languages (e.g., Native American languages) are part of the United States' cultural legacy and should be protected. The future of any language is with young people, and so education in heritage languages needs to be part of the education system.
- One strength of the US is its cultural diversity, and knowledge of heritage languages helps children to connect to both their ethnic cultures and to their parents and family. This supports strong family ties, which are essential for a functioning society.

Despite the advantages of bilingual education, there are often practical constraints limiting its viability. Some schools have classes with many different first languages. In an extreme case, a Birmingham UK primary school reported having a staggering 31 different languages spoken at the school. But even in less extreme cases, it can be infeasible to provide full bilingual education for each particular language, particularly if there are only a few students with each language.

Luckily, the choice does not have to be between pure English-only vs. full bilingual education. It is possible to blend the two, adjusting the proportions to suit the situation of each particular school. The crucial point is that most ESL students need some help transitioning into an English-only school environment, and anything that can be done to smooth this transition will help these students reach their full academic potential.

Power Point: There is little evidence that English-only instruction is very effective for ESL children. Conversely, there are many advantages to a bilingual approach for helping ESL children learn English while at the same time ensuring they also make progress in their other subjects. Most importantly, research shows that the time spent learning a heritage language is not time wasted in developing English. Unfortunately states that have put English-only policies in place, made worse by the NCLB/RTT's single-minded testing of just English (without giving credit for bilingualism and any academic knowledge known in another language), have put schools under pressure to teach in monolingual English, even though educators know that this approach may not be in the best interests of their ESL students.

1. Educational policy is a serious issue, and it is not possible to do it justice in a very short summary. Here is a detailed discussion of how English-only and NCLB policies have (often deliberately) eliminated or severely weakened heritage language and bilingual programs in several states.

http://www.international.ucla.edu/media/files/W_W_HLJ_5_1.pdf?

2. On the first website, Patricia Gándara (University of California, Los Angeles) discusses the emergence and problems of the English-only approach, and suggests how bilingual programs can be promoted in the future. The second website has a number of other discussions of government policies and bilingual education.

http://www.colorincolorado.org/article/50832

http://www.colorincolorado.org/article/c46

62

SHOULD I LEARN WITH A TEACHER IN A CLASS, OR WITH A COMPUTER PROGRAM?

There are lots of computerized language learning programs available. Should I just use one of these instead of attending a language class?

In order to answer this question, it is useful to think about the pros and cons of each approach. Going to a language class with a teacher is always a positive option, as it has a number of undeniable advantages:

- Language learning is a complex endeavor, and having the help and assistance of a trained teacher who understands the language learning process, and its potential problems, is invaluable.
- Speaking and listening are interactive skills, and can only be properly learned and practiced with other people, such as other students in a class. Oral learning is facilitated by

teachers who know how to design classroom activities that promote meaningful interaction.

- Reading and writing are literacy skills that are not just picked up (§51). They require explicit instruction, which should include expert guidance and feedback from an instructor trained to teach these skills.
- Teachers can tailor instruction and materials to your specific strengths and needs to a much greater degree than any learning software can. They can re-ask questions in different ways if you do not understand, and discuss the answers with you in a personalized way to help you think more deeply about how the language works.
- Using language is a social process, and so is best learned in a social collaborative environment with other people.
- Language learning is a long-term process, and so maintaining motivation is essential (§55). Working with other students in a class can make you feel part of a community, which many people find encouraging, because they can share both successes and problems with others in the same situation.

Overall, if instruction is available and you can afford it, it is worth investing in classes. But if for whatever reason this is not feasible, language-learning software programs can be useful, with real advantages:

- They are convenient, because you use them at the time and place of your choosing.
- You proceed at your own speed; although this can also be a potential disadvantage if you do not have teachers/classmates pushing you to learn a bit faster than your comfort zone.

- Extensive input is one of the key requirements for language learning. Language learning software offers the possibility of a great deal of language exposure, both oral and visual. Many of the better programs make extensive use of video input.
- Teachers have to keep their classes moving, even if you are having problems with a particular linguistic feature. Software allows you to go back and repeat a difficult section as many times as you like (although often without any variation or new examples). In fact, repetition is one of the strong points of software. For some aspects of language (e.g. vocabulary), this can be especially useful. Nobody learns new words from only one exposure, and so programs that build in scheduled repetition, reviews, and additional exposures can be very effective for learning vocabulary (e.g., with adaptive flashcards (§55).
- All of the software advantages can potentially also apply to Internet language learning sites and language learning apps.

Language learning software packages can be very useful in the initial stages of learning a language. But they typically become less effective as your proficiency improves. This is because language's ultimate purpose is social communication, which is inherently flexible, dynamic, and interactive. Software is simply not as good as live teachers for presenting and practicing the advanced, ever-shifting nature of real-world language use.

So both approaches have advantages, and can usefully be employed together. Language learning software can give you a good head start before beginning language classes, and potentially offers supplementary input while you are taking classes. But software programs are unlikely to be enough on their own to enable you to truly learn any language.

I will not recommend any particular brands of learning software, because they are constantly changing, and I don't know your specific needs. But what should you look for in a software package? You will not go far wrong if you find software that supports the principles of language learning described in §55.

First, the learning program should feature lots of *examples* of natural language, not just *descriptions* about it. Learning to analyze the new language is useful, but you also need lots of exposure to it in order to start "feeling" it. The software should maximize your exposure to the language.

Second, the software should focus on how to express meaning, rather than teaching too much about abstract grammar rules. This means it should emphasize vocabulary initially, as you will need to learn a range of words and phrases before you can do anything with the language. Once you know an assortment of vocabulary, the software can start showing you how they sequence together in meaningful ways, which is the essence of grammar.

Third, look for software that is as interactive as possible and that encourages you to produce the language early on. You want to learn the language by *using* it, rather than just *learning about* it. Also, the learning program must be enjoyable, because learning a second language is a long-term process, and you are unlikely to stick with any program that is boring or loses your interest.

Fourth, it will take many exposures and repeated practice to learn any language point, so make sure that the software has lots of review and recycling opportunities.

~

Power Point: Both computer programs and classroom instruction have advantages, but the best approach will depend on your preferences and situation. Computer programs can be useful for learning and practicing language outside the classroom, but most people will benefit from the specialist help that a trained teacher can offer, in a supportive social setting.

1. Here are three websites that review, rate, and rank various language learning software. All are informative and offer a basis for comparison. However, be aware that all their evaluations seem to be based on either a single editor (Jill Duffy for PC Magazine) or unnamed editor(s), and so your impressions may differ than theirs. The first is website from *PC Magazine,* the second from *Effective Language Learning,* and the third from *Consumers Advocate.*

https://uk.pcmag.com/education/8711/the-best-language-learning-software-for-2020

http://www.effectivelanguagelearning.com/language-course-reviews

https://www.consumersadvocate.org/language-software

2. Here are two language learning websites. The first is award-winning Duolingo, which offers instruction in many languages, and keeps a profile of your progress. It is very popular, with a reported 500 million total users. The Digital Dialects website has language learning games for a large number of languages.

https://www.duolingo.com

http://www.digitaldialects.com

63

WHICH ARE THE EASIEST LANGUAGES FOR ENGLISH SPEAKERS TO LEARN? HOW LONG DOES IT TAKE TO LEARN THEM?

I am a native English speaker. Will some languages be easier or harder for me to learn, or are they all the same?

Second languages are not all the same, and some will be easier and faster to learn than others. It is impossible to say how difficult any language will be for any particular person, because each person's background and learning environment is unique to them. But we know that one general factor that determines the difficulty of a second language is the relative similarity or difference to the learner's mother tongue. We also have the experience of language schools about how long it takes to successfully teach students.

For English speakers, perhaps the most informative guidelines are those of the US government's language school, the Defense Language Institute Foreign Language Center (DLIFLC). It trains military personnel, government employees, and various law enforcement officers in over a dozen languages. It offers elite courses to highly motivated students. The courses are intensive: five days a week, seven hours per day in class, with two to three hours of homework each night. As such, it may be considered an optimum learning environment. Over the years, the DLIFLC has developed a good idea of how long it takes its students to reach basic, intermediate, and advanced levels of proficiency in each language. The length of its courses can give us an indication of the relative difficulty of various second languages for English speakers, and how long it takes to learn them in full-time study.

You may have some ideas about which languages you think are easier or harder. Try the quiz below to see how good your intuitions are. First, rank the clusters of languages for difficulty (1 = easiest; 3 = most difficult). Then try to guess how many weeks long the DLIFLC courses run to achieve a basic level of proficiency.

	Difficulty Ranking	Weeks to basic level
___	Arabic, Chinese-Mandarin, Japanese, Korean, Pushtu-Afghan	_____
___	Hebrew, Persian-Farsi, Russian, Tagalog, Urdu	_____
___	French, Spanish, Indonesian	_____

One interesting point to take from the DLIFLC courses is that languages seem to cluster together in difficulty. Romance languages (French, Spanish) are generally the easiest for English speakers, with a 36-week basic course. (Indonesian is similar.) This means that it is possible to reach a basic functional level in a half-year of very intensive study. This is because Romance languages are the most similar to English. They are all *cognate* languages; that is, they all descended from the same ancestor language, *Indo-European*. This means they have similar sounds, and crucially, use a similar alphabet and writing system (e.g., they are read from left to right). Much of the vocabulary is also comparable, with some word sets being exact matches (English *generation* = German *generation*) and others being very similar (Spanish *generación*). There are also other word sets that are not quite so similar, but which still offer useful clues if learners know the correspondence rules between the languages; e.g. French *-té* = Spanish *-dad* → *nationalité* / *nacionalidad*.

There are a group of languages that take 48 weeks (e.g. Hebrew and Russian), and these have features which make them more difficult. For example, Hebrew uses a different alphabet, and it is also read right to left, which takes some getting used to for English speakers. Similarly, Russian uses a different alphabet.

The most difficult languages taught are Arabic, Pushtu-Afghan, and three Oriental languages (64 weeks). These three Oriental languages are unrelated to English and have completely different writing systems, so it is not surprising they are relatively difficult. English (and most languages) use alphabets, where writing symbols correspond with sounds (e.g. the letter *t* corresponds to the /t/ sound). But in Chinese (and to a large extent Japanese), the written ideographs correspond with concepts. This means that instead of needing to learn only the letters in an alphabet (e.g., English = 26, Arabic = 28, Ukrainian = 32), learners of Chinese and Japanese must memorize thousands of ideographs to read and write at a proficient level.

book *(noun)*	סֵפֶר	книга	本	书
English	Hebrew	Russian	Japanese	Chinese (simplified)

comparison of different written scripts

While the number of weeks required to reach a basic level may not seem so high, they add up to a huge number of learning hours. Each week of full-time study is at least 45 hours, and so the easiest group of languages (35-36 weeks) requires at least 1,575-1,620 hours. If you are learning on your own and consistently spend an hour a day studying, it would take well over 4 years to accumulate this number of hours. And this is only to achieve a basic level. Clearly, learning a second language takes a considerable amount of time and engagement.

Here is the complete course information for the languages listed earlier:

Language	Level		
	Basic	Intermediate	Advanced
French	36	18	18
Spanish	36	18	18
Indonesian	35	(not offered)	(not offered)
Hebrew	48	19	19
Persian-Farsi	48	19	19
Russian	48	19	19
Tagalog	48	19	19
Urdu	48	(not offered)	(not offered)
Arabic	64	19	19
Chinese-Mandarin	64	19	19
Japanese	64	(not offered)	(not offered)
Korean	64	19	19
Pushtu-Afghan	64	19	19

Power Point: Some languages will be easier or more difficult for English speakers to learn, but all will require a sustained period of study.

1. Here are language difficulty ratings based on the Foreign Service Institute, the primary training institution for the US foreign affairs community, including diplomats. It is interesting to compare their figures with those from the DLIFLC above, as there are some differences:

https://www.state.gov/foreign-language-training

2. Here is more discussion about the relative difficulty of learning second languages:

http://aboutworldlanguages.com/language-difficulty

64

CRAMMING FOR LANGUAGE TESTS: A WASTE OF TIME?

I am learning* [insert your second language here] *and want/need to take a test on it. But I haven't studied as much as I should have. I saw an ad that promised I could do well on the test by taking their two-week course. Is that really possible?

You have been studying a second language, and at some point, you might want to take a test to check your proficiency. There are many possible reasons for doing this. You might just be curious and want to see how you are doing. But there are many more formal reasons for needing a test score. You might need test score educational purposes, for example, to gain entrance to a good university, or to waive out of foreign language requirements once you are accepted. You may also need official documentation for employment purposes (e.g., a prospective job requires proficiency in Japanese).

Many languages have internationally accepted tests which show your level in that language; for example, French: the *Diplôme d'études en langue française* (*DELF*); Japanese: the *Japanese Language Proficiency test* (*JLPT*). If you are a speaker of English as a Second Language (ESL), there are many options available, with two in particular being well-known and widely-accepted world-wide: the *Test of English as a Foreign Language (TOEFL)* and the *International English Language Testing System (IELTS).*

But what if you suspect that your second language is not good enough to achieve the score you desire or which is required? Can you cram before the test, or go to a test preparation school, as a short cut to push up your score in a relatively short period of time?

Unfortunately, the answer is probably "No." Of course, any study is useful, and cramming might improve your score slightly. But true language proficiency is learned over extended periods of time (§63), and so short-term study like cramming is unlikely to lead to any substantial improvements in your language abilities.

Likewise, despite what the advertisements and salespeople might suggest, test preparation classes will generally not help you do well on a test if your language is not good enough. Internationally accepted standardized tests are carefully developed so people cannot pass them just by careful guessing or using test-taking strategies. So approaches like memorizing the questions from past tests or memorizing stretches of language to insert into your answers ("canned responses") are unlikely to help much. Most of these tests measure your knowledge of grammar and vocabulary, and the ability to communicate successfully when listening, speaking, reading, and writing. These skills and knowledge are complex and take a long time to develop. It is unlikely you can improve them to any great degree in short period of time, unless the course is truly intensive and focused on language development.

However, test preparation lessons can be helpful if they are designed to familiarize you with the test format and timing, and give you some practice with that format. Each of the major tests is different, and understanding the format can help you focus on your language rather than what is required on the particular test. Also, practice with sample tests can give you confidence that you know what to do, which can ease your nerves somewhat and help you perform to your full potential. Similarly, each test has its own timing, and understanding this can help you pace your efforts to the best effect.

There is limited direct evidence of how much score improvement you can get from familiarization and practice. But it seems that the advantage will be rather small, and mainly due to the effects of the drilling of language that is often part of test preparation courses. If your language proficiency is high enough, familiarization can help ensure that you do not receive a lower score simply because you get confused by the test format and that you get the highest score that your language proficiency allows. If you are borderline, the test preparation course may help you get over the threshold; but then you may not have the language necessary to be successful in the school or company you are trying to enter. However, if your proficiency is not good enough, then no amount of familiarization will compensate for your lack of language.

So familiarization is a good thing. But before spending money on prep classes, you should check out the test familiarization web pages that most test providers offer. These might be sufficient for you. If so, you can spend the money you save on additional language lessons, as improving your language is the surest way of doing well on these tests.

~

Power Point: You need to know the format of the language test you are taking and how it works in terms of timing and type of questions asked. You can familiarize yourself with many tests via information available on the internet (usually from the test providers themselves). Beyond this, if you want to get better scores, you need to get better at the language itself by studying the language, not the test.

1. These are the official sites for a sample of language tests: the Spanish DELE test, the Japanese JLPT test, the French DELF test, and the English TOEFL and IELTS tests. Each provides information and practice tests free of charge.

https://www.dele.org

http://www.jlpt.jp/e

http://www.ciep.fr/en

https://www.ets.org/toefl/ibt/prepare/

http://www.ielts.org/test_takers_information/test_sample.aspx

2. There are numerous websites giving tips on how to study for various language tests. This one gives advice on how to improve on the IELTS test. But the points should be useful for other language tests as well.

https://www.yeovilhospital.co.uk/wp-content/uploads/2016/04/IELTS.pdf

PART 9

LANGUAGE PROBLEMS FROM AGING, ACCIDENT, AND ILLNESS

WHAT HAPPENS WHEN LANGUAGE GOES WRONG OR IS LOST?

65

TIP OF THE TONGUE, SLIP OF THE TONGUE, AND SLIP OF THE EAR

AM I LOSING MY LANGUAGE?

I sometimes find myself searching for a word. I can almost remember it, and it seems like it was on the tip of my tongue. Is this a problem?

Everyone has experienced the feeling of trying to retrieve a word or phrase that they know but seems just out of reach. You know that you know the word for the meaning you are trying to express, you can feel it bouncing around in your mind, but you just cannot quite force it out. This is known as having the word on the *tip of your tongue (ToT)*. If this sounds like you, do not worry; you are not losing your marbles. It is a fairly typical phenomenon and happens to everyone occasionally.

During a ToT experience, it is not like you cannot remember anything at all about the elusive word. Typically, you can remember if it is a long word or a short word, how many syllables it has, the stress pattern of the word (i.e., the rhythm of pronunciation), whether it is a noun, verb, adjective, or adverb (word class), and probably the beginning of the word. This last point is interesting, and Jean Aitchison calls it the "Bathtub Effect" in her book *Words in the Mind*.

Imagine a person sitting in a bathtub. His head and shoulders stick up way above the tub, and his feet also do a little bit. This mirrors what happens with language: the beginning of a word, sentence, paragraph, or text is the most noticeable and usually best known. The end is so to a lesser extent, and the middle part is the least salient/known.

For example, if you had to memorize something when you were younger (e.g., Lincoln's Gettysburg Address, the Declaration of Independence), if you remember anything about it, it will likely be the beginning part. Likewise, learners of English usually start constructing negatives in English by adding *No* to the beginning of the sentence, where it is easiest and most obvious (*No speak English*). This also applies to words. Aitchison gives the example of *antidote*: if you remember anything, it will probably be *an-*, and then the ending *–dote,* but may not remember the middle (*anecdote*? *antipode*?)

Similar factors come into play in *slips of the tongue,* where you accidentally say the wrong word. For example, you might wish to say *She came yesterday,* but inadvertently say something like *She came tomorrow*. But as with ToT mistakes, slips are not random.

Research shows that there are patterns, as illustrated in more of Aitchison's examples:

1. I wonder who invented *crosswords* (jigsaws)?
2. There were lots of little *orgasms* (organisms) floating in the water.
3. I don't have much sympathy with rich-looking *burglars* (beggars).
4. I don't *expose* (expect/suppose) anyone will eat that.

As these examples illustrate, when you experience a slip of the tongue incident, the incorrect word is typically very similar to the intended word in either meaning (1), form (2), or both (3). Sometimes, the intended word is blended with another word that is similar in meaning and/or sound (4).

Such slips are not uncommon: Jena Pincott in a *Psychology Today* article reports that people make one or two slips for every 1,000 words spoken. With an average speech rate of about 150 words per minute, that suggests one slip every seven minutes of continuous talk, or between 7 and 22 slips a day.

ToT instances and slips of the tongue both have to do with producing language, but this type of thing can also happen when you are listening. In this case, they are called *slips of the ear*. This is when you are listening but mishear the words. Of course you do not listen to something like *That is a nice <u>bucket</u>* and mishear *That is a nice <u>refrigerator</u>*. What often happens is that you somehow miss where one word stops and another starts. (This splitting of continuous speech into its component words is called *parsing*.) So the incorrect parsing can give the mistaken interpretation of *an ice bucket*.

In every language, it is necessary to parse the speech stream. In English, this is done based on word stress. There is a very good chance that if a syllable has a strong stress, it is the beginning of a new word. The mind parses based on this probability, and gambles that a strong stress indicates the next word. This usually works, but when the strong stress occurs on a later syllable, the parsing strategy can misfire, and words can be misparsed at the wrong boundary. Notice in the examples below how the original word had a stress on the second syllable (*il lé gal*), but was misheard as a word with stress on the initial syllable (*éa gle*):

1. The parade was illegal. (*The parade was an eagle.*)
2. Acute back pain (*A cute back pain*)

This also explains why the following old joke works (sort of!): *Be alert! Your country needs Lerts!*

The mental lexicon of the average native English speaker holds many thousands of lexical items, and these need to be organized in some way; otherwise it is difficult to imagine how else the mind could find, retrieve, and use each item as quickly and automatically as it does. The results from ToT and slips research suggest that the mind uses many features to do this, but meaning, rhythmic pattern, and the beginnings of the words seem particularly important.

Power Point: It is normal to occasionally mishear or to misspeak words or phrases, so this is no cause for concern. An analysis of these mistakes gives interesting insights into the information that the mind uses to store and use vocabulary.

1. For more on slips of the tongue.

http://www.linguisticsociety.org/resource/slips-tongue-windows-mind

2. Slips of the ear also occur when listening to song lyrics. Professor Andrew Nevins (University College London) explains about these in videos on this site.

https://www.youtube.com/watch?v=6Ve6Fuxiedk

66

AUTISM: WHAT IS IT, HOW DO I CHECK FOR IT, AND HOW DOES IT AFFECT LANGUAGE?

My child is 18 months old, and I sense something is not quite right. Might they be autistic? What are the signs of autism?

Autism (and the more current term *Autism Spectrum Disorder - ASD*) are general labels for a group of complex disorders of brain development. The Centers for Disease Control and Prevention (CDC) estimated that among 8-year-old American children, 1 in 44 (2.3%) had autism in 2018. It affects boys more than girls at a rate of about 4 to 1. Likewise, the CDC estimates that 2.2% of American adults are autistic. In the UK, the National Autistic Society estimates that 1 in 100 people are on the autism spectrum, totaling about 700,000 children and adults. From these figures, we would expect that all countries are likely to have substantial numbers of autistic citizens.

Autism has its roots in very early brain development, where the connections and synapses between nerve cells are somehow disrupted or fail to develop. This causes problems with how the brain processes information. The mechanisms of this abnormal development are not well understood. Symptoms usually become evident in infancy or early childhood, usually within the first two years. Autism manifests itself by problems in three main areas: social interaction, restricted and repetitive behaviors, and verbal and nonverbal communication. Autism-help.org describes some of the following characteristics.

Problems with social interaction manifest themselves in a variety of ways, depending on the child's age. Early on, autistic children may be less responsive to social stimuli such as smiling, eye contact, or hearing their name, while 3-5 year-olds may be less likely to approach other people spontaneously, to respond to and imitate emotions, or to use non-verbal communication.

Autistic children are prone to repetitive behavior, such as hand flapping, body rocking, or head rolling. They may also exhibit behavior that highlights orderliness, such as lining up toys or cans in straight lines. They tend to dislike change, and prefer consistency (sameness) in their life (e.g., a consistent daily regimen and diet, an unchanging arrangement of their room furniture).

Language is also affected by autism, and many children do not develop a sufficient amount to get along in daily life (about one-third to one-half). As with social development, different language-related symptoms emerge at different ages:

1st Year

- delayed onset of babbling
- unusual gestures
- diminished responsiveness
- vocal patterns that are not synchronized with the caregiver

2nd and 3rd Years

- less frequent and less diverse babbling, and/or consonants, words, and word combinations than developmentally normal children
- gestures are less often integrated with words
- less likely to make requests or share experiences
- more likely to simply repeat others' words
- more likely to have problems with pointing gestures

Age 8 – adult

- High-functioning autistic children can have solid basic language skills, including vocabulary and spelling that are on par with developmentally normal children
- But they may perform less well on complex language tasks such as understanding or using figurative language, general comprehension, and inference

Parents usually have good intuitions about their children's behavior, including when things are not going so well (§44). If you suspect your child might be having some problems, it is best to take them to a doctor, because early diagnosis is important for any program of treatment and support. Pauline Filipek (University of California, Irving) chaired a large panel of autism specialists, and their consensus was that the following 'red flag' symptoms warranted further immediate tests for autism:

- No babbling by 12 months
- No gesturing (pointing, waving bye-bye, etc.) by 12 months
- No single words by 16 months

- No two-word spontaneous phrases (not just echoing what you say) by 24 months
- Any loss of any language or social skills, at any age

Section §43 in this book gives a comprehensive description of healthy child development at various ages, and if your child is not achieving these milestones, be sure to discuss this with your doctor.

In addition, the website of the Autism Center of Excellence (University of California at San Diego) lists the following signs of what toddlers at risk for autism (12-24 months) generally do and do not do, although normally developing children will probably exhibit some of these behaviors as well. See 1 for the complete list.

Toddlers MIGHT:

- Talk or babble in a voice with an unusual tone
- Display unusual body or hand movements
- Play with toys in an unusual manner
- Show low enthusiasm for exploring new things or appear underactive

Toddlers MIGHT NOT:

- Use common gestures
- Babble or talk back and forth with another person
- Try to gain the attention of others
- Show interest in other children

There are a number of diagnostic instruments available, including some that can be used by parents. The Autism Speaks website has an online version of the Modified Checklist for Autism in

Toddlers-Revised (M-CHAT-R). It asks 20 questions such as the following:

> If you point at something across the room, does your child look at it? (For example, if you point at a toy or an animal, does your child look at the toy or animal?)
> **Yes No**

> Does your child understand when you tell them to do something? (For example, if you don't point, can your child understand "Put the book on the chair" or "Bring me the blanket"?)
> **Yes No**

The M-CHAT-R is a quick initial screening tool for children, but tools for adults are also available.

Power Point: Autism is a developmental disorder that usually appears by age 2. It manifests itself in less active social interaction, restricted and repetitive behaviors, and difficulties with verbal and nonverbal communication. Luckily, diagnostic tools are available for early diagnosis.

1. The first site gives information on autism from the University of California San Diego School of Medicine. The second features a downloadable poster of early warning signs by the National Autism Center. The third provides a comprehensive list of autism warning signs to watch out for.

https://medschool.ucsd.edu/som/neurosciences/centers/autism/treating-early-autism/Pages/signs.aspx

http://www.nationalautismcenter.org/autism/early-signs

https://www.autismspeaks.org/what-autism/learn-signs/develop mental-milestones-age

2. The first site has the M-CHAT-R test in many languages. The second site has an autism questionnaire geared towards adults.

https://www.autismspeaks.org/what-autism/diagnosis/mchat

https://psychology-tools.com/test/autism-spectrum-quotient

67

DYSLEXIA: PROBLEMS WITH READING AND SPELLING

I've often heard about dyslexia, but don't really know what it is. Is it a disease, a disability, or what? Is it curable?

Dyslexia is a combination of abilities and difficulties that particularly affects the learning and use of written language in people with normal intelligence. It sometimes affects the ability to work with numbers as well. It includes a range of problems and can be more or less severe, but it is essentially a condition where the brain has difficulty learning and processing the relationships between the sounds and symbols of language. In English, this involves difficulties making connections between the sounds of English (e.g., the /e/ sound in *bet*) and the written letter that represents it: *e*. The eye and brain can see the letters (i.e., it is not a visual problem), but the connections with their corresponding sounds are somehow difficult to make.

Dyslexia occurs worldwide and can affect people of all backgrounds and intelligence levels. Speakers of other languages may also have problems, but they can differ. For example, with the word *student*, readers of Chinese may have problems matching the symbols with their meaning.

student	学生
meaning	*symbols*

The Chinese word for "student"

Dyslexia is not uncommon, with the University of Michigan Dyslexia Help website reporting that 5-10% or more of the population are dyslexic (with some estimates as high as 17%), and the Dyslexia Association giving figures of up to 10% of the population being dyslexic to some degree, with 4% being severely dyslexic.

Dyslexia is not an illness or disease, and is not characterized as a medical condition. This means that it is not typically diagnosed by general doctors – specialist developmental pediatricians are better equipped – and unfortunately it is not usually covered by medical insurance.

Dyslexia can better be thought of as the result of a different pattern of "wiring" in the brain. This difference sometimes leads to non-language advantages (e.g., strong visual/spatial, creative, and problem-solving skills), but importantly, it also leads to information-processing problems when it comes to written language. Dyslexia is a lifelong condition that cannot be cured. Because it is part of the brain's infrastructure, those affected will not grow out of it.

Symptoms of dyslexia are varied, and can include the following:

- When a child does not learn to read although their other abilities are progressing normally
- Difficulties in understanding the individual sounds in words
- Missing parts of words or sentences when speaking
- General difficulties with written language, but no problems with listening comprehension
- Omitting words while reading
- Missing punctuation in written text
- Difficulties in reading different styles of type
- Difficulties in copying from a book or from the whiteboard
- Reversing letters and numbers past the age of 7 or 8 (It is common for all children to do this when initially learning to write.)

There are also emotional consequences of dyslexia. Children sometime appear to lose interest in school (or are considered lazy) because they do not want to be embarrassed by their difficulties or do not want to risk failure. But dyslexia is not just a childhood condition. Adults also suffer from dyslexia. Because it varies greatly in its severity, many people with less obvious impairment may not be diagnosed until adulthood, if at all.

Unfortunately, dyslexia does not go away, but once diagnosed, dyslexics can learn a range of language strategies that can usually help them lead normal, and even exceptional, lives. Robin Williams, General George Patton, Woodrow Wilson, and Agatha Christie were all dyslexic. Explicit instruction into the relationship between sounds and letters is usually helpful.

Some examples of instruction and strategies include:

- Focusing on the initial sounds and letters of words. An example exercise would be sounding out the initial sounds of animals beginning with the same letter (*turtle, tiger, turkey*) and explicitly relating the sound /t/ to the letter *t*.
- Giving the first sound of a word (/b/), and the second part (/ug/), and then having the learner blend the sounds together into a single word (/bug/), either with or without cards to illustrate the letters and objects.
- Showing that some sounds (e.g., /sh/ - the "Be quiet" sound) are represented by clusters of letters: *sh*.
- Explicitly teaching the spelling patterns and rules of the language (e.g., "I before E except after C, unless it sounds 'ay' as in 'neighbor' and weigh'" – as in *tier* and *receipt*)
- Using technology and software as an aid to language learning and use.
- Learning reading strategies, such as not worrying about every unknown (or unrecognized) word on the page, as long as the main points can be understood.
- Learning writing strategies, such as composing several drafts, each with its own emphasis (e.g., content, organization, punctuation). Using aids, like outlines, help to get the overall organization in place before worrying about the details.
- Learning vocabulary strategies, such as using flashcards, and using a systematic method of recycling the words so that they are seen enough times to be learned (probably 10+).
- Approaching the challenges of dyslexia with a systematic plan, with goals and measures to see how much progress is being made.

~

Power Point: Dyslexia is not a disease but a condition of atypical brain development. Happily, dyslexics can learn strategies and techniques to deal with their condition, which can allow them to lead productive and fulfilling lives, especially as they often have non-written-language strengths that non-dyslexics do not. But diagnosis is essential to begin early sound-letter instruction and training in language strategies.

1. The first University of Michigan website gives a more detailed description of many aspects of dyslexia, including its signs and symptoms. The second is the Sightwords website with a number of exercises that work on phonemic awareness.

http://dyslexiahelp.umich.edu/answers/faq

http://www.sightwords.com/phonemic-awareness/curriculum

2. Here are two more University of Michigan webpages. The first gives links to a number of games and puzzles that are good practice for dyslexics (and a lot of fun!). The second lists apps that dyslexics might find useful.

http://dyslexiahelp.umich.edu/tools/fun-games-for-dyslexics

http://dyslexiahelp.umich.edu/tools/apps

68

TESTING FOR DYSLEXIA: MIGHT MY CHILD (OR I) BE DYSLEXIC?

My child seems to be having trouble learning to read. Might they have dyslexia?

Dyslexia is a common condition (§67). Around 80% of people with learning disabilities have dyslexia, making it the most common learning disability. Although many dyslexics have no family history of learning problems, genetics do seem to play a part. It is estimated that about 40% of all dyslectic people come from families with a previous history of it, so family history should definitely be considered a risk factor. Dyslexia also commonly co-occurs with other learning disorders, particularly Attention Deficit Hyperactivity Disorder (ADHD). About 25%-40% of people with dyslexia also have ADHD, and vice-versa.

Dyslexia can have long-lasting negative consequences if not addressed. In a report for the American Academy of Pediatrics, Sheryl Handler and Walter Fierson identify a number of cumulative problems for children that can stem from dyslexia. They report that children with poor oral language skills in kindergarten often become poor readers, and unless help is given, they will probably remain so. Poor readers in 1st grade usually continue to have problems, and most (>88%) will still have difficulties as they finish 4th grade. The effect can be long-lasting, as 74% of 3rd-graders with reading problems will still have trouble reading in the 10th grade.

Dyslexic readers have to work harder to read, which makes reading difficult, inaccurate, tiring, and unpleasant. As a result, they often read less, which means less reading practice. This in turn leads to lower levels of word-identification skills and vocabulary growth, with the deficits only increasing over time. As schooling progresses into the "reading to learn" stage (§51), reading-impaired children will not be able to fully benefit from new knowledge presented in print about such important subjects as science, mathematics, literature, and history.

Encouragingly, if dyslexia is identified early, children can be given special instruction on sound-symbol relationships and taught strategies to deal with their dyslexia (§67), which mean many of the dire consequences outlined above can be avoided.

But this all depends on diagnosing dyslexia before it becomes a major problem. Because dyslexia is so common, a number of tests have been developed to diagnose it. Equally encouraging is that early diagnosis is now very possible: children who are at risk can be identified as early as preschool, and conclusively diagnosed in the early grades. Since dyslexia is essentially a problem of relating sounds to letters, the tests focus on exploring these sound-symbol connections. The University of Michigan website gives examples of typical test items found in dyslexia tests:

- What rhymes with *cat*? → *bat, mat, rat*. An early sign of dyslexia is a child's difficulty in learning to rhyme. Children with dyslexia often do not want to play rhyming games.
- Say *sand* without saying /s/ → *and*. Dyslexics may have trouble separating the individual sounds or syllables of a word from each other.
- How many sounds are in *sleigh*? This is a tricky one! There are only 3 sounds in sleigh—*s, l,* and *long a*, with that *long a* represented by 4 letters (*eigh*).

Dyslexia can take many forms, and varies greatly in severity, and so the most accurate diagnostic tests need to be given and interpreted by trained professionals. In most cases, there will be a fee for this.

However, there are a number of checklists available on the internet which can give an initial indication of whether you or your child might be at risk and whether further, more formal, testing might be needed. These checklists are convenient and can be completed at home, but all of them stress that they are not diagnostic tests and only provide guidelines for information.

If they indicate the possibility of dyslexia, the results should be discussed with a knowledgeable professional (doctor, school psychologist, teacher trained in literacy difficulties, a learning disabilities specialist, or speech pathologist).

Power Point: Dyslexia is the most common learning disability, and if left undiagnosed, can lead to serious long-term learning difficulties. Early diagnosis is important to begin special training before these difficulties become problematic. Dyslexia

is complex, and so diagnostic tests need to be carried out by a trained professional, but checklists available on the internet can give an indication of whether more formal testing is warranted.

1. This site provides age-specific checklists from the University of Michigan website and lists some behaviors which may indicate dyslexia.

http://dyslexiahelp.umich.edu/dyslexics/learn-about-dyslexia/what-is-dyslexia/clues-to-dyslexia

2. Here are two checklists from the British Dyslexia Association website. The first is for children, and the second for adults.

https://www.bdadyslexia.org.uk/advice/children/is-my-child-dyslexic

https://cdn.bdadyslexia.org.uk/uploads/documents/Dyslexia/Adult-Checklist-1.pdf

69

LOSING LANGUAGE BECAUSE OF STROKE OR INJURY: APHASIA

My aunt just had a serious stroke. The doctor said this might affect her language ability. What changes might I expect?

Aphasia is the deterioration of language ability due to damage to the language centers of the brain. For most people (particularly right-handed people), these centers are primarily in the left hemisphere of the brain. Aphasia is not uncommon, with the National Aphasia Association (NAA) estimating that it affects over 2 million Americans (1 in 165 people), with around 180,000 new cases per year. In the UK, over 350,000 people have aphasia. The risk of aphasia increases with age.

Aphasia can be caused by a number of things: traumatic brain injury, brain tumors, brain infections, and brain surgery. However, by far the most common cause is stroke. The NAA reports that about one-third of stroke survivors suffer some form of aphasia. Similarly, a study in Ontario, Canada found that 35% of patients who went to hospitals with stroke were diagnosed with aphasia before they left.

Aphasia can take a number of forms. The most severe type is *Global Aphasia,* where patients cannot read or write, and can understand little or no spoken language. At the milder end of the spectrum, patients with *Anomic Aphasia* can understand speech and reading, but have trouble finding words when they speak or write. The two prototypical forms of aphasia are *Broca's Aphasia* and *Wernicke's Aphasia.*

Broca's Aphasia was first identified by the French neurologist Paul Broca in the 1860s, and is also known as "expressive" or "non-fluent" aphasia. Patients may be able to comprehend language fairly well (listening and reading), but have trouble in expressing it (speaking and writing). In this type of aphasia, the language produced makes sense, but is very labored, and patients are usually aware of their communication problems. These problems include:

- Difficulty in retrieving words
- Difficulty producing grammatical sentences, because "grammar words" like *the, and, she,* and *there* are often omitted.
- Language output limited to short utterances of less than four words
- Halting and effortful language, with difficulties in producing sounds and words
- Problems with understanding more complex grammatical constructions, although simple speech is understood relatively well
- May be able to read, but will be limited in writing

When asked about his leg problems, here is how one patient responded (one minute): "Ah, No good, Ah … ache … and … Ah …

Ah … Ah … knees … and ankles … Ah …"

About the same time as Broca, the German scientist Carl Wernicke was studying aphasic patients who had difficulties in comprehending language. Sufferers of Wernicke's Aphasia (also known as "receptive" or "fluent" aphasia) are fluent, but have problems understanding meaning, with vocabulary choice and grammar being affected. This kind of aphasia is associated with fluent, but nonsensical language. Patients are often not fully aware that what they say does not make sense. Typical problems include:

- Difficulties in understanding the meaning of words and sentences, so patients say many words that do not make sense
- Speech is fluent, with normal prosody and speed
- Sentences can be grammatically correct, but might not make sense
- Serious difficulties with language comprehension
- Difficulties with reading and writing

When asked about what he is doing with an iPad, a Wernicke's patient responded: "I'd like my change for me and change hands for me. It would happy. I would talk with Donna sometimes. We're out with them, other people are working with them. I am very happy with them. This girl was very good."

Aphasia can last a lifetime, but the brain can also heal itself by creating new pathways, and so improvement is often possible. The important thing is that those affected continue to try to communicate and socialize. The American Stroke Association gives aphasia patients a number of suggestions for ways to begin communicating again. These include realizing that new ways of communicating may be necessary, starting the process with one-on-one conversations with sympathetic partners; compensating with writing, drawing, or gestures to complement oral expression; practicing common expressions to use; and persevering in trying to get their points across even when difficult.

Aphasia patients typically retain their intellectual capacity; it is just their ability to communicate that has been compromised. Thus, an essential requirement is for friends, family, and caregivers to help the patient express their thoughts in whatever way they can.

Power Point: Aphasia patients typically keep their intellectual capacity, but have problems with using language to communicate. Language deficits vary, but Broca's and Wernicke's Aphasia represent typical patterns of difficulties.

1. The first website is for the National Aphasia Association. The second site presents a poster from the American Stroke Association talking about stroke and aphasia.

http://www.aphasia.org

https://www.stroke.org/-/media/Stroke-Files/Lets-Talk-About-Stroke/Life-After-Stroke/LTAS_StrokeandAphasia_2020.pdf

2. Here are videos of Broca's and Wernicke's Aphasia patients trying to communicate.

https://auditoryneuroscience.com/vocalizations-speech/broca-aphasia

https://auditoryneuroscience.com/vocalizations-speech/wernicke-aphasia

https://www.youtube.com/watch?v=3oef68YabD0

70

DEMENTIA AND ALZHEIMER'S DISEASE 1: LOSING YOUR MENTAL ABILITIES

I know that dementia is something about losing mental abilities with age. But what is dementia exactly, and how can it affect my later life?

Everyone grows older, and hopefully your later years will be interesting and active. After all, Picasso and Michelangelo were still creative in their late 80s. But virtually all parts of your body will eventually start showing signs of age. With the mind, almost everyone will experience some deterioration of memory. However, if your mental abilities degrade more than would be expected from normal aging, this is called *dementia*.

Dementia is common but certainly not inevitable. A 2022 report from the Alzheimer's Association reports that about 11% of people aged 65 and older in the USA had Alzheimer's dementia (the most common type). The likelihood increased with age: 5% of people between the ages of 65-74 had dementia, 13% for those between 75-84, and 33% for people aged 85 and older.

Dementia is usually caused by the degeneration of brain cells in the cerebral cortex, the part of the brain (left and right hemispheres) that is responsible for thinking and acting, as well as containing personality traits and memories. Most dementia (about 50-70%) is related to Alzheimer's disease (AD). Vascular dementia (caused by a rupture of blood vessels in the brain) is the second leading type, accounting for between 15-20%.

How can you tell if you or a loved one has dementia/AD? The death of brain cells in the cerebral cortex causes a range of problems, and some of the warning signs include: asking the same question or repeating the same story again and again, forgetting how to do everyday activities like cooking or playing cards, and difficulty doing things like managing your finances. Dementia/AD usually progresses slowly, and by the time you become aware of it, the gradual deterioration in your brain has probably been happening for a long time.

The symptoms of dementia/AD vary, but one of the main ones is frequent and progressive memory loss, which makes most things more difficult. Other symptoms include the following:

- general confusion
- the inability to perform familiar tasks
- difficulty with abstract thinking and problem solving
- misplacing objects
- balance problems, tremors
- vision / perception problems

Of course, language and communication problems are also common symptoms, and these are covered in more detail in §71. Given the damaging impacts on lifestyle, it is not surprising that many sufferers also have depression (estimates vary between about 30-50%) and/or anxiety (5-21% with anxiety disorders and 8-71%

showing some anxiety symptoms). Other behavioral changes can include apathy, irritability, delusions, rapid mood swings, and even psychosis.

If you notice any of these in yourself or a loved one, it is worth seeking professional help. Your medical team have a number of ways of screening you for dementia/AD. They will probably start by asking about your medical history, your family history of dementia, the medications you take, and then give you a complete physical exam to make sure that your symptoms are not due to some other cause. They will also want to check for other problems that can cause dementia symptoms, such as hypothyroidism (underactive thyroid), vitamin B12 deficiency, Lyme disease (from tick bites), and neurosyphillis (from untreated syphilis). All of these are treatable, and can be checked with blood tests.

There are a number of short cognition and memory tests (5-15 minutes) that explore possible problems with memory, planning, attention, and language. The most common is the Mini Mental State Examination (MMSE). It has 30 items that include repeating lists of words, stating what day it is and the location of the test, writing a sentence, and drawing geometric shapes accurately. Finally, in some cases, your doctor may take an image of your brain, for example with an MRI scan.

Unfortunately, there is still no treatment for dementia/AD. Luckily, there are some things you can do to reduce the risk of developing the disease. Most of these relate to staying healthy in general.

- First, eat a healthy diet that includes lots of fruit, vegetables, and dietary fibers, and which is low in sugar, saturated fat, cholesterol, and salt.

- Second, exercise. It does not have to be overly strenuous, but needs to be regular; e.g. 30 minutes a day. It should include elements of both cardiovascular activity (which strengthens your heart and lungs), and strength activity (which keeps your muscles and bones strong).
- Third, stay mentally active. Try learning and doing new things, which forces the brain to adapt and create new connections.
- Fourth, stay socially active, as this also keeps the mind functioning. Perhaps the best approach is participating in social activities that also include physical and mental elements, such as walking with a friend while talking about something that requires serious thought.

Interestingly, speaking multiple languages is one of the things that can help delay the onset of dementia. Ellen Bialystok (York University, Toronto) and colleagues have found that people who have consistently used two or more languages throughout their lifetime retain more white matter in their brains (which transmits signals from one region of the brain to another) than monolinguals. It might be that the requirement to systematically switch between languages serves as exercise for the part of the brain that controls mental operations (executive control), and so strengthens the connections and pathways in the brain. This appears to make the brain more resistant to dementia/AD, and on average seems to delay the onset of symptoms by about 4-5 years. This is just one more convincing reason to learn one or more second languages (§58).

~

Power Point: Dementia and Alzheimer's Disease are debilitating diseases that will afflict many of us as we grow

older. Although there is no cure, a healthy lifestyle lowers our risk, and speaking a second language can delay its onset.

1. This website by Janssen has a range of information on dementia and Alzheimer's disease.

http://www.dementia.com/index.html

2. This newspaper report gives more information on Bialystok's dementia/bilingualism work. It also reports Judith Kroll's (then at Penn State University) related research.

http://www.theguardian.com/science/2011/feb/18/bilingual-alzheimers-brain-power-multitasking

71

DEMENTIA AND ALZHEIMER'S DISEASE 2: LOSING YOUR LANGUAGE

My grandfather has been diagnosed with Alzheimer's Disease. How might this affect his language abilities when I go to visit him?

This section will focus on the language-related symptoms associated with dementia/Alzheimer's Disease (AD). They are varied, and concern both the ability to comprehend and produce language; for example:

- difficulty in finding the right words
- inability to understand instructions
- difficulty in following the logic of moderately complex sentences
- inability to understand the sentences one has produced
- tendency to repeat oneself
- challenges with reading and writing

One of the key symptoms of dementia/AD is loss of memory, and this directly affects patients' ability to use language. As we age, it is normal for everyone to have their memory weaken. We may forget part of an experience (*What was the name of that restaurant we went to last week?*), but might remember it later, especially if given some hints. But people with dementia/AD may forget the whole experience entirely (*I don't even remember going to a restaurant*), and might not be able to remember it at any later point either. So the memory loss for dementia/AD sufferers is much more severe. For example, it is normal to sometimes have to search for words and the names of people you do not know so well. But one of the signs of early AD is forgetting the names of common objects and family members. Likewise, briefly forgetting details of a conversation is normal, but frequently forgetting entire conversations may indicate early AD.

One of the most noticeable results of memory loss is difficulty in recalling and choosing the right words to express one's thoughts. While it is normal to experience increased difficulty in recalling low-frequency words (§86), problems with common words are a hallmark of dementia/AD. It might be that the person is not able to recall the words at all, as in the Tip of the Tongue phenomenon (§65), or they may experience a slowness in retrieval, leading to long hesitations that affect their fluency.

Alternatively, they might have difficulty in finding the right words. They may produce instead a synonym which is not quite right, or a completely wrong word which has the same beginning letters (e.g., *blanket* instead of *blossom*, as in the Bathtub effect - §65). Or they may resort to giving a paraphrase of what the word means (*You know what I mean—the machine you use to clean carpets*).

The verywell health website offers the following advice when talking to someone with word-finding problems. First, if you know the word the person is trying to come up with, it is fine to help them out and say it. But if you are unsure, it is best not to offer multiple guesses, as this may confuse the person further. Second, ask for clarification if you cannot follow the person. For example, if they say that they like their "banger," point to their burger and confirm they like it. But the most important thing is to be patient. The person will probably already be frustrated with their difficulties in communicating, and rushing them or showing impatience will only increase their stress and anxiety, which is counterproductive to whatever level of communication they are able to achieve.

Language impairment typically extends beyond just word-finding, and so you will have to adapt to the person's overall communicative attempts in a number of ways. It can be frustrating, but persevere, because chatting with family and friends is probably the best way of reinforcing their language skills. The HelpGuide and verywell health websites suggest a number of do's and don'ts when communicating with people suffering from dementia/AD.

DO

- The problems are not the person's fault, so try not to get frustrated. Make them feel comfortable and safe, and this will make things easier. Stress is counterproductive for everyone, so take a break if you feel yourself becoming impatient.
- Speak to the person by name, and tell them who you are if there seems to be any doubt.
- Speak slowly and make sure what you say is short, simple, and clear. For example, only ask one question at a time and give directions one-by-one.
- Ask Yes/No questions (*Did you enjoy the TV program?*), which are easier to answer than open-ended ones that

require more complex responses (*What is your opinion of the program?*).

- Find simpler ways of saying things if they were not understood; e.g., a simpler statement with fewer words. Be explicit. Instead of using pronouns for people (he), use the full nouns (Mr. Jones). The same goes for locations and directions: *Sit in the red chair* is better than *Sit there.*
- Skirt around issues that might upset the person. This might entail telling white lies to avoid saying something that might be painful.
- Some patients cannot remember information for more than a few minutes at a time, so be prepared to say the same things over and over.
- Use various techniques to attract and maintain the person's attention: smiling, using gestures, touching, and keeping eye contact.

DON'T

- Don't say things that highlight the person's problems; e.g. *How could you forget that?* or *Try to remember.*
- Don't ask questions that tax the person's memory. They probably will not be able to answer, which is awkward for you both. And if they cannot remember what you have just said, just repeat it over and over.
- Don't give too much information at one time. Rather, offer one idea at a time.
- Don't ignore the person and talk to somebody else as if they were not there. Include them in the conversation to the extent possible.
- Don't use vocabulary that might be difficult, like low frequency vocabulary, idioms, or slang. Sarcasm and irony can also cause comprehension problems.

- Don't be patronizing or use baby talk. The person will probably be aware enough to be hurt by this.

Power Point: Dementia and Alzheimer's Disease can severely impact a person's ability to communicate, largely due to memory impairment. Being aware of the person's linguistic limitations can help make visits more successful and satisfying.

1. This website has more information on word-finding difficulties.

http://alzheimers.about.com/od/symptomsofalzheimers/a/Alzheimer-S-Disease-And-Word-Finding-Difficulties.htm

2. Here are more suggestions for communicating with people suffering from dementia/AD from the HelpGuide and verywell websites.

http://www.helpguide.org/articles/alzheimers-dementia/dementia-and-alzheimers-care.htm

https://www.verywell.com/how-to-talk-to-someone-with-dementia-97963

https://www.verywell.com/tips-visiting-people-dementia-97960

PART 10

LANGUAGE FOR SPECIAL PURPOSES

72

CSI LANGUAGE: SOLVING CRIMES AND CATCHING CRIMINALS WITH FORENSIC LINGUISTICS

The various* CSI *television series show many investigation techniques. Are there any that work for language?

The various *Crime Scene Investigation* television series have enjoyed long runs and high ratings. One of the attractive features of the CSI programs is their demonstration of forensic techniques involving everything from DNA analysis to insect growth rates showing time of death. Language is an essential part of crimes, criminal investigation, and courtroom procedure, so what real-life tools are available to police and the justice system? In fact, there are a range of linguistic analyses available, and this area is usually referred as *forensic linguistics.*

A common question in criminal investigation is whether a person actually said or wrote the sample of language in question. The importance of this issue is highlighted by a murder case from 1952. Two teenagers were trying to burgle a London warehouse, but were stopped by the police. The older one, Derek Bentley, was soon captured, but the other one, Chris Craig, had a pistol and killed a policeman. Under British law, Bentley was also charged with murder. The prosecution's case relied heavily on Bentley's statement of the events. It seemed to indicate that Bentley knew in advance that Craig had the pistol and might have encouraged him to use it. Bentley was eventually convicted and hanged. The statement was supposed to be an exact, unprompted and unedited, word-for-word account of Bentley's interview, and the police testified that it was.

However, a linguistic analysis carried out later by Malcolm Coulthard (Aston University, Birmingham) found that this was very unlikely to be true. Coulthard compared Bentley's statement with statements from other witnesses and with statements from police officers, and found that Bentley's was stylistically much more similar to those of the police officers.

This was particularly true of the use of *then* (a marker of time sequencing). Witness statements generally used it as it is typically used in everyday discourse: *Then I did something*. It was also not a very common feature, occurring only once in 930 words. Conversely, it was a very common feature of police statements, occurring 29 times in 2,270 words. Also, the way police tended to use *then* was different from everyday usage: *I then did something*. This analysis showed that the police almost certainly helped Bentley (who had a low IQ and was illiterate) with his statement, even though they testified that they did not. This cast doubts on the rest of the police testimony and on Bentley's previous knowledge of the gun, and so his murder conviction was quashed by the Court of Appeal in 1998.

In the US, one of the most famous cases that forensic linguists helped to solve was that of the Unabomber, Ted Kaczynski, in

1996. Between 1978 and 1995, Kaczynski sent 16 bombs, which killed 3 people and injured 23 more. Kaczynski had promised to stop bombing if his anti-technology manifesto was printed. After being published by the *New York Times* and the *Washington Post,* his brother noticed similarities in the writing style of the manifesto and Kaczynski's previous writings, including the expression *You can't eat your cake and have it too,* which is much less common that the more typical *You can't have your cake and eat it too*. FBI analysts compared a range of letters and papers provided by his brother with the manifesto, and found enough similarities to convince a judge to issue a search warrant for Kaczynski's cabin in Montana, after which Kaczynski was convicted and imprisoned.

Of course, criminal cases can also involve spoken language. Forensic linguists are often called on to do *Speaker Identification*—determining whether the recordings of speech from a criminal (e.g., from a telephoned ransom demand) match the recordings from a suspect in question; i.e., are they the same person? They can also narrow the search area for police by creating speech profiles based on the regional and local speech patterns of the criminal.

This can be effective, as was unfortunately demonstrated in the famous UK "Yorkshire Ripper" case in the late 1970s. When searching for the Ripper, police received a cassette tape and three letters purportedly from the killer. Although the forensic linguists were suspicious of the tape, they successfully narrowed the language down to Sunderland (a coast city in northeast England), to where the police shifted much of their efforts. But the tape and letters were a hoax, and the real killer, Peter Sutcliffe, was living some 80 miles away in Bradford in north central England. Luckily, Sutcliffe was eventually captured, though the hoax delayed this. In a bit of poetic justice, the hoaxer (John Humble) was caught in 2006, aided by forensic scientists who matched his DNA to that left on the envelope of a hoax letter.

Interestingly, forensic linguistic techniques can be used for more than catching criminals. For example, they can be used to identify the authors of anonymous or disputed texts. For example, a series of political letters critical of the government of King George III were written in 1769-1772 under the pseudonym of "Junius," with much speculation over who the author might be. Eventually, a linguistic analysis of the vocabulary in the letters (for example, whether *on/upon* or *among/amongst* were used) showed that it was very similar to the vocabulary used in the writings of Sir Philip Francis (a British politician), who was then identified as the probable author.

Power Point: While not quite as clean-cut as portrayed on television, forensic linguistics can be very useful in helping the police and courts investigate and decide criminal cases. It also has applications in determining authorship attribution of anonymous or disputed texts

1. This VICE site has interviews with two academics from the Centre for Forensic Linguistics at Aston University: Dr Nicci Macleod and Professor Tim Grant.

https://www.vice.com/en_uk/read/forensic-linguists-use-spelling-mistakes-to-help-convict-criminals

2. Another term for the study of linguistic style is *Stylometry*. Wikipedia's page on stylometry describes a number of examples of author attribution using stylometry.

https://en.wikipedia.org/wiki/Stylometry

73

THE LANGUAGE OF FLYING: AVIATION ENGLISH

How can pilots and air traffic controllers from all around the world communicate with each other?

Imagine a large international airport like Los Angles International (LAX). Planes are taking off and landing every minute from countries all around the world. The pilots of these planes speak a wide variety of mother tongues, while the air traffic controllers probably only speak English. The pilots of these planes are likely to fly into other large international airports, and the situation would be similar there, although the controllers would speak other mother tongues. Clear and effective communications are essential for flight safety, but how do all of these pilots and air traffic controllers speak to each with no misunderstandings?

Clear communication is promoted in two ways. The first was the establishment of English as the *lingua franca* (common language) of the aviation world in the early 1950s. The second was the introduction of standardized wording for communicating about specific actions, for example giving permission to land.

To ensure English as a lingua franca, the International Civil Aviation Organization (ICAO) requires pilots and air traffic controllers to have a functional level of English ability that covers pronunciation, grammar structure, vocabulary, fluency, comprehension, and the ability to interact. This need for this functional level is highlighted by a 2003 ICAO document that reported that communication problems played a significant role in 70% of accidents investigated. To confirm a functional level of English, aviation professionals must take an Aviation English proficiency test, although a review by Charles Alderson (University of Lancaster) suggests that the various tests available still vary widely in quality.

Introducing standard ways of saying things is the other way to avoid misunderstandings. For example, a controller could potentially tell a pilot that landing is permitted in a number of ways: *It is OK to land now, You are permitted to land, Landing is now acceptable,* and many more. But, in reality, there is only one phrase that officially gives permission to land: *Cleared to land.*

There are standard phrases for most everyday flight operations. The use of these phrases has many advantages, including that 1) there are a limited number of phrases to learn and understand, and 2) pilots and controllers can predict upcoming phrases, and so comprehend them better.

Here is a sample list of some common aviation phrases:

Aviation English	Everyday English
Taxi to X	Taxi your plane to position X and then stop there
Line up and wait	Taxi your plane onto runway ready for takeoff, but then stop there
Cleared for takeoff	You have permission to takeoff
Cleared to land Runway #	You have permission to land on Runway #
Affirm	Yes
Negative	No
Wilco	I **will** **co**mply with your instructions
Unable	I cannot comply with your instructions
Say again	I did not understand. Please say message again.
Mayday, mayday, mayday	I have an emergency

Although much aviation language is made up of set phrases, it is important to be able to communicate in unexpected situations, because not every situation can be anticipated with predetermined phrases. For example, there was no predetermined language that pilots Chesley Sullenberger and Jeffrey Skiles could have used to report and cope with an extremely unlikely multiple bird strike which took out both of their engines on US Airways Flight 1549. In such unpredictable and highly stressful emergency situations, it is critical that pilots and controllers are able to fall back on their English ability to supply essential information and to solve problems.

Even with a common language and standard phraseology, misunderstandings can still happen, as illustrated by these extracts from the communications between the cockpit of KLM Flight 4805 and a Tenerife air controller. It was just before the KLM 747 crashed into a Pan Am 747 in what became the largest air disaster of all time (583 died).

> **KLM:** Uh, the KLM ... 4805 is now ready for take-off ... uh and we're waiting for our ATC clearance.
> **TENERIFE TOWER:** KLM 4805 uh you are cleared to the Papa Beacon climb to and maintain flight level 90 right turn after take-off proceed with heading 040 until intercepting the 325 radial from Las Palmas VOR.
> **KLM:** Ah roger, sir, we're cleared to the Papa Beacon flight level 90, right turn out 040 until intercepting the 325 and we're now (at take-off).
> **KLM CAPTAIN:** We gaan. (We're going)

There were many causes of the crash (e.g. fog, many planes diverted into Tenerife airport, simultaneous messages causing radio distortion so the KLM crew could not hear that the Pan Am jet was still on the runway), but the main reason was that the KLM pilots took off without a takeoff clearance. The clearance they received was for their flight plan (*cleared to Papa Beacon*), and not takeoff (i.e., no *Cleared for takeoff*).

At small airports, the local language can still be used, and this is common at airports serving only small private planes like 4-seat Cessnas. But at international airports, pilots and air traffic controllers need to be able to speak English if necessary, and use of English is the norm for all communications in most cases.

Power Point: Clear, unambiguous communication is crucial for flight safety. The use of standard phrases and English as a common language helps ensure comprehensibility. But these sometimes break down, and pilots and controllers need to be able to revert to everyday English to resolve problems in emergency situations.

1. The first YouTube audio clip shows how communication problems can occur if pilots do not have a sufficient level of English. The second clip shows how fast air traffic control communications can be (in this case ground control), along with some of the humor that can be inserted.

https://www.youtube.com/watch?v=3AFv48IWhJw

https://www.youtube.com/watch?v=UXE-CFraGX8

2. Here is a Flightgear webpage that gives some common phrases with explanations.

http://wiki.flightgear.org/ATC_phraseology

74

ENJOYING POETRY: HOW AUTHORS USE LANGUAGE TO INTEREST YOU

How do poets create language that keeps you interested, entertained, and intrigued?

Throughout this book, you have hopefully seen that language is very flexible, and that there are many ways of saying things. Consider the following three examples:

1. Every language is alive and changes according to the needs of its users.

2. Languages have consistently evolved diachronically according to the requirements of their speakers, developing new syntactic patterns and lexis as needs warranted.

3.

Language likes to vary
Depending on the meaning you want it to carry
But no matter what you want to say
Language will change a little every day

Sentence 1 is an example of relatively straightforward English, the kind I have tried to use in this book. Sentence 2 is a contrived example of more academic/technical language (§19). Example 3 is a (not very good) poem saying basically the same thing as 1 and 2.

Which did you find the most interesting? Example 1 might have been the easiest to understand, 2 might carry the most precise information, but perhaps 3 caught your attention more and maybe even amused you slightly. Language varies depending on the purpose for which it is used, and sometimes the purpose is mainly to be entertaining and interesting, such as in poetry and novels.

Poets and authors know this, and they manipulate language in ways that make it more emotive and stimulating. Much of this has to do with word selection (§30). But it also has to do with the written and spoken forms of the language. If you know more about how poets and authors do this, you might even enjoy their writing more. Below are some of the common techniques.

Rhyme

Rhyming is simply using words that sound the same (typically in the last syllable), and every child has played rhyming games. The most common type is for the end of the lines to rhyme, and in my poem, lines 1 & 2 and 3 & 4 include rhyme. But there are many other patterns, such as in the following limerick (1 & 2 & 5 and 3 & 4):

The limerick packs laughs anatomical
Into space that is quite economical.
But the good ones I've seen
So seldom are clean
And the clean ones so seldom are comical.
Roger Gordon

Alliteration

Alliteration is the repetition of the same or similar consonants. This can be seen in the following example:

Writers weave their wonderful, witty words into webs.

Alliteration is used in poems, but is also a common technique in newspaper headlines (§30) to capture attention and create interest:

Teary Tara to Keep her Tiara

Alton Attorney Accidentally Sues Himself

Assonance

This is repetition of vowel sounds to create a phonological harmony. We can see this in an extract from William Wordsworth's poem "Daffodils":

A host, of golden daffodils;
Beside the lake, beneath the trees,
Fluttering and dancing in the breeze

Rhythm/Meter

Most things in life have a rhythm (music, marching, the four seasons), and language is no exception. The rhythm of English is counted by *stress.* You can check this by tapping a pencil when you hear strong stresses in the following sentence:

A woman can never have enough vocabulary.

Surprisingly, the stresses are not always at the beginning of the words, and are not evenly spaced according to number of letters or syllables. English is a *stressed-timed* language, where strong stresses are spoken at equal intervals. In the above sentence, it goes like this:

A w**ó**man can n**é**ver have en**ó**ugh voc**á**bulary.

A w**ó**man can n**é**ver have en**ó**ugh voc**á**bulary.

Authors can change the feeling of language by how they pattern the stresses in their language, and here are four examples. The most common is *iambic pentameter,* which has a weak stress + strong stress pattern, happening over 10 syllables (*penta* = Greek '5', so five sets of weak + strong syllables). (A tiny circle over a letter [å] indicates a weak syllable.)

No̊ l**ó**nge̊r m**ó**urn fo̊r m**é** whe̊n **Í** åm d**é**ad (Shakespeare, *Sonnet 71*)

Conversely, there is the strong + weak pattern:

D**ó**uble̊, d**ó**uble̊, t**ó**il ånd tr**ó**uble̊ (Shakespeare, *Macbeth*)

Then we have a pattern of three syllables, with two weak and the last one strong:

> Fo̊r the̊ móon ne̊ve̊r béams wi̊tho̊ut bríngi̊ng me̊ dréams (Edgar Allen Poe, *Annabel Lee*)

We can also put the strong stress at the beginning of the three syllables:

> Hálf å le̊ague, hálf å le̊ague, Hálf å le̊ague ónwård,
> Áll i̊n the̊ válle̊y o̊f Déath, Róde the̊ si̊x húndre̊d.
> (Alfred Lord Tennyson, *The Charge of the Light Brigade*)

Power Point: Authors and poets can change the mood of language by manipulating phonological patterns of language, including rhyme, alliteration, assonance, and rhythm. Knowing about these might help you appreciate their writings more.

1. Here are two sites to find poetry.

http://www.poetryfoundation.org

https://www.poets.org

2. If you want to write some poetry, here is a site that explains rhyme, and helps you find words that rhyme in different ways.

http://www.rhymer.com

75

THE LANGUAGE OF HUMOR

How can we use language to make a joke funny?

1. *"Do you believe in clubs for young people?" "Only when kindness fails."* (W.C. Fields)
2. *I'm on a seafood diet. I see food and I eat it.*
3. *I wouldn't say her new hat was pretty, and I wouldn't say it was ugly – just pretty ugly.*
4. *"My daughter was involved in a terrible train accident." "Yes, the trains are terrible round here."*
5. *What's the difference between a bad marksman and a constipated owl? One shoots but can't hit, and the other...*

Everyone likes to laugh, and a good joke is a pleasure to both hear and tell. But what makes something funny? Part of humor is the unexpected twist, where the joke leads you in one direction but then switches direction at the end.

A man was tried and acquitted of armed robbery. He turned around and said, "Great! Does that mean I can keep the money?"

The first sentence sets you up to think that he was innocent. The second one shifts this to show he is actually both guilty and an idiot.

In order to achieve this shifting of perspective, many jokes make use of ambiguity in language to set up one meaning and then change to another. There are a number of linguistic ways this ambiguity can be created.

• **Polysemy** (multiple meanings) A lot of jokes play on the fact that many words have more than one meaning. This is the case in #1 above where the "organization" meaning of *club* is expected, but then it is switched to the "weapon" meaning. We also see this in the following short gag, where the meanings of *strike* ("catch attention" and "hit something very hard") are mixed:

The first thing that strikes you in Mexico City is the traffic.

This one plays on the polysemy of the words *hard* and *drive*:

What do you get if you cross a computer with an icy road? A hard drive.

• **Similar Sounds** Some jokes switch one word (or more) that sounds similar to another to create humor, as #2 above (*seafood/see food*). Other examples using *pause/paws* and *wife/life* are:

How did the cat stop the DVD player? It pressed the paws button.

Shotgun wedding: a case of wife or death.

• **Parts of Speech** Joke #3 gains its humor from changing the word *pretty* from an adjective where it means "attractive" to an adverb where it means "quite" or "for the most part." We can also see this happen unintentionally in the following newspaper headline, where the *poor* was meant to be interpreted as "poor people," but can humorously be seen as "low quality":

Lawyers give poor legal advice.

• **Grammar** The grammar of a sentence can be manipulated to cause humorous ambiguity, as in #4, where *terrible* would usually modify *accident*, but is twisted to modify *train*. Pronouns (e.g., *it, he, we*) only have meaning when connected to other nouns in the surrounding context, and since they are not fixed, they are especially open to humorous misinterpretation. We see this in the following joke, where *they* does not refer to *friends* as expected, but rather *bombs*:

"My friends are trapped in Grand Central Station. There's been a bomb scare."
"Are they safe?"
"No, bombs are really dangerous."

• **Spelling** A popular type of joke relies on listeners being able to change the spelling of an unremarkable sentence in way that creates an unspoken, but amusing, alternative. We see this in #5, where *One shoots but can't hit* is changed from *shoots* → *hoots* and *hit* → something naughtier. These transpositions (sometimes called *spoonerisms*) are often used to imply a more risqué sentence that is never explicitly said. A couple more examples:

What is the difference between a TV evangelist and a bottle of fix-a-flat?
One heals souls.

What's the difference between an angry rooster and a lawyer? One of them clucks defiance.

George Carlin used the same transposition idea to come up with the following quip:

Don't sweat the petty things and don't pet the sweaty things.

So language is often manipulated to create humor in jokes on a wide range of topics. But is can also be the subject of the joke. Here are three language jokes I found amusing.

The past, the present, and the future walked into a bar. It was tense.

Two translators on a ship are talking.
"Can you swim?" asks one.
"No," says the other, "but I can shout for help in nine languages."

A mouse is in his mouse hole and he wants to go out to get something to eat, but he's afraid there might be a big cat outside. So he puts his ear by the opening and all he hears is "Bow wow." He thinks, "Well, there can't be a cat out there because there's a big old dog." So he goes out of his mouse hole and is promptly caught and eaten by a cat, who licks his lips and says, "It's good to be bilingual!"

• **Analogies** Although not strictly about manipulating language, analogies are another method of creating humor. It involves making comparisons between two things. Here we have the comparison between mind and steel trap, but with an amusing twist at the end:

Even in his last years, Granddad had a mind like a steel trap—one that had been left out so long it had rusted shut.

Power Point: Ambiguity in language can be manipulated to create the surprising misdirections that make many jokes amusing

1. The first website has a number of amusing sentences using polysemous words. The second has some very funny analogies. The 'Grandpa' example comes from here.

https://www.plainlanguage.gov/resources/humor/why-english-is-hard-to-learn

https://writingenglish.wordpress.com/2006/09/12/the-25-funniest-analogies-collected-by-high-school-english-teachers

2. Here is a website with many language jokes, although some of them are a bit racy. Two of the language jokes come from this site.

http://french-to-english.net/translation-and-language-jokes/nondescript-linguistic-madness

PART 11

HOW IS ENGLISH PUT TOGETHER?

THE GRAMMAR AND VOCABULARY OF GOOD ENGLISH

76

HOW HAS ENGLISH CHANGED OVER TIME? IS IT STILL CHANGING?

Sometimes there seems to be more than one way to say things. For example, is the past form of the verb* sneak *either* sneaked *or* snuck*? Why doesn't English just stay the same, with one correct way of saying things?

Every language serves the needs of its users, and when it does not, it is either discarded in favor of another language or adapted to be more useful. This means it is in a constant state of evolution.

Some changes happen so quickly that they are very obvious. Slang is a good example of this. Any parent with teenage children can testify that their informal language seems to change from month to month (§84). There seems to be a constant drive to coin new ways of saying things. This kind of vocabulary change can be quite rapid, but changes in the grammar system are typically much slower, and not very noticeable as they happen over time.

English has been changing since it was first spoken on the British Islands. It was originally a "word part" language, relying on suffixes to provide most grammatical information. But it gradually evolved to a language dependent on word order and prepositions, and by 1500-1700, the resulting grammar was such that it would be recognizable today.

As part of this shift, the number of suffixes and other grammatical items declined. For example, the Old English spoken by the Anglo-Saxons contained around 12 forms of articles, but now we have only three (*the, a, an*). Verbs changed from mainly irregular verbs, where they change their spelling to indicate past tense (*swim, swam, swum*), to regular verbs where the suffix *–ed* is added (*walk, walked, walked*).

Spelling in the days of the Vikings, William the Conqueror, and Chaucer was very flexible, and each scribe tended to handwrite his manuscript according to his own customs and regional dialect (*book, boke, booke*).

The introduction of the printing press to England by William Caxton in 1476 meant that books soon became much more commonplace, which had the effect of freezing spelling. (Every book couldn't have different spelling conventions! §77.) By the early 1600s, the first English dictionaries began appearing, which further standardized spelling. By the time of Samuel Johnson's *Dictionary* of 1755, English spelling had essentially been fixed to what we know today.

Likewise, the vocabulary of English has been in constant flux. About 85% of the original 24,000 or so Old English words have disappeared, but the remaining 15% are hugely important, because they represent the most essential things in life (*man, wife, house, good, high, live*). Most of the lost words were replaced by loanwords from a range of languages, but primarily from French, Greek, and Latin.

Usually the old words just disappeared, but sometimes they remained in the language and took on slightly different senses of formality or style: *kingly* (Old English: general), *royal* (French loanword: formal), *regal* (Latin loanword: intellectual). English continued to add large numbers of words, and Shakespeare by himself is credited with using around 2,000 words for the first time in print. Conversely, lots of other words continued to be lost (*anda* → envy, *galdor* → song, *cohibit* → to constrain, *temulent* → drunk).

English change continues today. Terms like *groovy* will instantly identify someone as being young during the 1960s/1970s, simply because they are not usually used by anyone from another time period. Other words were displaced; for example, *wireless* was displaced by *radio*, and then came back with a new life and a completely different usage in the computer era.

As I mentioned before, vocabulary changes like these are relatively noticeable, but the grammar changes happening today are less apparent. One is the trend of irregular verbs becoming regular verbs. For example, the past form of *chide* was traditionally *chid*, but the more regular *–ed* version *chided* has now become the norm. But sometimes the opposite is true: while *sneaked* continues to be a common past form of *sneak*, the irregular form *snuck* has shown an increase in usage since 1980, and now is the dominant form. Evidence for these changes comes from counting their occurrences in books published between 1800 to 2019 (see graph).

There have also been changes in verbs that end in *–t* vs. *–ed*. For example, while *burned* is typically considered the American spelling and *burnt* the British spelling, in fact *burned* is now used just as much as *burnt* in the UK, and it looks as if *burned* will eventually take over.

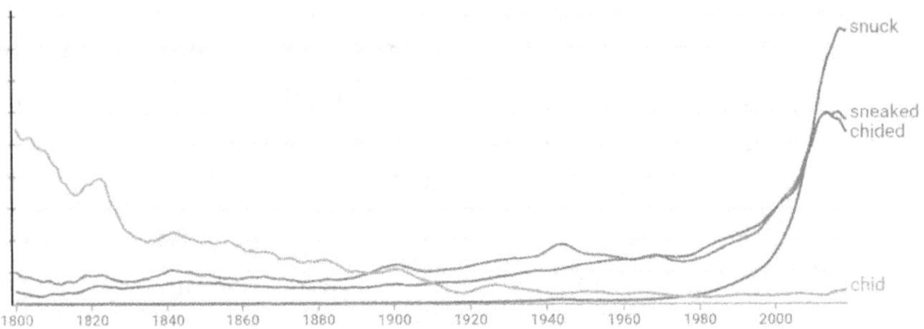

Some language commentators writing in newspapers are overly prescriptive and may rail against such new usages as *snuck*, referring solely to precedent, and maintaining that the old forms are the only correct ones. But we have seen that language is living and ever evolving, and so the only reasonable way to describe good language is to identify what forms people are actually using.

Language changes because people find the new forms useful, and language gurus need to accept these new forms once they have become integrated into use in society. Anything else implies that the commentator knows better than the millions of people using English.

Power Point: Every language is alive and changes according to the needs of its users. English is no different, and has evolved dramatically over the 1,500 years or so of its existence. This change continues today, and some English features are in the middle of this change with both old and new alternative versions in concurrent use.

1. This website has lots of fascinating material, much of it presented in attractive illustrations and graphs to show the historical development of English. It also has a great deal of information on English as it is used today.

www.thehistoryofenglish.com

2. Google Books Ngram Viewer. We have seen this before in §54 looking at the development of Teen Talk, and it remains a very useful and interesting site for examining language change over time.

https://books.google.com/ngrams

77

WHY ARE THERE SO MANY EXCEPTIONS AND IRREGULARITIES IN ENGLISH?

My child has trouble pronouncing and spelling words with silent letters, such as* de<u>b</u>t. *Exceptions like this seem harder to learn. Why isn't English more regular and logical?

Language is alive, and so grows and develops (and sometimes dies) like any living being. But living beings are not machines and so grow up in ways that are not completely logical. With people, this is no bad thing; how boring it would be if all children grew up in exactly the same predictable way. Languages can also develop in ways that are not completely predictable. Unfortunately, this makes them more difficult to both describe and learn than would be the case if they were completely consistent and regular. So where do the exceptions and irregularities come from?

The first source of irregularity is English's incomplete evolution from a word-part language to word-order language.

Old English had numerous word parts (*prefixes, suffixes*) that provided grammatical information, but as word order took over, most disappeared. A few remained because they continued to be useful: e.g., *–ed* (indicates past activity—*talked, exaggerated*) and *–s* (indicates plural— *odors, skunks*). But one suffix persisted even though it adds no meaningful information: the third person singular present tense –s: *Charlie likes to drive expensive cars.*

Sometimes the word part that changed was actually inside words. For example, the singular *man* was changed to plural by changing the internal vowel: *man men*. Similarly, verbs changed from present tense to past tense by vowel changes: *swim swum*. The irregularities come from some words keeping the old forms (*goose/geese; run/ran*) while most changed to more regular forms using suffixes (*boy/boys; kick/kicked*).

Another confusing feature of English is the "silent letters," like the *g* in *gnarl* and the *b* in *debt*. Some of these letters used to be pronounced, like both the *k* and the *gh* in *knight*. Unfortunately, by the time the sounds ceased to be pronounced in the 16th and 17th centuries, the printing press had been invented, and tens of thousands of books had already been published that included spellings with those now missing sounds. Any attempt to start over with revised spellings would have made all of those expensive books obsolete, and so English spelling was effectively frozen with the silent letters.

In the 16th century, there was also a move to respell some loanwords to bring them closer to their historical origins. For example, *debt* was borrowed from French (*dette*). However, scholars of the time added a *b* to show the ultimate Latin root (*debitum*), even though the *b* had never been pronounced in English. Other examples of added silent letters include the *p* in *receipt* (Latin *recipere*) and the *c* in *indict* (Latin *indictum*).

Another source of English's irregularities is the way the first grammar books were written. Grammar books began appearing after 1750, were eagerly bought, and were printed in many editions. Unfortunately, we now judge these books to have a number of serious shortcomings. It was the Age of Enlightenment, and Latin was held up as the language least corrupted by human use. So when grammars of English were written, most had the implicit intention of purifying English by using Latin models as a reference. This was a time of prescription, when learned people took it on themselves to decide correct usage and condemn what seemed to them to be improper.

The problem is that English is a completely different language from Latin, and its grammar is word-order-based, while Latin grammar relies mainly on suffixes. Trying to describe English in terms of Latin grammar was like trying to fit a square peg into a round hole. The grammarians were forced to fabricate a number of "rules" for English that made little sense, in order to follow the Latin model. Some of these misjudged rules still cause problems and controversy today; for example, "split infinitives" and "double negatives" (§78).

These old grammar books show the folly of trying to prescribe grammar rules from logic or intuition. Happily, most modern grammar books are no longer written by prescriptive grammarians dictating what they think should be correct usage. Rather, linguists refer to numerous examples of language use collected in multi-million-word databases of English called *corpora,* and then try to describe actual English usage. These evidence-based books offer a much more realistic representation of how English is used in the real world. The *Cambridge Grammar of English* is a good example, but there are many others (§78).

Power Point: Most of the exceptions and irregularities in English were caused by its historical development, which was not always even and consistent. Some of this inconsistent development was caused by the English's incomplete evolution from a word-part language to word-order language, its sound system changing but its spelling being frozen by the printing press, and early prescriptive grammars that were not evidence based.

1. Here is a more detailed explanation of silent letters and rules for how they occur in English.

http://www.myenglishteacher.eu/blog/list-of-words-with-silent-letters-in-english

2. If you would like to try using a corpus for yourself, this is one of the best: Mark Davies' one-billion-word *Corpus of Contemporary American English* (*COCA*). The basic website is free to use; all you need to do is register. If you like it, the paid version is still inexpensive. It will take a short time to learn how to use it, but you will then have access to the same language tool that specialists use.

https://www.english-corpora.org/coca

78

I CAN'T EXPLAIN ENGLISH GRAMMAR AT ALL. DOES THAT MEAN I HAVE POOR GRAMMAR?

I am helping my child with an oral presentation for school. There is a sentence that sounds wrong, but I can't really explain why. Does this mean that I have poor grammar myself because I do not know the correct grammar rule?

If the situation in the box above sounds like you, don't worry! Actually, this is quite normal, as there is a fundamental difference between the ability to *use* grammar accurately and appropriately, and the ability to *explain* it. This difference mainly comes from the way people acquire their language.

Native speakers acquire their mother tongue from the exposure they get to it as young children, hearing thousands of hours of it in their early years. Each instance of this input leads to an incremental improvement in their developing knowledge of the words and pattering in the language. Frequency of exposure is key, with more exposures leading to faster and deeper learning. This process is largely unconscious, and it occurs without much, if any, explicit instruction. The result is the ability to use language correctly and relatively automatically, with intuitions about what works in the language and what does not.

But this unconscious acquisition process does not necessarily provide the ability to describe the grammar of the language. Of course, native speakers can learn the rules of a language through explicit study, and many schools do teach this. But this involves teaching the rule-based explanations for the language to native students who already know and use it. This means that the resulting knowledge of the mother tongue's grammar is likely to be partial at best, because it was not a prerequisite for the initial learning and is not necessary to actually use the language.

Let us contrast this with someone learning a second language as an adult. Typically, they will get rather limited amounts of exposure, and much of their instruction will concentrate on explicit explanations of the grammar of the language. Unless they study for a long time, their ability to use the language will likely never reach the levels of a native speaker. But since they largely learned the language by studying its "rules," they are more likely to be able to explain those rules compared to a native speaker.

Consider the following example sentences. Are they correct or incorrect? If they are incorrect, can you explain the problem?

1. Fat cats eat fat rats.
2. Guitar cheap my sounds awful.

Anyone with any proficiency in English will know that Sentence 1 is correct and Sentence 2 is incorrect. This is true whether that person is a native speaker or a second language learner.

The real difference is the ability to explain *why* the sentences are correct or not. Native speakers will have gained intuitions that suggest that 1 is correct, but may have problems explaining why. Likewise, they may sense that the word order of Sentence 2 is simply all wrong, but not be able to give the specifics. But since most second language learners have been taught grammar rules explicitly, they are much more likely to be able to explain the structural issues. For example, description words (*adjectives*) like *my* and *cheap* usually come before the things (*nouns*) they describe. This is not the case in Sentence 2, which should be *My cheap guitar sounds awful.* The correct word order (*fat* before *cats* and *rats*) is maintained in Sentence 1.

Language teachers need to have a clear understanding of their language's grammar and vocabulary, and they need to be able to describe this clearly and confidently to their students (§62). An important implication of this discussion is that natives cannot be assumed to have this explicit knowledge. Therefore, all language teachers, regardless of whether they are native or nonnative, need to have training in their language's grammar in order to be able to explain it.

Another issue that makes grammar less easy to explain is that grammar rules are often not black and white. Consider Sentences 3-6 for correctness:

3. How are you? I'm good.
4. The team are confident.
5. To boldly go where no man has gone before.
6. Badges? We don't need no stinking badges!

Speakers of American English would probably judge Sentence 3 as perfectly acceptable in informal speech, and indeed, *I'm good* is a very frequent way of indicating a positive state of being. There is also the common variation of *We're good,* which means that a relationship is on good terms, particularly after a period of tenseness, or that an interaction, negotiation, or business transaction is agreed and finished. But speakers of British English may have judged this as incorrect, preferring *I'm well* in its place. Although the vast majority of grammar does not vary across national varieties (e.g., British English, American English, Australian English), there are a few differences, and this is one of them. There is also the issue of speech versus writing. While this form is acceptable in American speech, it is much less likely to be used in more formal writing in any national variety.

You might have judged Sentence 4 as incorrect based on the grammar rule that *team* is a single thing, and so the verb needs to be singular (*is*) instead of plural (*are*). But things are no so clear-cut here either. If the meaning is that the team as a whole has confidence, then *team is* should be used. But *team are* means that all of the individual players are confident. So both versions can be correct, and it is more a question of intended meaning than following grammar rules. There is also a national variety issue as well, because American English (unlike British English) prefers using singular verbs with collective nouns like *team* and *government.*

The correctness of Sentences 5 and 6 depends on whether you follow a prescriptive grammar that insists on fixed (and sometimes old-fashioned) rules, or believe that actual usage should inform grammar norms. The famous saying from *Star Trek in* Sentence 5 violates the archaic rule that you should not split an infinitive (*to go*) by putting a word in between (*to <u>boldly</u> go*), but such usage is common and is perfectly correct in Modern English. The quote in Sentence 6 from the movies *The Treasure of Sierra Madre* and *Blazing Saddles* has a double negative (*don't* + *no*). It is also in common usage in informal spoken English to create emphasis, but could be considered inappropriate in more formal speech, and definitely in standard written English (§79).

We can see from the six sentences that although grammar can sometimes be just plain wrong (Sentence 2), in many cases, "correctness" is not so straightforward. What is perceived as correct grammar can vary depending on what country one comes from, whether one is using an overly prescriptive grammar book, and most importantly, whether the language is written or spoken. In other words, you must be skeptical about the idea of one correct grammar for all cases.

Power Point: Just because you cannot explain grammar, this does not mean that your grammar is deficient. If you have good enough intuitions to use a language appropriately with the people you communicate with, then you have good grammar. But to explain grammar well, most people require additional study about the mechanics of grammar.

1. The Cambridge Grammar of English is a reliable grammar book that describes the way English is actually used today.

http://www.cambridge.org/gb/cambridgeenglish/catalog/grammar-vocabulary-and-pronunciation/cambridge-grammar-english

2. This website gives 10 grammar "rules" you can forget, spiced with references to movies and music.

http://www.theguardian.com/science/2013/sep/30/10-grammar-rules-you-can-forget

79

WHO DECIDES WHAT "GOOD GRAMMAR" IS?

I'd like to use good grammar, but often I get conflicting advice. Sometimes grammar experts tell me something is forbidden, but I see and hear people using it all the time. Is there some official source I can go to so I can be sure what is right?

The short answer for English is that no one officially dictates what proper grammar usage is. This is in contrast to many other languages, which have institutes that control and regularize them (see below).

But because there is no official organization to decide on good usage, who or what does control English? While "control" is too strong a term, English does have a cluster of influences that guide accepted usage, including grammar books, dictionaries, publishing conventions, and style guides. But the extent to which all of these guide usage largely depends on the context of use and the people you are communicating with.

In everyday spoken situations, when using language informally with people you know (such as with friends in a bar), there is nothing to stop anyone from using English as unusually or creatively as they wish, as long as the people they are speaking with go along with it. This creativity could include coining new words from word parts. For example, if you are thirsty and want a drink of a cool, refreshing beverage, you might say you are feeling "beerish" Your friends might find this wordplay amusing once or twice, but if you persisted in doing it for too long, they would probably soon tire of it. So although there are no official constraints against novel and atypical uses, language tends to be self-regulating towards conformity, as people communicating together will naturally tend towards language that is known and easier to understand and use.

The situation is usually more constrained in more formal contexts, particularly when writing for wider audiences. Published texts can be read by a variety of readers, almost all of whom the author will not personally know. In order to communicate most efficiently with this wide variety of people, the most effective approach is to use a type of language that is common to greatest number of people. This is *Standard English,* the kind that you see in newspapers, books, and academic textbooks.

Standard English does not consist of one unvarying set of conventions, but is rather the amalgamation of several influences. First, there are reference sources such as grammar books and dictionaries. Grammar books are influential because they are used in schools and so instill the idea that certain conventions are "correct" in a wide range of students. Dictionaries mainly focus on vocabulary, but modern ones also include a great deal of grammatical description. Writers of these reference sources do their best to explain English, but they will never be able to fully describe its nuances in these books (§80, §77, §83). Nevertheless, these sources tend to be seen as the final authority on English usage by many people.

Another major influence is publishing conventions. Standard English needs to be consistent between users within a country, and also internationally. You have no doubt read books, newspapers, and magazines in English written by authors from many different nationalities and published in different parts of the world. If you compared these various texts, you would find little difference in the grammar and use of vocabulary because publishers follow norms and guidelines that are remarkably similar across the world. These publishing conventions developed over time, and are based largely on grammar books and dictionaries. Most published material is edited according to these conventions, and the resulting material serves as a model of good writing. The conventions are codified in style guides and are required for writing in outlets like newspapers and academic journals. They are also constantly reinforced by being taught in schools and universities.

Thus, English is regulated by the conventions of use agreed on and used by its writers, publishers, teachers, and other people of influence. Critically, these conventions remain open to change, allowing language to remain relevant in an ever-changing world. (There was little language 40 years ago to talk about computers, and no way to cite Internet sources like Wikipedia!) It is also important to remember that Standard English is intrinsically no better or worse than any dialect or slang form of English, but it has the major advantage of being familiar to the widest range of English users, and so is the most effective form of communication for the greatest number of people.

In contrast to English's unofficial conventions of use, many languages have institutes that control and regularize them. In fact, over 100 do, ranging from Afrikaans to Chinese to Spanish to Yoruba.

Perhaps the best known is the *Académie Française* (French Academy), which advises on matters pertaining to the French language. The Académie, which was created in 1635, is made up of forty members who try to regulate French grammar, vocabulary, spelling, and usage. I say "try" because language is alive and ever-changing, and is not easily constrained by prescribed rules. As with many languages, French has been heavily influenced by English. The Académie has tried to resist this English influence, but with mixed success. It is powerless to stop the international exchange of loanwords between languages, and a large number of English loanwords have become common in French usage (*week-end, ticket, email*). Still, the Académie retains considerable influence, partly through the official dictionary it publishes (the *Dictionnaire de l'Académie Française*).

The idea of an English academy has been discussed at various times, but never gained much support. This is a good thing, because the lack of "official" oversight has allowed English to grow freely and adapt to the changing world without artificial constraints.

Power Point: There is no official organization that controls and regulates English. Rather, written English usage is guided by conventions, which are codified in grammar books, dictionaries, and style guides. Spoken English usage is less constrained by these conventions and so is more amenable to creative usage.

1. This website gives a balanced view of what Standard English is, and is not.

http://grammar.about.com/od/grammarfaq/a/standardeng lish.htm

2. Here is a listing of institutes controlling languages all across the world.

http://en.wikipedia.org/wiki/List_of_language_regulators

80

THE VOCABULARY OF A LANGUAGE IS MORE THAN JUST THE WORDS IN A DICTIONARY

The vocabulary of English consists simply of the individual words that appear in a dictionary. Doesn't it?

Dictionaries are a great resource, but there is no way that any dictionary can contain all the vocabulary of a language, particularly a language as large, rich, and diverse as English (§81).

Dictionaries cannot list all of the names and places we might come across, or the *technical words* that are specialized for particular fields. In my area of applied linguistics, a term like *illocutionary force* is useful. It refers to the intended meaning of an utterance. For example, if someone says, "It's warm in here," the meaning is not typically a literal statement of fact, but an indirect request to open the window. This is a useful concept when talking about language and meaning, and so the term is found in specialist linguistic dictionaries. But a general dictionary of English would not usually have the space to include it, nor the many thousands of other technical words like it from various fields: e.g., *trinitrotoluene* (chemistry = the explosive TNT), *deponent* (law = someone who testifies under oath to the truth of facts), or *natremia* (medicine = the presence of sodium in the blood).

The best attempt at creating a comprehensive dictionary is the *Oxford English Dictionary (OED)*, although the editor is quick to point out that it can never be truly all-inclusive. It is advertised as having over 600,000 words spread over 1,000 years of English.

But even the OED misses one of the key aspects of vocabulary: the *lexical patterning* that exists in language. Sometimes the patterning is obvious when a meaning is connected to *multi-word units* (*MWU*), where several individual words combine together to make up a "big word," as in the case of idioms. Idioms have a meaning that cannot be understood from the meanings of the individual words in the idiom: *kick the bucket* has nothing to do with kicking or buckets, but means "to die." Unless you understand that the three words kick+the+bucket combine together into one MWU, it is impossible to understand the meaning of death.

But most lexical patterning is somewhat less obvious and involves the way words work together to sound natural. Let us take the case of rain pouring down. You would call this *heavy rain,* but not **powerful rain* or **strong rain*. (* = not standard or common usage) Conversely, you would say *strong coffee,* not **heavy coffee* or **powerful coffee*. All of these words (*heavy, strong, powerful*) give the idea of strength or density, so why does *strong coffee* sound natural but **powerful coffee* sound wrong and awkward? This is due to a language characteristic called *collocation,* where some words just seem to partner together and others do not, regardless of meaning. When we look at large language databases called *corpora* (§77), we find that most words have these preferred partners, and collocation is one of the things that holds language together and makes it more predictable.

The lexical patterns extend beyond 2-word collocations, and can be several words long. Douglas Biber from Northern Arizona University has studied these longer patterns extensively, and finds that although they may not always have obvious meanings in themselves, they are typical ways of achieving some language functions. Some examples include:

- *I don't want to* = a way of saying you do not want to do something
- *in the case of* = a way of giving a particular example
- *I see what you mean* = a confirmation of understanding someone
- *from the point of view of* = a signal that an opinion comes from a particular perspective

Perhaps the most interesting types of lexical patterning are the patterns that build around words and have some fixed elements and some open slots. Let us take the example of *think*. As an individual word, it can be used in many ways:

- *I think that is a good idea.*
- *She thinks I'm fat.*
- *I did not have time to think.*
- *He belongs to a think tank.*

But when *think* becomes part of a longer lexical pattern (*think nothing of*), its usage becomes more specific and constrained. It has slots both before and after and looks like this:

________ *think(s) nothing of* ________

But what can go in the slots? Anything? Does this sentence sound right to you?

The house thinks nothing of standing in the rain.

No, this sentence is nonsensical, because the first slot must be animate, normally human or an organization:

Rob thinks nothing of studying until three in the morning.

The government thinks nothing of taking all my money in taxes.

How about this sentence?

She thinks nothing of eating lunch every day.

This sentence sounds funny because the action in the second slot must be something unusual or unexpected, not a common or everyday thing.

She thinks nothing of eating caviar for lunch every day.

Diane thinks nothing of practicing piano for three hours before breakfast.

So the slots are actually constrained in what can be inserted. The complete lexical pattern this looks something like this:

(animate, normally human/organization) *think(s) nothing of* (something unusual or unexpected)

It is used when you want to remark that someone or something regularly does something unusual. This is the meaning of the phrase, but since it has slots, it has the flexibility to refer to a very wide range of situations, as illustrated by these examples from a Google search:

> *Going from an inactive couch potato to marathon runner in just 10 months... Now I think nothing of just popping out for a 10k if I have some spare time.*
>
> *Heroes think nothing of wearing a silly outfit to change the world.*
>
> (Headline) *Wealth squeeze for couple who think nothing of [spending] £6m for party*

Power Point: Lexical patterning is essential to the way language forms meaning and sounds natural. But dictionaries are largely unable to describe the complexities of this patterning. Although dictionaries can define most of the individual words in a language, they fall far short of being able to describe how the more extended vocabulary of a language works.

1. Here is the homepage of the *OED* from Oxford University Press.

http://public.oed.com/about

2. Here are two sites for collocation. The first is an especially accessible introduction because it was written for English as a Second Language learners. The second is an online collocation dictionary: type in a word and see what words partner with it.

https://www.englishclub.com/vocabulary/collocations.htm

https://www.freecollocation.com

81

HOW MANY WORDS DO YOU KNOW?

Sometimes I struggle to find the right word for what I want to say, and I feel like my vocabulary is too small. What is a typical vocabulary size, anyway?

English has one of the largest vocabularies of any known language. It has many more words than German, Italian, French, or Spanish. But trying to determine the exact number of words in English is an impossible task. Estimates I have found in the popular press range from 200,000 words in common use to totals stretching into the millions.

The different counts depend mainly on whether you count individual words or "families" of words. Consider these words: *size, sized, sizing, sizes, sizable, sizably*. They could be counted as six separate words, or as one "word family" with the same underlying meaning. The total count also depends on whether you added technical/specialist words; e.g., medical and rodeo terms: *tibia* (shinbone) and *lariat* (rope used to catch cattle). The same thing holds for whether you added the almost unlimited number of names (*Golden Gate Bridge, Microsoft, Chicago Blackhawks, Abraham Lincoln*) to the count.

Overall, everything points to there being easily over one million different words in English. But a great majority of these will be very infrequent and specialized. If we disregard technical words, proper nouns, and dialect/transient words, the number is much smaller and more manageable. Furthermore, if we restrict ourselves to words that are common/useful enough to make it into mainstream dictionaries, we still come up with over 50,000 dictionary entries (essentially word families).

This is still a substantial number, and most native speakers will know only a fraction of these. Just as it is difficult to count all of the words in English, it is difficult to measure all of the words a person knows. The best estimate we have is that typical educated native speakers of English are likely to know between 10,000 and 13,000 word families. (Most vocabulary size tests are counted in word families.) But this depends on a person's age. In a study by linguist Marc Brysbaert and colleagues, the median score of 20-year-olds was 11,100 word families, while it was 13,400 families for 60-year-olds. However, there is a great deal of variation among individuals. The low end of the 20-year-old group only knew 6,100 families, while the high end knew 14,900. Similarly, the low end of the 60-year-old group knew 9,000 families, and the high end 16,700. Of course, figures for the number of individual words known would be much higher. Brysbaert and colleagues suggest that a rough estimate for 20-year-olds is around 71,000 words, while for 60-year-olds, it is about 82,000 words.

Note that all of these estimates are for *receptive vocabulary* (vocabulary that a person can recognize when heard or read). The amount of *productive vocabulary* a person knows (vocabulary that a person can use in their speech or writing) would be considerably less. That is because people can typically understand more words when listening or reading than they can independently produce in their own speaking or writing. Measuring productive vocabulary is tricky for a number of reasons. For example, should words only be considered productively known if they can be used in both speech and writing, or is one mode enough? Or can close misspellings be considered known (*ocassion*), rather than only fully accurate spellings (*occasion*)? Because of these reasons, no good estimate of productive vocabulary size yet exists.

Learners of English as a Second Language will typically have much smaller vocabularies, and sizes of 2,000-3,000 word families or fewer are not uncommon. However, highly proficient second language users can have large vocabularies rivaling those of native speakers.

If you are interested in seeing how many word families you know, take the test below. It has been used to obtain estimates of native speaker vocabulary size in a number of research studies. The words are sampled from *Webster's Third New International Dictionary* and then placed in frequency order (e.g., *bag* is among the most frequent words in the dictionary and *matelasse* among the least frequent). To take the test, check (√) each word that you know at least one meaning for. If you are not sure, consult a dictionary to confirm if your impression of the word's meaning is correct or not. Multiply all of the words you actually know meanings for by 500 to obtain an estimate of your vocabulary size in word families.

Note that vocabulary size estimates will always vary depending on the type of test used. Brysbaert and colleagues used an Internet-based test, and this one is based in a book, so comparing your results to their results can only be approximate. Good luck!

Vocabulary Size Test[8]

___ 1 bag
___ 2 dog
___ 3 improve
___ 4 cow
___ 5 hostile
___ 6 immense
___ 7 cavalry
___ 8 resen
___ 9 sprig
___ 10 microscope
___ 11 abstract
___ 12 firmament
___ 13 accede
___ 14 bagpipe
___ 15 chowder
___ 16 commissary
___ 17 marquise
___ 18 monologue
___ 19 untoward
___ 20 asperity
___ 21 aviary
___ 22 countermarch
___ 23 gloaming
___ 24 nominative
___ 25 planking
___ 26 punkah
___ 27 asphyxiate
___ 28 embolism
___ 29 appositive
___ 30 chomp
___ 31 comeuppance

___ 32 draconic
___ 33 golliwog
___ 34 nighthawk
___ 35 repartition
___ 36 setout
___ 37 brazenfaced
___ 38 carboxyl
___ 39 corvette
___ 40 dactylology
___ 41 cupreous
___ 42 paraprotein
___ 43 rigorism
___ 44 apertometer
___ 45 capsulectomy
___ 46 sporophore
___ 47 axbreaker
___ 48 doombook
___ 49 matelasse
___ 50 sparrowbill

_____ (number of words known) x 500 = _________ (your vocabulary size in word families)

~

Power Point: There are over 1 million words in English, but if you count in word families based on dictionaries, there are over 50,000. Average educated native speakers will know about 10,000-13,000 word families.

1. This BBC site gives more information about the amount of vocabulary required to use English. Note that when Stuart Webb talks about *lemmas,* he is referring to a base word and only its

grammatical inflections (e.g., *size + sized, sizing, sizes*), rather than the complete *word family* package (e.g., *size + sized, sizing, sizes, sizable, sizably*).

https://www.bbc.co.uk/news/world-44569277

2. Here is an expanded vocabulary size test similar to the one above, but which will probably give somewhat higher scores, because it counts words differently than in word families.

http://testyourvocab.com

82

HOW MANY WORDS ARE NECESSARY TO USE ENGLISH WELL?

I know that English has a huge vocabulary, but many of its words are quite rare or used only by specialists. How many words are needed to do everyday things in English, like participate in daily conversation or read the newspaper?

We saw in Section §81 that adult native speakers of English typically know between 10,000-13,000 word families, and this amount is clearly enough to be proficient in the language. But what about people who are still learning English? How much vocabulary does it take to become functional in English?

For native children, this is a largely a question about how soon they can start accessing 'adult' reading materials like newspapers, before they eventually acquire an adult-sized vocabulary. But for English as a Second Language (ESL) learners, this is a key issue, as most will never reach an adult native vocabulary size. In fact, one of the main hurdles ESL learners face is acquiring enough vocabulary to operate in English. So for ESL learners, a very practical question is, *How many words do I need to learn in order to do things in English?* Happily for them, it is only a fraction of the total words which native speakers typically know, and it depends on what they want to do in English.

In order to understand how much vocabulary is needed to use English, it is first necessary to understand how vocabulary works. All vocabulary is not the same, and some words occur much more frequently in discourse than others. Also, we know that language learning is strongly linked to exposure of a language, so more frequent words are typically learned before less frequent words. This makes word frequency a key factor in both the acquisition and use of vocabulary.

The importance of high frequency vocabulary is clearly illustrated in the two graphs below.[9] They show the relationship between frequency and *text coverage*. Text coverage is the percentage of words in a written text that a reader would recognize if they know a particular set of words. For example, if a person knew these words (*vocabularies, reading, faster, and, much, more*), this would allow a text coverage of 60% for the following sentence (6 known words ÷ 10 total words):

> Larger <u>vocabularies</u> make <u>reading</u> easier, <u>faster</u>, <u>and</u> <u>much</u> <u>more</u> enjoyable.

The first graph shows that the most frequent *content words* (words that have meaning—*dog, walk, bright, quickly*) are extremely common, and that they account for a disproportionate percentage of text coverage. The most frequent 1,000 content word families by themselves make up around 40% of an average text. The next 1,000 word families (i.e. 1,001-2,000) make up about 8%, and the percentages go down from there.

The second graph shows the cumulative percentages of text coverage. *Grammatical words* (also called *function words* – §30) are few in number (only about 150 depending on how they are counted), but they make up about 40% of an average text. This is because these words (e.g., *the, a, its, and*) are the grammatical "glue" of English and occur in every text regardless of the topic. (For example, the underlined words in this sentence are the grammatical words.)

If we add the text coverage of function words and the text coverage of content word families together, we find that the first few thousand content word families plus function words make up a large percentage of any text. For example, the first thousand content word families plus function words make up about 80% of an average text, while the first three thousand plus function words make up around 92%. In order to get to 95% text coverage, it takes around 5,000 word families plus function words.

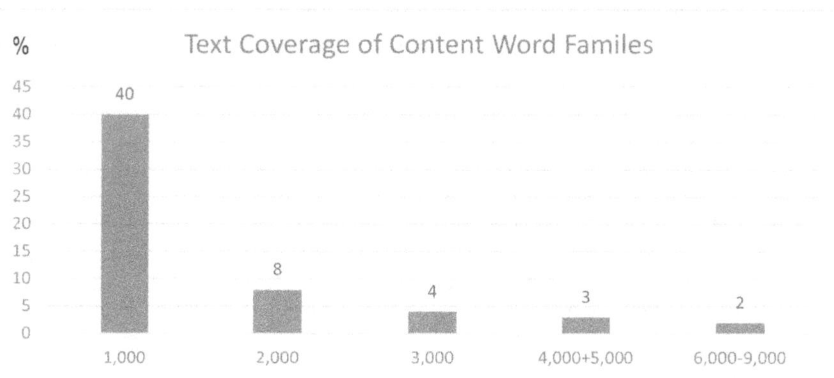

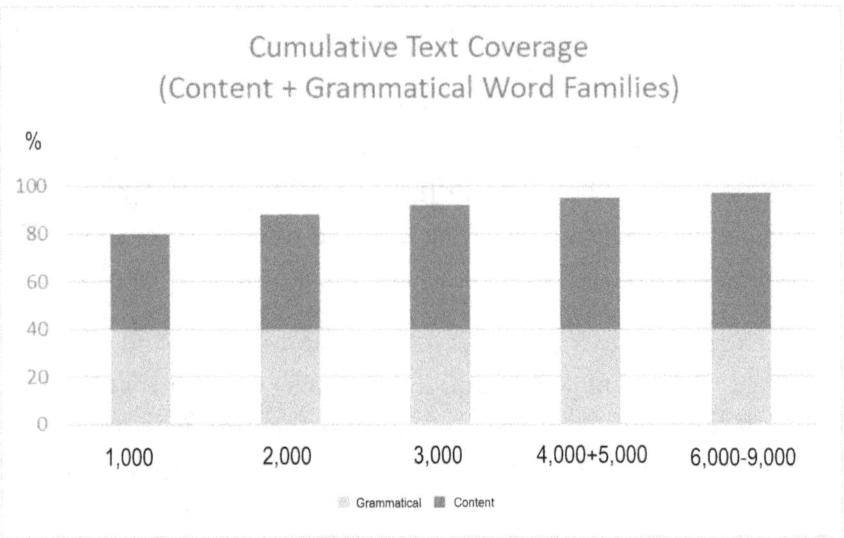

With this background of frequency and text coverage in mind, let us now consider the vocabulary size requirements to use English. One of the most basic things people might want to do in English is to participate in daily conversation. Between about 2,000 and 3,000 total word families (including grammatical words) can provide enough vocabulary to do this. Of course, speakers will not be able to discuss everything, but they will have enough vocabulary to get their ideas across for everyday purposes (e.g., shopping, describing their last birthday party). In order to engage in discussion about a wider range of more complex topics (e.g., politics, precise directions about how to fix a faulty computer), something closer to 6,000 to 7,000 word families is necessary.

Written texts are denser than spoken discourse and contain more lower-frequency words (§92), and so require a larger vocabulary to read. To begin accessing everyday texts like newspapers and magazines, something like 3,000-5,000 word families are required. But this size will still leave a lot of unknown words (perhaps 1 in 20), and reading will be constantly interrupted by the need to guess the meaning of those unknown words from the surrounding context or to consult a dictionary. To read more fluently, and to read a wider range of texts, the vocabulary size requirement goes up to 8,000-9,000 word families. Even at this level, there will still be some unknown words, but only about 1 in 50. These few can be more easily skipped without losing too much meaning or can be successfully guessed. To give you some sense of this, it would take knowledge of the most frequent 8,000 word families to read this section of *Language Power* and know all the words.

So in broad terms, we can say that a vocabulary size of about 9,000 word families should provide the lexical resources to use English effectively in most contexts (§52). Thus, the most frequent 9,000 or so word families can be considered the essential vocabulary of English. Of course, more vocabulary provides a greater range of expression, and native speakers will typically have more vocabulary than this. But these minimum size requirements are especially important as the fundamental learning goals for ESL learners.

For those of you working with either emerging native child readers or ESL learners, here is a task to give you a feeling for what reading is like with a barely-adequate vocabulary. Below is a passage taken from a book I co-authored on the development of the English language.[10] I have replaced 5% of the lower-frequency words with blanks. (See §52 for another example of this.)

- How well can you comprehend the passage?
- Can you guess the missing words?

It is a curiosity of language use that speakers who understand each other perfectly well may nevertheless speak in dissimilar ways: Their _____ may be different, and they may pronounce specific words in quite distinct ways. The authors of this book come from two separate continents and say some words in different ways, but we have no difficulty in communi-

> *cating. Most languages are _____ of variation; it is not the sounds themselves, but their relation to other sounds that determines the level of success in communication. The degree of _____ varies. To communicate the word* 'often', *for instance, it is only necessary that we _____ the pair of _____* 'ft' *clearly and supply a _____ before them: We could supply almost any _____ and there would be no comprehension problem because there are no even remotely similar words to cause possible confusion.*

Most people feel that knowing only 95% of the words in a text (i.e., 5% unknown) is as low as they can go and still read comfortably. This example shows that knowing most of the words in a text really is necessary to comprehend and enjoy what you are reading. While you can stop and guess some of the unknown words or look them up in a dictionary, it disrupts reading and makes it less pleasurable. Having a large vocabulary is important!

Power Point: Knowing around 2,000-3,000 word families allows participation in daily conversation, and 6,000-7,000 word families makes it possible to understand a wider range of speech (e.g., talk radio, academic lectures, political speeches). Between 3,000-5,000 word families are the minimum needed to begin reading everyday texts like newspapers and magazines, but to read fluently and read a wider range of texts, 8,000-9,000 word families are necessary.

1. Whether you are a native speaker or an ESL learner, there are a number of internet sites that can help you improve your vocabulary in a more systematic way. Here are two, to give you a taste of what they can do for you. The first gives ten games for practicing and increasing children's vocabulary. The second site is geared more towards adults.

https://mumslittleexplorers.com/word-games-for-kids-vocabulary

http://www.vocabulary.com

2. Here are two websites that provide a wealth of tools for analyzing, teaching, learning, and testing vocabulary. The first site (Lextutor) is presented by Tom Cobb (Université du Québec à Montréal). The second site is the software page of Laurence Anthony's (Waseda University) website. If you are interested in vocabulary, you will love these sites. I use them all the time.

http://www.lextutor.ca/

https://www.laurenceanthony.net/software.html

Answers: accents, tolerant, toleration, articulate, consonants, vowel, vowel

83

NEW WORDS IN ENGLISH

I am constantly seeing new words in English, like* "bromance." *Where do they all come from? Are they real words?

Languages are alive, and they change to meet the needs of their speakers. So as the needs of the speakers evolve, it is not surprising that new words (*neologisms*) are developed that support these needs.

Historically, most new words in English have been borrowed from other languages as loan words. In fact, much of the English lexicon consists of imported words, especially from French and Latin, which together account for over 50% of English vocabulary.

But English has also created a large number of words. You might think that most of these are simply made up, but in fact this seldom happens. Rather, most new words tend to be created by using previously existing words and word parts in various ways. Three common methods are:

Compounding: Here two or more existing words are combined to build a new word.

> *Hypebeast*: A person obsessed about acquiring fashionable items, especially clothing and shoes

Blending: When two or more words are combined together with only parts of each included in the new word.

> *Pelfie* (p[et] + [s]elfie): A self-taken photograph of one's pet

Word parts: Creating new combinations of word roots and affixes

> *Nerdify:* To make or render something nerdy

Where do neologisms like this come from? Surprisingly, they are not usually originally from dictionaries and journalism. These tend to be conservative, and only pick up new words once they are in common usage, rather than creating them. Mainstream media, like newspapers and magazines, are constrained by Standard English norms (§79), and so favor vocabulary that is established and easily understood by a wide variety of readers.

Conversely, spoken discourse is more spontaneous and interactive, which allows (and even encourages) speakers to be more creative. Social media like Facebook and blogs mirror this freer oral language, and so neologisms tend to get taken up in these media rather easily. Once new words become commonly used in this more open environment, they come to the attention of journalists and lexicographers (dictionary writers), who then include them in their more formal publications, and in doing so, validate them as recognized, useful vocabulary.

But until this happens, and a neologism makes it into print and/or a dictionary, is it truly a real word? The answer is *Yes* if it is used by enough speakers. There is a lingering idea that words are only "correct" or "real" if they appear in a dictionary. But we need to get away from the idea of dictionaries as the foolproof arbiters of usage. As Anne Curzan and Erin McKean make clear in their TED talks, dictionaries are compiled by humans, who can only make subjective judgments about which words are worth putting into a dictionary and which ones are likely to disappear too quickly to be worth the effort. Besides, there will always be a lag period between new words being commonly used and when they are finally judged worthy of dictionary inclusion. In addition, traditional paper dictionaries will always be constrained by size limitations. All this means that many new words may be in common use but not (yet) in mainstream dictionaries.

Would you consider the following as real words: *cyberbullying, e-waste, hyperlocal, sodcasting*? You may not be inclined to, if you have never heard of them before, or perhaps simply because you do not like the way they sound. But at the time this book was written, a Google search showed millions of hits on the Internet for the first three words. Even *sodcasting* had over 5,000 hits. Clearly these new words are filling a need in English and are being quite widely used, at least by certain segments of society. On this basis, the only reasonable conclusion is that they are indeed practical words that have a real presence in the English language.

Where can you find neologisms like these before they finally make an appearance in a traditional dictionary? One answer is in internet-based dictionaries, which are not constrained by size and are open access, and have thus been much more responsive to neologisms like these. One good example is Wiktionary, from which all definitions in this section were taken. Another source is the lists of neologisms that have been compiled by linguists, such as the Rice University Neologisms Database.

Whether you like neologisms or not, language will always develop new words. So it is best to embrace language's creativity and vitality and enjoy the new words. But if they are really not your taste, there is no reason to fret about language decay, because if any neologism proves to be valueless, it will simply disappear without any action required.

Power Point: New words come from you, and millions of creative people like you. As long as a neologism fills a need in English and is in common use, it must be considered "real," even if it has not yet made it into a traditional dictionary.

1. The TED talks at this site by Anne Curzan and Erin McKean discuss how lexicographers decide which words make it into dictionaries and what limitations dictionaries have in dealing with neologisms.

https://www.ted.com/playlists/117/words_words_words

2. Here are the websites for the Wiktionary neologism page and the Rice University Neologisms Database.

https://en.wiktionary.org/wiki/Category:English_neologisms

http://neologisms.rice.edu/index.php?a=index&d=1

84

SLANG

I've always been told to avoid slang, but yet I hear it around me all the time. Is it OK to use slang? Why do people use it so much?

In 2020, some popular slang words included:

- *bae*: a term of endearment for your romantic partner, which is a short form of "babe/baby" and also an acronym for "before anyone else"
- *flex*: before it was showing off your muscles, but now it is showing off in general, especially with money
- *on fleek*: being perfect

What is the difference between these slang words and neologisms (§83)? There are no hard-and-fast distinctions, but slang dictionary editors describe a number of the characteristics of slang, noting that it is humorous and entertaining wordplay and that it is direct, earthy, and quaint.

Slang gives colorful alternative ways of saying things. It is a feature of spoken discourse, and gives the sense of informality. It is commonly used by young people and college students. Much of it is defiantly politically incorrect and often carries overtones of prejudice. It often concerns topics like race, sex, and ethnic origins, and can be offensive, even extending into the realm of what might be considered *taboo words* (§85). Its natural home is informal conversation, and it is frequent in movies, TV, and radio. But it also appears in newspapers and magazines. My favorite depiction of slang is by John Ayto and John Simpson (editors of the *Oxford Dictionary of Modern Slang*), who say, "The slang of English is English with its sleeves rolled up, shirt-tails dangling, and its shoes covered in mud."

Ayto and Simpson describe three stages in the development of slang. The oldest is from the mid-18th century, when it was the vocabulary of persons of "low or disreputable character." This was the language of the underworld, of thieves, gangs, and drug users. Later, slang also included the language of professions like printers, doctors, and lawyers, which we would now characterize as *jargon* (the technical vocabulary of a field). The above criminal and professional uses were essentially a mark of identity and showed someone as belonging to a particular group. By the early 19th century, slang came to be thought of as any language that was highly colloquial and below standard usage.

Looking at lists of slang can be amusing, but perhaps it is more interesting to understand the reasons slang exists in the first place. One of the most obvious reasons to use slang is to lower the formality of your message, compared to Standard English. The two following sentences have the same meaning, but the second is clearly more colloquial. It is also shorter, as the slang word carries a lot of information that would take many additional words to spell out in Standard English:

Standard English: *Mike is so introverted that he will only express his feeling via texts.*

Slang: *Mike is such a* ***textrovert****.*

The second reason is to show your attitude or stance towards something. For example, it is easy to say that a person is a bit boring in Standard English, but the following sentence clearly shows the speaker's disdain for Jane's unsophisticated conformity (*basic* = liking the things that everyone else stereotypically likes, therefore not being very original or interesting; or engaging in obscenely obvious behavior):

I don't really like Jane. She's so ***basic****.*

Another reason for using slang is simply about fun; to use language in more interesting and innovative ways, often flouting the standard way of saying something. Whether you like the slang in the following sentence or not, it is difficult not to be amused by the wordplay of *grey* + *vacation* (*greycation* - going on family holiday with grandparents, in order to share costs and babysitting):

We're going on a ***greycation*** *this year, so we'll have a lot more free time.*

However, one of the most important reasons for using slang concerns one's identity and showing that one belongs to a particular group. This is an extension of the idea of criminal and professional group membership mentioned above. Eugene Landy, the editor of the 1970s *Underground Dictionary*, comments that criminals and hard-core drug addicts in the 1920s and 1930s who did not want to be infiltrated by the police or informers used slang as sort of an "in-house" code, which outsiders did not know. This led to slang becoming a calling card of criminal identity. It is still used in this way today, although in less immoral ways.

Now young people use slang as an in-house code among their peers. Use of the same language leads to group cohesiveness and identifies them as a separate generation from their parents. It is interesting that while slang is rarely considered prestigious, it is in this case, because it signals desirable group affiliation. This reason also explains why much slang is so short-lived; once the code is broken or becomes widely used, it loses its value as an identifier, and new forms must be developed that are exclusive to the group in question.

Slang often quickly falls out of use, and by the time you read this, *bae, flex,* and *on fleek* may well have already been discarded. But sometimes slang is so useful that it becomes part of standard language. Two good examples of this are *wet blanket* and *on the level,* which were slang in the 1920s but are in use as common phrases today.

Power Point: Slang is much more than just non-standard language. It has several specific uses, including allowing you to be informal when you want to be, showing your attitudes toward someone or something, indicating your group affiliation, and simply having fun with language.

1. The Urban Dictionary is a popular crowd-sourced online dictionary of slang words and phrases. The second site describes slang from a British perspective.

http://www.urbandictionary.com

http://www.peevish.co.uk/slang

2. This website gives 30 examples of slang words and phrases, and provides a short explanation of the various ways slang is created.

http://examples.yourdictionary.com/20-examples-of-slang-language.html

85

SWEAR WORDS (TABOO WORDS)

My mother taught me not to swear. But if swearing is so bad, why are there so many swear words around, and why do people swear so much?

Warning! This section contains words that some readers might offensive.

Swear words. Also known as "dirty words" or *taboo words*. We all know what they are. We also know the general prohibitions against them, because most of our parents and teachers made their inappropriacy very clear to us. Yet most of us use them at some point, to a greater or lesser degree. Why is this? The simple answer is that they communicate particular meanings in ways that no other words can quite match.

Most people think that the meanings of words are basically fixed, because you can find them in a dictionary. For example, *loser* has the meaning of a person who has lost a game or competition, and this meaning does not change. But meanings can be interpreted differently depending on the context they are used in. In the context of life in general, *loser* takes on the very negative connotation of someone who is a dismal failure, due to incompetence, laziness, or lack of character. This idea of context-specific meaning is useful when thinking about taboo words; it matters who says them and in what situation. That is, to understand why taboo words are used, we need to understand the contexts in which they occur.

Many taboo words relate to awkward topics like sex, some body parts and bodily fluids, and religion. But sometimes these topics need to be brought up. So language has several levels of "naming" that allow us to refer to these topics depending on the context. For example, when might you use the each of the following synonyms?

feces – poo – shit

coitus – bonking – fucking

penis – dick/willy – cock

toilet – bathroom – shithouse

It is obvious that the words in the three columns have very a different impact, even though they mean essentially the same thing. The first contains the most neutral version, which would be used in formal, legal, and academic contexts. You might even think these terms are somewhat bland. They would seem out of place in more informal contexts, such as when talking to your family or friends. Imagine taking your child to the restroom to "drop some feces." In fact, the phrasing is so alien that I had trouble deciding what verb to put in this example! You would almost certainly say something like "Do you need to poo?" The words in the second column are *euphemisms*, which allow us to talk about these things in a nicer way that is not overly offensive but is still more informal than the terms in the first column.

The last column contains the taboo terms that are typically dispreferred (often causing shock or giving offence), and which carry the greatest impact. But there are still a number of reasons why they might be used:

1. The main reason is to add emphasis or to intensify what you are saying. They are used to express strong feelings. For example, *fuck* (the infamous 'f' word) is one of the strongest taboo words, but referring to sex is not its most frequent usage. Rather it is more often used to add intensity to an utterance. If I smashed my thumb with a hammer, I am not likely to merely report, "That hurts." Instead I would be much more likely to exclaim something like "Dammit! That fucking hurts!" This exclamation not only reports a sense of pain but strongly reflects its intensity and also my feelings about my inept hammering technique. The following examples also show this strength of feeling:

- *Shit! I've forgotten my wife's birthday.*
- *Why the hell is he turning here?*

Of course, the same sentiments can be expressed by people not wanting to use taboo words, as there is usually a more euphemistic synonym available. But usually much of the intensity is lost:

- *Darn! I've forgotten my wife's birthday.*
- *Why the heck is he turning here?*

2. Another reason is show membership in a group, or to show that you have, or want to have, a close personal relationship with the people you are talking to. This is similar to the group solidarity function that slang often performs (§84). Swearing to show affinity

might seem strange to you, but if your family, friends, or gang habitually swear, you would seem like an outsider if you did not conform and do the same. Similarly, you would not normally use taboo words with strangers, but rather with people familiar to you who you know will not be offended. I am a goaltender on the local recreational hockey team, and if I let in a particularly bad goal, I am almost sure to be subjected to good-natured jeers from my teammates on the bench along the lines of *"You useless fuck! Stop the puck next time!"*

3. Taboo words can also be used in a much more sinister way, if you want to insult another person or even threaten them.

- *You stupid shit-for-brains!*
- *I'm going to break your fucking neck!*

So ultimately, the use of taboo words is about choice, and about creating a particular impression with a particular set of listeners. As with all language, taboo words are not good or bad, but rather tools to be used in particular situations to convey particular communicative meanings.

Power Point: Although they must be used with caution, taboo words exist in language because they allow the expression of strong feelings and attitudes, and can potentially indicate cohesion between speakers. They can also add intensity to insults and threats, if that is your communicative intent.

1. This website has a short extract from *English Grammar Today* which describes swearing and taboo expressions and gives a number of examples.

http://dictionary.cambridge.org/grammar/british-grammar/swearing-and-taboo-expressions

2. The first website shows the top 15-20 swear words on Facebook, listed according to gender, age, region of the US, and country. The second discusses swearwords on Twitter.

http://www.slate.com/blogs/lexicon_valley/2013/09/11/top_swear_words_most_popular_curse_words_on_facebook.html

https://www.theguardian.com/technology/shortcuts/2014/feb/23/most-popular-swearwords-on-twitter

86

THE POWER OF BIG AND SMALL WORDS

I often feel that I need to use big words to sound official, intelligent, or important. But is that right?

In the song *Big Time,* Peter Gabriel sings that he comes from a small town where people think small and use "small" words, but that he is smarter than them, and uses "big" words. With these lyrics, Gabriel plays with the idea that big words are somehow more impressive and valuable than smaller or shorter words. But nothing could be further from the truth. In the following extract, author Richard Lederer makes the case for using short words:

> When you speak and write, there is no law that says you have to use big words. Short words are as good as long ones, and short, old words — like sun and grass and home — are best of all. A lot of small words, more than you might think, can meet your needs with a strength, grace and charm that large words do not have. …

> Small words cast their clear light on big things — night and day, love and hate, war and peace and life and death. ... Short words are bright like sparks that glow in the night, prompt like the dawn that greets the day, sharp like the blade of a knife, hot like salt tears that scald the cheek, quick like moths that flit from flame to flame and terse like the dart and sting of a bee.

If you found Lederer's argument persuasive and well-written, you might note that he used only single-syllable words in the extract. So clearly it is possible to communicate powerful and complex ideas with short words. So why is there the idea that big words are more sophisticated?

One reason might be the historical origins of English vocabulary. Many of the short, one-syllable words in English come from Old English and represent the basic things in life (*child, leaf, meat*) (§76). Later loanwords from French, Latin, and Greek were often longer and referred to more specialized concepts (*grammar, enzyme, judicial, claustrophobia*). So shorter words are often the most appropriate to speak of everyday matters, with longer words referring to more complex ideas. With the prejudice that daily issues are somehow less important, shorter words can also be seen as relatively unimportant.

This brings up the idea of *appropriacy of use*: big or small words are neither better nor worse in themselves—what matters is the context in which they are used. Consider the following sentence:

> *Pachyderms never forget the locus of succulent verdures.*

I suspect you probably do not know some of the words in this sentence, and I had to look up *verdures* myself. So although it includes several big words, which some people might think make me sound more knowledgeable or authoritative, in fact this sentence is completely inappropriate for this book, which is meant to be accessible to the general public. A word like *pachyderm* would be more appropriate in a zoology text, where its more precise meaning (mammals such as elephants, rhinoceroses, and hippopotamuses, usually with a thick skin) would be understood and would be a useful distinction in a scientific discussion. Big words exist for a reason; often to make finer, subtler distinctions than are possible with everyday words. But if they used in the wrong situation, they can just sound pretentious.

In contrast, do you find the following equivalent sentence more comprehensible?

Elephants never forget the location of juicy green leaves.

I suspect that you do, partly because some of the words are shorter (*succulent – juicy*). But you might have noticed that *locus* is shorter than *location*, yet still seems harder. So length is not the only thing that defines "big" words. In fact, their frequency of occurrence (or more precisely rarity) probably makes more difference. Consider the following pairs of near-synonyms and think about which seem "harder":

locus (3) / location (48)

nil (1) / nothing (384)

big (471) / humongous (0.7)

joyful (3) / rapturous (0.4)

I bet you chose *locus, nil, humongous,* and *rapturous*. In some cases, the longer word seems more difficult, but not always. The figures in parentheses indicate how often the words occur in every 1 million words of English discourse. You will see that the words that occur less often always seem harder. Overall, research shows that lower-frequency words are generally learned later, have more specific meanings, and are used in more specific contexts. Thus, "big" words are essentially less frequent words. In terms of communication, if you want most people to understand you, it is better to use mainly higher-frequency words.

Similarly, there might also be something about the exclusiveness of longer words that make them seem intellectual. That is, they are often connected to specialist topics rather than everyday situations. This makes them less common in language, and the longer they are, the less frequent they are. We can see this in the following table. Bengt Sigurd and colleagues[11] counted the percentages of words with varying numbers of letters in English and Swedish. Other than very short words with 1 and 2 letters (*a*, *to*), the longer the word, the lower the percentage. We can also see that, although the percentages are slightly different, the trend is consistent across the two languages.

Number of letters in word	% of English	% of Swedish
1	3.2	3.4
2	17	12
3	21.2	24.7
4	15.7	11
5	10.9	11.1
6	8.5	9.2
7	7.7	6.2
8	5.6	5.4
9	4	4.5
10	2.8	3.7
11	1.6	2.6
12	0.9	1.9
13+	0.9	4.3

The longer words can thus sound more intelligent or educated simply because fewer people know and use them, which gives them an air of sophistication.

Power Point: Big words have their place for making finer nuances of meaning, but most communication will inevitably use mainly shorter words. Frequency of occurrence has a larger impact than word length on what words people are likely to know and use, but frequency and word length are strongly related in any case.

1. Here are three pages from Richard Lederer's *Verbivore* website (for people who devour words). The first gives links to numerous sites dealing with language, many of them quite amusing. The second gives the complete text from which the above Richard Lederer extract was taken. The third presents a convoluted history of humankind made up of comical student bloopers collected by Lederer.

http://verbivore.com/wordpress/language-sites-on-the-net

http://verbivore.com/wordpress/the-case-for-the-strength-and-grace-of-short-words

http://verbivore.com/wordpress/american-history-according-to-student-bloopers

2. These are two websites dealing with frequency lists. The first site allows you to either scroll and see words in in their frequency order, or to type in words to search for. The second site provides a

wider range of lists derived from the one-billion-word *Corpus of Contemporary American English* (§77). They require purchase, but are among the most accurate frequency lists currently available for English.

https://frequencylist.com

https://www.wordfrequency.info

87

SIGN LANGUAGE

Is sign language merely a "gesture" translation of English, or is it a completely separate language? How difficult is it to learn?

Humans have always communicated with signs formed by their hands and arms. In fact, there is one hypothesis that the earliest human spoken language grew out of the connection between sounds and gestures and physical movement, which eventually became attached to meaning. You might remember watching classic Hollywood Westerns where Native Americans communicate with cowboys or other Native Americans using sign language. This really did occur, with different tribes using a system of "Hand Talk" (American Indian Sign Language) as a *lingua franca* to trade among themselves, as most tribes spoke different languages. (It has been estimated that there are between 150-200 Native American languages in the US and Canada today.) In modern times, some of the most iconic symbols are still hand signs; for example, the two-fingered peace sign and the raised clenched fist that symbolizes solidarity and support.

While hand signs can carry powerful messages for the general population, the most comprehensive use of physical signing must be by deaf people. It is estimated that about 2% of people in the United States are deaf, and around 15% report some hearing problems. The World Health Organization reports that over 5% of the world's population (more than 430 million people) would require rehabilitation to address their hearing loss. Many of these people will use some type of sign language (§3).

Sign language is not simply physical gestures representing the letters in a language such as English. While it is true that English words can be spelled out with hand signs (see Figure 1 for the letter 'B'), this is not typically how sign language is used, just as speaking people do not typically spell out words (P-L-E-A-S-E). Rather, just as in English where complete words represent concepts (*please*), sign language is a unique and different language, in which particular signs represent particular concepts (Figure 2 for American Sign Language (ASL)). These signs-for-concepts need to be put in sequence, and sign languages have their own distinctive rules for word order and complex grammar.

Also, just as spoken languages can have national varieties and dialects (§91), so can sign language. Notice how British Sign Language has a different sign for *please* than American Sign Language (Figure 3).

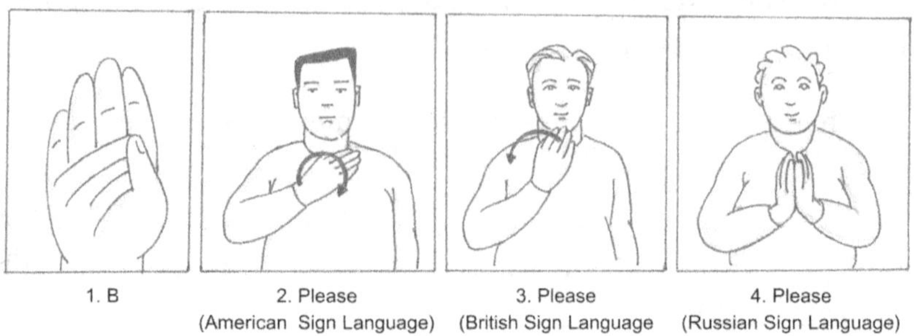

1. B　2. Please (American Sign Language)　3. Please (British Sign Language　4. Please (Russian Sign Language)

I have discussed sign language in terms of English, but there are sign languages corresponding to many other spoken languages. Sometimes the signs for concepts are the same or similar across sign languages, but sometimes they are different. For example, the sign for *please* in Russian is two hands held together in front of your chest (Figure 4). This is different from American or British sign language, but quite similar to the sign languages used in the Czech Republic, Bulgaria, Romania, Poland, Lithuania, Latvia, and Estonia.

Like any language, sign language has native speakers and non-native speakers. Children who learn from an early age (with the sign language being their mother tongue) typically become more proficient than signers who learn later in life. It is therefore important to have deaf children diagnosed early, which allows them to begin learning sign language as soon as possible (§44). Later learners can become fluent, but much depends on becoming immersed in the Deaf community. Deaf children born to speaking parents (who learned sign language as a second language and so are usually not so proficient) may not reach their full signing potential until they have consistent interaction with other deaf people, which gives them consistent and intense exposure to advanced levels of signing.

Learning sign language takes about as long to learn as any new language; that is, a number of years. Exactly how long will depend on many things (e.g., amount of exposure, language learning aptitude, motivation), so it is difficult to say how long it would take you personally. However, the Handspeak.com website suggests that it takes at least 6 ASL courses over the span of 2-3 years to attain a beginning-intermediate level of skill. To progress to an intermediate-fluent level, it takes another 2 years in ASL/English interpretation training. Achieving true fluency requires at least a few more years of practice. So like any second language, sign language offers many benefits, but requires considerable time and effort to learn.

Power Point: Sign languages do not just mime spoken languages, but are separate languages with their own vocabulary, grammar, and ways of expression. It takes as much time, effort, and motivation to learn a sign language as it does any other language, typically measured in years.

1. Here are three sites dealing with sign languages. The first is from the National Institute on Deafness and other Communication Disorders describing American Sign Language. The second is a British Sign Language dictionary. The third is old footage of Native American sign language taken in 1930.

http://www.nidcd.nih.gov/health/hearing/pages/asl.aspx

http://www.british-sign.co.uk/british-sign-language/dictionary

https://www.youtube.com/watch?v=bfT2a5SGDFA

. . .

2. Here is a website where you can type in a word or phrase and get short videos illustrating the corresponding signing in numerous different languages.

https://www.spreadthesign.com

PART 12

LANGUAGE MYTHS, INTERESTING LANGUAGE FACTS, AND LANGUAGE TRIVIA

88

LANGUAGE MYTH #1: LANGUAGE IS GOING TO THE DOGS

"[Adults'] language is deteriorating. They are lowering the bar. Our language is flying off at all tangents, without the anchor of a solid foundation." —Marie Clair, of the Plain English Campaign

Is current language use really that bad?

In 2014, *Intelligence*[2] hosted a debate on the question of whether English is going to the dogs. Some commentators lamented that knowledge of English is declining and that it is being used in incorrect ways. For example, some words are being used with meanings that are different than their original ones; e.g., *decimate* originally meant "destroy one in ten," but now it is being used for the more general meaning "to destroy large numbers of people, animals, or other creatures, or to harm something severely" (Cambridge Dictionaries Online). Likewise, they complained that grammar rules are being used incorrectly; e.g., the use of *who* vs. *whom*.

Of course, views like this are nothing new. Every generation seems to have language snobs who moan that language is being ruined by bad usage and that people just cannot use language as well as they could in the good old days. But when were those good old days, when language use was so excellent? If we look at complaints through the ages, evidently there has not been good language use for centuries! In his TED talk on texting as a new form of language (§39), John McWhorter (Columbia University) presents a number of quotes stretching across the centuries that lament the decline of language knowledge:

> Many do not know the alphabet or multiplication table, cannot write grammatically, and seem to have been trained to hate mental exercise … often they cannot read intelligently, and dislike any reading. —*1956 English professor at a small college*

> Bad spelling, incorrectness as well as inelegance of expression in writing, ignorance of the simplest rules of punctuation, and an almost entire want of familiarity with English literature, are far from rare among young men of eighteen otherwise well prepared for college studies. —*1871 Charles Eliot, Harvard President*

> For a long time I have noted with regret the almost entire neglect of the art of original composition in our common schools … hundreds graduate from our common schools with no well-defined ideas of the construction of our language. —*1841 County superintendent of schools*

> Spoken Latin has picked up a passel of words considered too casual for written Latin, and the grammar people use when speaking has broken down. The masses barely use anything but the nominative and the accusative … it's gotten to the point that the student of Latin is writing in what is to them an artificial

language, and it is an effort for him to recite in it decently. *—63 A.D. pedant writing in Latin*

In today's media, it is not difficult to find grumbles of a similar sort. But is language really in crisis? Or are some people just too picky? I believe the evidence clearly shows that language is alive and prospering. Yes, it is constantly adapting to people's needs, which irritates many traditionalists. Take *decimate,* for example. How many times do we really need to express the meaning of losing one in ten of anything? Rather, the word has taken on the much more useful meaning of general destruction. It is important to remember that language has never lost its ability to communicate the ideas that people want to express. Because of this, language needs to be described and taught as it is *used* by the general population, not according to how a few self-proclaimed experts assert we *should* use it (§76-§79).

In fact, the number of items disputed by language grumps is actually very small, while there is consensus on the vast majority of language use. The points the grumps tend to focus on are relatively picky; for example, the distinction between *disinterested* and *uninterested.* While these words traditionally had different meanings ("impartial" and "not interested" respectively), *disinterested* is increasingly being used for the "not interested" meaning. However, English is not losing its capacity to describe impartiality; it is simply finding different means to express it. In addition, while the grumps approve of fixed black-and-white "correct" rules, they often cannot agree on what those rules are.

The truth is that language is alive, growing, and evolving, regardless of whether language snobs like it or not. And language has always evolved. You probably have noticed that we no longer talk like Shakespeare, and even Shakespeare was changing the language of his time by adding hundreds of new words and phrases to the

English vocabulary. Language constantly changes to meet the needs of society, and is one of the most adaptive things we know of. There is an ever-increasing diversity of scientific, cultural, and philosophical ideas for language to express.

There is also the widest range of media ever for expressing these ideas: a variety of traditional print media (e.g., books, magazines, comics, graphic novels, brochures), electronic writing media (e.g., email, texting, blogs), a range of speech outlets (e.g., radio, music lyrics), television and movies, and internet and social media outlets (e.g., Facebook, TikTok, YouTube). It is not surprising that distinctive styles of language are used in these different media. If they are not all the same (i.e., conforming to the traditional formal written language style), then so much the better. Diversity is strength. Most people become proficient in a range of these language styles, and are not bothered in the least if they differ from one another, as each style has its own advantages and optimal situations of use (e.g., texting in the space-limited confines of portable electronic devices – §38).

Overall, it is not unreasonable to claim that we are in a Golden Era of language use, with more people communicating more widely and effectively, about more things, on more different language media, than ever before. Is language going to the dogs? I don't think so.

Power Point: It seems a popular pastime to moan about language's demise, but people have never used language in more vibrant ways than today, across an increasingly wide range of media.

1. In this essay, David Shariatmadari discusses how language snobs have always complained about language decline.

https://www.theguardian.com/science/2019/aug/15/why-its-time-to-stop-worrying-about-the-decline-of-the-english-language

2. Here is a site by Maggie Browning (Princeton University), illustrating some more gripes about how language is in dire straits, along with some bullet points about why we should not be flustered.

https://www.princeton.edu/~browning/decline.html

89

LANGUAGE MYTH #2: PEOPLE SHOULD BE STRAIGHT TALKERS AND JUST SAY WHAT THEY THINK

I'm tired of people hedging and waffling when they talk to me. It would be a lot better if everyone was a straight talker, wouldn't it?

The simple rebuttal to this myth is that the world would be a lot *less* harmonious place if everyone always just said what they thought. Let us consider a number of situations and what might happen if people were completely direct:

1. Can I help you?
Can you annoying sales people just leave me alone for once?

2. Would you like to go out with me tonight?
I wouldn't go out with you if you were the last man on earth.

3. Doctor, is the disease serious?
Yes, you'll probably be dead in three weeks.

So from trivial situations to quite serious ones, there are good reasons for not always being direct with the truth. In Example 1, it is just common courtesy and politeness not to insult a salesperson when they are just trying to do their job. Here, a standard phrase like "[I'm] just looking, thanks" is enough to deflect their attention without causing any offense. In the second, everyone knows that asking for a date is a potentially embarrassing undertaking, and anyone with any class will decline the invitation gracefully if not interested. The person being asked might use a white lie to make an excuse, with the intention of saving the asker's face (§90): "Thanks, but actually I'm already seeing someone." In Example 3, brusquely telling the full truth might lead to so great a shock that it severely reduces any chance of recovery.

So *indirectness* turns out to be an important aspect of being able to use language appropriately and well. It is often related to politeness, with longer and more indirect forms usually considered to be more polite. Compare the following:

1. Close the window.
2. Please close the window.
3. Would you please close the window?
4. Would it be possible for you to close the window?
5. Could you possibly consider closing the window for me, please?

The five requests are listed in in ascending order of indirectness/politeness, but of course which form to use depends on the situation. Most people would find 5 far too indirect for such a simple request, the same as they would find 2 far too direct for a major request such as *Please lend me your car for a week.* The key is adjusting your language to the person/people you are communicating with (depending on their age, gender, social status, how well you know them, etc.) and the degree to which you are imposing on them. Greater social distance and greater imposition generally requires more indirectness. For example, imagine you need to ask your boss for time off from work at short notice, even though it is a busy time at the company. This nightmare scenario requires very indirect language:

> *Excuse me, could I please talk to you for a minute? I've just had a family emergency. I know it's a bad time to ask, but could I possibly get a week off to deal with it? I'm sorry, and I'll make up the time once I'm back.*

This example has plenty of politeness features (*excuse me, I'm sorry, could I possibly, please*), plus an important additional element: a reason/explanation why the boss should grant you the time off. An indirect formulation like the above is likely to be much more effective than a more direct request like *Please give me the next week off.*

How much indirectness needs to be included in communication? It depends on the situation, but Paul Grice, a philosopher of language, gives us a way to think about this question. He said that successful communication depends on us cooperating with our partner, by making our contributions conform to the following four principles:

- **Truthfulness** Do your best to make contributions that are true.
- **Informativeness** Give as much information as required, but not more.
- **Relevance** Make your contributions relevant.
- **Style** Avoid obscurity and ambiguity; be appropriate and orderly.

Grice's principles can be applied to the "time off" example above. First, the request should be *truthful*: there really should be a family emergency and not just a desire to sneak away for a week's vacation. Second, there should be enough *information* to justify the request, and the person would probably follow up with additional information about the family emergency. Third, the request is *relevant* to both the requester's family needs and the boss's desire to keep the company's workflow moving.

For our discussion of indirectness, the fourth principle of *style* is crucial. Where the previous three principles are mainly concerned with *what* is said, the principle of style is more about *how* it is said; i.e., appropriateness. The requester knows that their desire for time off is a serious imposition and therefore needs to be expressed in indirect language that would be perceived as polite and unpresumptuous. This offers the greatest chance for success. In general, any request, disagreement, or imposition to your speech partner requires the inclusion of indirectness, and the greater the social distance and imposition, the greater the indirectness necessary.

Power Point: Indirectness is the social lubricant that helps people maintain harmony even when talking about potentially controversial issues. The greater the imposition to your partner, the more indirectness is required to maintain the appropriate level of politeness.

1. Here is a more detailed explanation of direct and indirect communication by Cynthia Joyce (University of Iowa).

https://conflictmanagement.org.uiowa.edu/sites/conflictmanagement.org.uiowa.edu/files/2020-01/Direct%20and%20Indirect%20Communication.pdf

2. Here are some materials from Lancaster University that explain Grice's principles in more detail, and give you a chance to do a bit of language analysis using them.

http://www.lancaster.ac.uk/fass/projects/stylistics/topic12/14cp1.htm

90

LANGUAGE MYTH #3: SOME LANGUAGES ARE MORE POLITE THAN OTHERS

I've heard that some languages like Japanese are more polite than English. Is this true?

There is a myth that some languages are more polite than others; for example, that Japanese is more polite than English. But politeness is a social requirement in all cultures, and so all languages have ways of demonstrating politeness in one form or another. Thus, it is very difficult to argue that one language is more polite than another. So why does the myth persist?

One reason may be that some languages have more overt markers of politeness, while others perform their politeness more indirectly. For example, many languages have "familiar" and "formal" forms of address. Some languages use separate words for the English pronoun *you* (e.g., French [*tu/vous*], Russian [*ty/vy*], and German [*du/sie*]), and this distinction is partly used to indicate respect and politeness. In French, for example, *vous* is used for superiors, while *tu* is reserved for peers or people of lower status. The distinction is also used to indicate social solidarity or intimacy. *Tu* is used to indicate a close and friendly relationship, while *vous* indicates distance, or that one does not belong to the group. So the use of the appropriate *tu/vous* forms for friends or superiors makes politeness very obvious. Similarly, Japanese has a wide range of linguistic forms that show different degrees of formality and respect; for example, more and less formal verb endings (e.g., *ikimasu* = formal "to go" / *iku* = informal "to go"). Some people might feel that languages with these kinds of overt distinctions are more polite simply because the politeness markers are more apparent.

Every language has politeness forms (more or less overt), but of course it is people who are polite, and not language itself. Still, it seems that some cultures use politeness forms more than others. For example, David Crystal notes that speakers of many European languages do not use their word for *please* as often as English speakers do.

To understand why different cultures tend to use different degrees of politeness, we must first become familiar with the notion of *face*. Face is everyone's desire to feel good about themselves and not to feel imposed on. All cultures encourage you to "save the face" of people you are talking to, but do so to different degrees. David Morand (Pennsylvania State Harrisburg) describes some cultures, particularly Asian cultures like Japanese, as having a relatively high social distance between people, and so place an especially high emphasis on protecting face. This means that there is more obligation to use forms of politeness when Japanese do something that is face-threatening to the person they are talking to. The politeness is realized by extremely indirect language. For example, a straightforward "No" is seldom used, but rather more indirect forms such as "Maybe" or even "Let me think about it."

Other cultures, e.g. Israeli, assume less social distance and more equality, and so it is possible to be more direct without being seen as impolite. This was shown in a study of English and Hebrew speakers making apologies, where the Hebrew speakers often expressed a lower intensity of regret than the English speakers. Another study found that Chinese speakers often voiced a much higher intensity of regret than English speakers. Thus, from an English speaker's perspective, Hebrew speakers might appear somewhat rude, while Chinese speakers may appear overly polite. But when speaking with their compatriots, the respective levels of politeness would seem appropriate. It is when speaking with people from other cultures that the politeness differences become evident.

But it is not only about cultural differences; different situations also require varying levels of politeness. Everyone would phrase a big request to borrow someone's car for a week much more politely than a small request to borrow someone's pen for a minute.

To illustrate the importance of situational context, let us try one of the situations that Elite Olshtain and Shoshana Blum-Kulka (Hebrew University of Jerusalem) gave to English-speaking university students in Israel, and some possible responses. Which would you rate Very Appropriate (√), More or Less Appropriate (+/-), or Not Appropriate (X)?

Ruth, a friend of yours at the university, comes up to you after class and tells you that she has finally found an apartment to rent. The only problem is that she has to pay $200 - immediately, and at the moment she only has $100. She turns to you and says:

1. *How about lending me the money?*
2. *So do me a favor and lend me the money.*
3. *Do you want to lend me the money?*
4. *I'd appreciate it if you could lend me the money.*
5. *Could you possibly lend me the money?*
6. *Lend me the money, please.*

85% of their students rated the non-presumptuous, indirect (5) as Very Appropriate, with 60% rating the somewhat more formal (4) the same way. Conversely, (2), (1), and (6) were rejected (Not Appropriate) by 73%, 53%, and 53% respectively. However, you may have judged the responses differently. The point is that the language of all of the responses clearly asks for money, but the one you would choose depends on both your cultural background and on your sense of the level of politeness required for this situation.

Power Point: Every language has ways to be polite, but these politeness features are more overt in some languages than in others. But most perceived differences in politeness are due to people from various cultural backgrounds having different preferences for more direct (less polite) or more indirect (more polite) language use. Various situations require differing levels of politeness. Thus, the main differences in politeness come not from language itself but from the strategies that we prefer to use to communicate.

1. This page reports an unscientific, but interesting, experiment into courtesy worldwide by Reader's Digest Canada. You might note that English is spoken in some of the most- and least-polite cities, according to the Reader's Digest rankings.

http://www.readersdigest.ca/health/relationships/how-polite-are-we

2. Here is probably more than you want to know about politeness forms in Japanese, but it does show how linguistically complicated politeness can become.

https://kimallen.sheepdogdesign.net/polite

91

LANGUAGE MYTH #4: PEOPLE FROM SOME PARTS OF THE COUNTRY SPEAK BAD ENGLISH

***"Y'all come back now, y'hear." —Line from the 1960s television show* The Beverly Hillbillies**

Do people from some parts of the country really speak better or worse than people from other regions?

People judge other people based on a number of things, including physical attractiveness, age, and gender. But one of things that influences our judgments most powerfully is language, particularly the way people speak. Written language is relatively consistent in published texts like newspapers and magazines, regardless of where they are written (§79 – Standard English). But where people are from has a great effect on spoken language. These regional differences are called *dialects*.

So you might ask, if you want to make a good impression, "What dialect is best?" Dennis Preston from Oklahoma State University has been studying people's perceptions of dialect for decades, and his investigation of folk linguistics has uncovered some interesting patterns.

One is the enduring myth that some dialects are not as good as others. Let us see how this works in the United States. Linguists have identified a number of dialects in the US, with the largest in terms of geographical scope being the West, the South, the Midland, and the North, as shown below:[12]

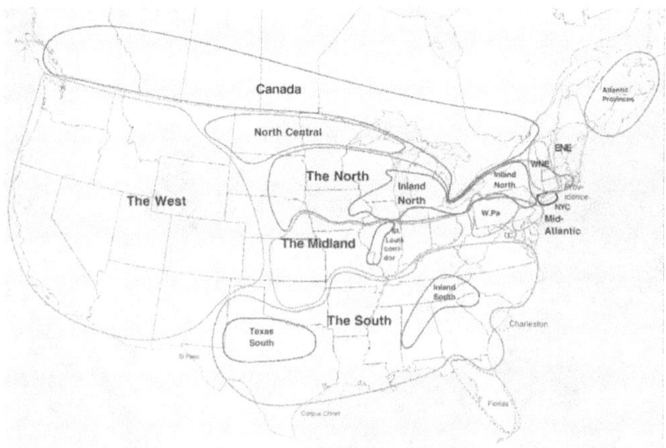

Dialects are determined by systematically recording and analyzing speech differences. The analysis makes no value judgments; it simply demonstrates that dialects use different pronunciations and some different words in the various regions. But when we ask people about their *perceptions* of these dialects, we get a much different picture.

Preston asked 147 residents of Michigan to rate the *correctness* of the English spoken in various parts of the country on a 10-point scale (1 = least correct, 10 = most correct). As you can see from his figure below, they rated their own dialect as the most correct, with an average of 8. The rest of the North and West was rated 6 or 7, but the South (and New York City) generally fared badly, with the

English spoken in Alabama rated as a dismal 3. The pattern is clear: the respondents in Michigan rated themselves as the most correct speakers, and the scores generally decreased as one moves South.

When a similar survey was done with university students from Alabama, they did not rate the South particularly highly either (Alabama = 5), with Texas, Louisiana, and Mississippi given a lowly 4.

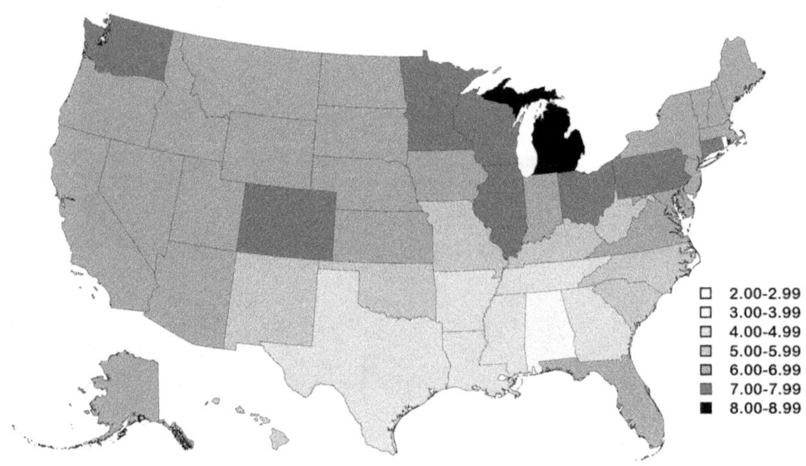

However, the opposite is true when the Alabama students were asked to rate English according to *pleasantness*. Here Alabama came out on top with an 8, while people from Michigan were given a 4. So even though the Southerners were not quite sure of their correctness, they felt that their local dialect was the most pleasant to listen to.[13]

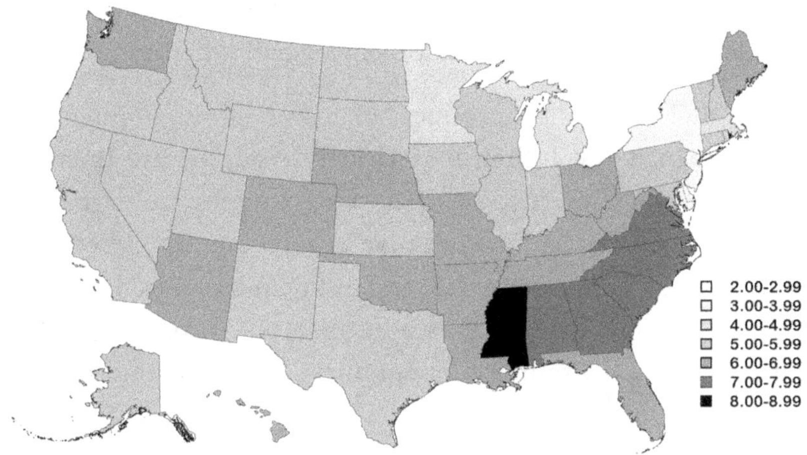

These results show that rather than having a single spoken dialect that everyone agrees is best, we largely judge people based on whether they speak like us. Moreover, these kinds of findings hold for other countries as well; we find similar results in Japan, Germany, France, and Turkey.

While it is useful to be aware of these stereotypes, it is important to understand that dialect does not relate to intelligence or ability. Rather, dialects are largely connected to language change, which happens all across the world. In cases where there is relative isolation between regions, the language changes in one region may develop independently from other regions, and eventually become a distinct dialect.

In the US, the dialect regions are relatively large. But in the UK, the regions are much smaller, with distinctive dialects developing even from one town or valley to the next.

The historical development of an area also affects dialect. For example, the Pennsylvanian dialect still reflects the influence of early English and Irish settlers. Of course, individual people within a dialect region will also exhibit variation in their speech, with social standing and education having an influence.

Because dialects are the products of historical development and natural language evolution, it is clearly wrong to use them as a basis for personal evaluation. Dialect stereotypes are particularly harmful when they lead to negative evaluations of less educated people, people from rural areas, and ethnic minorities. In the end, we need to think of dialect as a regional variation of language, with each being as useful for communication in its home region as another is in its own region.

Power Point: People have strong stereotypes concerning dialect and accent, but in reality, they are not a good indicator of ability or intelligence. It is important to listen to <u>what</u> people say, rather than the <u>dialect</u> they say it in, when judging their value.

1. This website shows color dialect maps where you can see how various parts of the US respond to questions like "What is your generic term for a sweetened carbonated beverage: *soda, pop,* or *coke?*"

https://www.businessinsider.com/22-maps-that-show-the-deepest-linguistic-conflicts-in-america-2013-6

2. A fuller explanation of the dialect maps in this section can be found at this website:

http://www.pbs.org/speak/speech/prejudice/attitudes

92

LANGUAGE MYTH #5: I SPEAK WITH BAD GRAMMAR

I pride myself in writing well. But when I speak, I feel that I cannot express my ideas as precisely, and that I am always pausing to think. Why isn't my speech as polished as my writing? Do I speak with bad grammar?

There is a common misconception that although a person can write well using Standard English norms, their speech is somehow malformed and ungrammatical because it does match their written language. You hear this idea in statements like "I think my grammar when I speak is terrible." This misconception is based on the assumption that spoken English is merely the oral form of written English. Nothing could be further from the truth. Spoken English has its own characteristics, and to judge it based solely on written norms is a mistake.

The main reason for the differences between written and spoken English is that the mind has difficulty listening to, taking in, and understanding written English if it happens to be spoken. Written English discourse is denser than spoken English, containing extended, complex sentence structures, lower frequency vocabulary, and little repetition. This is fine if you are reading, because you can re-read a text as many times as necessary. But try listening to a friend reading an academic book or magazine article to you for a few minutes. You will almost certainly begin to struggle straight away, because there will be a lot of information and precious little time to process it. There will not be much repetition and no hesitations to provide thinking time. It is simply too much information, too fast.

Because spoken English must be processed in real time, it has a number of features that make it easier to digest. The features of spoken and written English are illustrated in the following examples, both focused on taxation in different countries:

> SPOKEN: *and then she says my goodness are there any other countries* **UM** *that also have* **UM** *such liberties as the United States? and* **UM** *and then I <u>bel-</u> <u>U-</u> either it's John or Sue <u>that-</u> that I believe it's Sue that says that the Netherlands and Denmark also have* **UM** *high taxes*

> WRITTEN: *Income tax burdens vary so much by country because of the rates at which each country funds social insurance programs, such as old-age pensions and healthcare. In some countries, such as the Netherlands, social insurance taxes are significantly higher than basic income taxes. Each country provides different levels of benefits to its citizens, and individuals get different returns on the sums they pay into social insurance programs based on personal factors like income, age, and health status.*[14]

Spoken discourse generally uses a smaller range of vocabulary, with most of the words being highly frequent and generally well-known. In the spoken passage above, virtually all of the words are among the most common 1,000 words in English, and so are frequently used and easy to understand (§86). On the other hand, only 77% of the words in the written text are from the most common 1,000 words in English, which makes the written text somewhat more difficult. But the less common words also allow a precision and conciseness not possible with the simpler spoken vocabulary. For example, the word *status* requires seven words to define in the Cambridge online dictionary ("state or condition at a particular time"), while a word like *altruistic* requires 18 words.

The grammatical structures of spoken English are also generally simpler than those of written English. While the written example has relatively complicated grammar, with long sentences (26, 17, and 34 words) containing many ideas, the spoken extract has its ideas packaged in shorter, easier chunks, consisting mainly of clauses/phrases, rather than complete sentences. Ideas are strung together sequentially using the conjunction *and*. This illustrates a crucial difference between spoken and written English: while written English is structured around the full sentences, spoken English revolves around clauses/phrases.

The information content of spoken language is usually less dense than in written language, as speech is usually about main ideas rather than numerous specific details. It is also often more about the social act of interacting with someone rather than the actual message. For example, the common utterance *How ya doin?* is not usually seen as a request for information about one's well-being, but rather as a friendly greeting.

But perhaps the greatest difference between spoken and written English is that spoken language has many cases where it is not fluent; e.g., pauses, hesitations, and false starts. We see several of these disfluencies in the spoken extract. There are four pauses, where the sound **UM** is inserted to indicate the person is formulating what say next. The speaker also has false starts, as when they start to say *believe* (bel-), but then hesitate before mentioning John and Sue. This happens again with that-, but in this case, there is the repetition of *that* to get the discourse started again. In fact, repetition is another common hallmark of spoken language. Such disfluencies are normal and are a part of everyone's speech to some extent. With such disfluencies, spoken discourse can seem less polished than written language, which is often revised several times under no time constraints. But these disfluencies and clause/phrase structure are the norm for spoken language and should not be seen as a sign of poor grammaticality.

Of course there is more formal speech (e.g., lectures) and less formal writing (e.g., personal letters) than this example shows, but the differences described above will still apply to a large degree. However, newer methods of electronic communication (e.g., blogs, text messaging) are starting to blur the spoken/written distinctions (§40).

Power Point: Spoken language is different from written language, and is generally less complex because of the need to comprehend and produce it in real time.

1. Another short description of the differences between spoken and written language is available here

https://www.omniglot.com/writing/writingvspeech.htm

. . .

2. Andreea Calude (University of Waikato) discusses how grammar differs between written and spoken language from a New Zealand perspective.

http://theconversation.com/the-slippery-grammar-of-spoken-vs-written-english-92912

93

LANGUAGE MYTH #6: ANIMALS HAVE LANGUAGE

Webpage headline: "Dolphins have a 'Highly Advanced' Spoken Language." Can that be true?

Can animals use language? The answer to this question largely depends on how you define language. If you believe language is any form of communication, then yes, many animals communicate using sounds, physical gestures, or even changes of skin color (e.g., chameleons and cephalopods like squid and octopuses). This communication typically revolves around survival, such as warnings about predators, or mating behavior. Animals that have been claimed to have this kind of communication include elephants, prairie dogs, dolphins, and apes, among others.

A very good example is vervet monkeys, who have three distinct types of danger call, each eliciting a different escape behavior. A call for "eagle" leads the monkeys to hide in the tree branches. A "snake" call makes them stand up and check the ground for danger.

A "leopard" call causes them to climb out on the smallest branches of a tree, where a heavy cat cannot follow them. Clearly, animal behavior such as this carries meaning, and so animals can certainly communicate to some extent.

The question is whether this should be considered "language" or simply some kind of instinctual language-like behavior that is useful for staying alive and reproducing. Linguists conceive of language as permitting the communication of varied, abstract, and complex information, and have clear descriptions of what makes this possible. Stephen Pinker (Harvard) gives a good definition of this, with three requirements.

First, language is a system (described in Point 2 below) which can represent an infinite number of ideas, including ones from different times and places, or even imaginary ones. Second, it does this by combining discrete parts (e.g., sounds or written letters/symbols) in systematic ways (called *grammar*) to be able to produce an infinite number of words, phrases, and sentences. For example, the letters *o, p,* and *t* can be arranged in different orders to make the words *opt, pot,* and *top*. Third, the different combinations of sounds/letters/morphemes/words have meanings which can be derived from the grammar rules that govern the combinational possibilities.

These rules govern how the pieces of words go together in meaningful ways (called *morphology*): e.g., the prefix *re-* means "do again," and so when combined with the word *read,* can be understood to mean "to read again." The rules also show how words combine in ways that create meaning (called *syntax*). Compare, for example, the following sentences with the same words, but very different meanings based on the different grammatical sequencing: *Sam has what Joe wants* vs. *Sam wants what Joe has*. Overall, language allows flexible, innovative, and nuanced communication of both basic and complex ideas.

Given this description, it is clear that humans have language. Yes, like animals, humans can communicate with non-linguistic behaviors such as laughing, crying, pointing, etc., but we can do so much more with language. We are able to discuss an infinite range of ideas, many of which have no basis in reality. Anyone familiar with science fiction will know what warp drive or a light saber is, even though they do not exist. Reading through an encyclopedia (or perhaps more likely Wikipedia nowadays) throws up a mind-boggling diversity of topics that language is able to capture. We have a range of ways of saying the same thing, but with slightly different shades of meaning and often different levels of directness/politeness (§90): *Shut up! / Be quiet / Please be quiet / Would you please let me speak now?*

It also seems clear that the communicative signals that animals use cannot be considered language. Pauline Foster (St. Mary's University) in her Bad Linguistics blog gives a convincing and lively account of the reasons why not. Using the vervet monkey example, she points out that they only have three signals for three predators, and do not create new signals for new dangers, such a man with a rifle. A special feature of language is that new things can be discussed, and animal communication does not seem capable of this. Evaluating claims that prairie dogs whistle differently depending on the description of the predator or person, such as whether they are wearing brown or yellow pants, Foster explains that if this were indeed true, it should be possible to isolate particular sounds for particular concepts, such as "brown" vs. "yellow." Then the meaningful sounds could be analyzed to see how they combined into longer meaningful strings (i.e., how prairie dog grammar works). There seems to be no evidence that has been done, or even that it could be, and so many of the claims about animals possessing language remain assertions without proper evidence.

Further, even if the prairie dogs could connect a particular whistle with a color, they only do it in warning signals, and not for any other communicative purpose. Animal communication is always about the immediate situation (e.g., warning off potential rivals) and they cannot use their signals to communicate about past or future events. Conversely, humans routinely use language to communicate about situations displaced in both time (not now) and space (not here). Foster says that it is grammar (morphology and syntax - §78) that makes this communication about abstract ideas possible. Thus, when looking for animal language, you need to identify a grammar, and not just a few signals that map onto some very constrained meanings. Or as Foster succinctly summarizes: No grammar, no language.

Power Point: Many animals can certainly communication simple messages of warning or mating, but it is too generous to call this language. True language is a system in which discrete sounds/symbols are combined in rule-based ways, which allows reference to an infinite number of meanings. No animal is known to use communication patterns even approaching this level of flexibility and complexity.

1. Pauline Foster's blog Bad Linguistics gives a rebuttal to many of the ill-informed (or just downright wrong) portrayals of language in the media. It covers a wide range of topics, from the ever-popular moan about why English is going to pot to a punctuation analysis exploring the madness of King George III. The web address below brings up her blogs on animal language.

https://badlinguistics.wordpress.com/?s=animal+language

2. There have been a number of studies attempting to teach apes language, but all of the apes have plateaued far short of the definitions of language discussed in this section. This video is of the bonobo Kanzi showing he can relate spoken words to symbols on a lexiboard.

https://www.youtube.com/watch?v=wRM7vTrIIis

94

LANGUAGE IS NEVER COMPLETELY LOST

I lived in Germany for a few years and learned to speak German. I haven't been back for many years and now can't seem to remember much of it at all. Have I lost a language I once knew?

It is a common enough experience: you learned a second language to some level of proficiency either in school or when visiting a foreign country, but now, years later, you can't seem to speak it at all due to non-use. Laypeople usually call this "language loss," but scholars who research this issue tend to use the term *language attrition*. This is because languages are not usually completely lost.

The "lost" metaphor conjures up the sense of something almost physical, which can disappear, cease to exist, or be misplaced. However, this is probably not the best way to describe the deterioration of language knowledge. We do not have a full understanding of the physiological basis of language, but we do know it must be made up of brain cells (neurons) and the chemical/electrical connections and pathways between them. The incredibly complex network of neurons and pathways that make up a language probably never completely disappears, and so it seems better to talk about the ability to use the language (or not).

It is actually quite easy to show that remnants of a second language remain even if not used for decades. A good example of this is from research carried out by Lynne Hansen at Brigham Young University–Hawaii. The Mormon church trains some of its young members (typically in their early 20s) in a second language to prepare them to go overseas to preach. Many of these missionaries come back and never use that language again.

Hansen studied the language knowledge of these returned missionaries, sometimes after decades of non-use, to determine whether attrition has occurred. She taught her participants a number of words from the languages they had previously studied. Some were words they had previously learned (but had forgotten/thought were lost), and others were words they had never known. Her aim was to find out if relearning previously known words would take the same amount of time and effort as learning completely new words. She hypothesized that if the old words were learned faster and more easily than the new words (saving time and effort), this would indicate that some knowledge remained, even if the informants were not consciously aware of it. Over a series of studies, Hansen found there was always some savings, whether the missionaries had returned home 1 year ago or as long ago as 45 years. This indicated that some language knowledge remained.

Similarly, Harry Bahrick (Ohio Wesleyan University) found residual vocabulary knowledge in his informants even after 50 years of language non-use.

It therefore is probably best to think of attrition in terms of languages becoming inactive rather than in terms of a complete loss of knowledge. People relearning a previously known language, even after a very long time and with no apparent knowledge still evident, will enjoy a substantial advantage over people learning the language for the first time. Also, if you re-immerse yourself in the language again, you should expect that it will come back far more easily than if you were starting from scratch.

Other studies, especially in the Netherlands, suggest that attrition is not just simple forgetting of language as a whole. Vocabulary knowledge seems to be more prone to attrition than other aspects of language, such as pronunciation or grammar. The ability to use vocabulary productively (i.e., for speaking or writing) is even more likely to become inactive than the ability to use it receptively (i.e., for listening or reading). When even receptive knowledge is forgotten, peripheral words will be the first to go; these include low-frequency words (§86) that are not cognate (i.e., from the same language family) with your mother tongue. The extent of attrition seems to be connected to your proficiency level: if you had a relatively larger vocabulary to start with, when many words become inactive, you will still have more left than if you started with a relatively smaller vocabulary. Finally, attrition is not nice and steady; rather, most of the attrition occurs within the first few years (perhaps 3-6) and then levels off.

The above discussion talks about second language attrition, but it is also possible to lose proficiency in your mother tongue. This is not uncommon when people live in a country where their first language is not widely used for a period of time. However, there are situations where first language attrition can potentially be virtually complete. This may occur when children younger than 8-10 years of age emigrate to another country with their families or through international adoption, and the second language becomes the dominant (and often sole) daily language. Language attrition occurs for these younger children partially because the first language was incompletely acquired, and partly because the children's lives now revolve around the language of the country they live in, and they need and want to fit in. That is, the second language becomes part of their identity, while the first language no longer plays a role in that identity. However, this situation of "complete loss" will always be the exception in the overall scheme of language attrition.

Power Point: With the exception of some cases of young migrant/adopted children, previously known languages do not become totally lost but rather become inactive. People relearning a previously known language will almost always find it easier than people learning it for the first time.

1. Wikipedia has a reliable description of second language attrition.

https://en.wikipedia.org/wiki/Second-language_attrition

2. Here is an amusing YouTube video showing international students trying to say something in their mother tongue about their American college. It is not always as straightforward as you might think. Signs of mother tongue attrition?

https://www.youtube.com/watch?v=y8Bz9GnLalo

95

WHO OWNS ENGLISH NOW? EVERYONE!

English is now being spoken all around the world. But who should be the authority on how it should be spoken?

Section §2 described how English is now the global lingua franca. Where historically English was largely the domain of the British and Americans, it is no longer the preserve of native speakers. Rather, people all around the world are using it for communication, and increasingly making it their own. In fact, the number of people who speak English as a Second Language (ESL) far outstrips the number of native speakers.

It is difficult to estimate how many ESL speakers there are because this involves judgments about what level of proficiency would qualify. Nevertheless, the web site Ethnologue estimates there are 753 million users of English as a second language worldwide. If we included students who are learning English as a second language, the figure might approach one billion people. But even if we take the more conservative Ethnologue figure, we find that around 67% of the people who use English around the world are second language speakers.

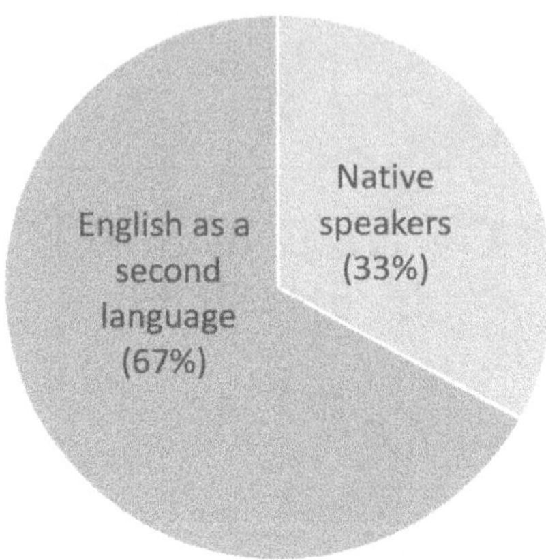

Furthermore, the gap between ESL speakers and native speakers (now 67%-33%) is likely to increase in the future, as more and more people use English as a lingua franca.

This idea of widespread ESL use was expanded on by Braj Krachu from the University Illinois at Urbana-Champaign, who analyzed global English use and concluded that there are three "circles" of English use. The Inner Circle consists of native speakers who live in countries where English is the dominant language, like the United States, the United Kingdom, Canada, and Australia. The Outer Circle is made up of second language speakers who live in countries where English is established and perhaps has some special status; for example, India, Nigeria, and Singapore. The Expanding Circle has second language speakers who live in countries where English has no special status, such as China, Egypt, and Indonesia.

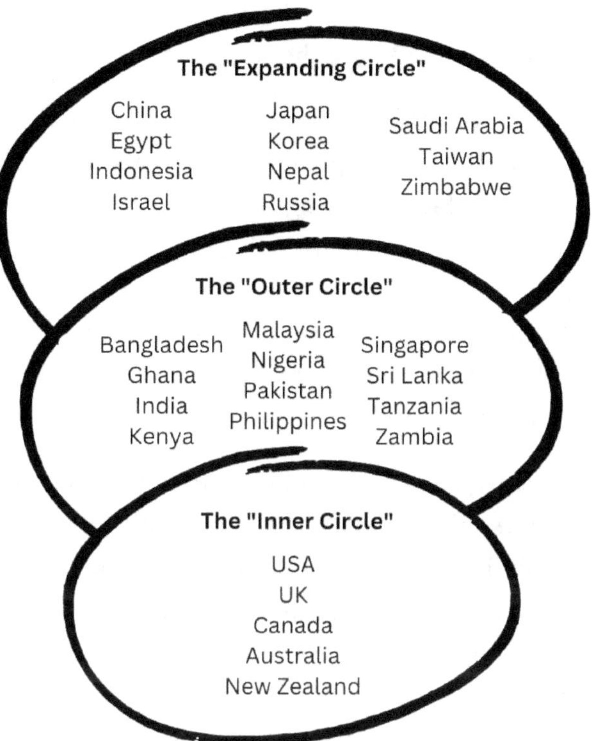

The model[15] is not perfect, because it does not take into account countries where English has no official status yet its use is widespread; e.g. Denmark and Sweden. But it is useful in highlighting the idea of *World Englishes,* where there is not one correct, native variety of English but rather a large number of Englishes shaped by the countries and cultures that they serve.

Still, the increased use of English worldwide poses an interesting question: How do we ensure that these various World Englishes remain mutually intelligible? Unless there is some type of standard to refer to, the different Word Englishes could slowly diverge. This raises the next question of who gets to set the standard. Traditionally, the Inner Circle produced the varieties of English looked on as models, and particularly, though not exclusively, British and

American English. But which of these countries should be considered most influential in setting the standard?

We could think about this in terms of historical birthplace, which would give British English primacy. Or we could consider the number of native speakers of English around the world. It is quite difficult to get precise figures, because in a multi-lingual world, it is often hard to tell whether English is a person's mother tongue or a proficiently spoken second language. Also, the figures often rely on self-reported information, such as from census data. As a consequence, various sources report somewhat different figures.

Nevertheless, based on a combination of these sources, the following figures give a reasonable portrait of native English speakers worldwide. We find that there is something like 379 million native speakers of English in the world. The United States has the bulk of these, around 231 million. The UK comes a distant second with about 60 million. Canada and Australia come next with around 19 and 17 million respectively. South Africa (5.5), Ireland (4.5), and New Zealand (4.6) add another 14.6 million between them. So in terms of numbers of speakers, the US far outstrips the historical British homeland of English, and so could claim precedence. But the UK would surely not like this size argument, and the speakers of the other national varieties of English (e.g., Canadians and Irish) would also be rightly upset with an argument that allowed the Americans (and British) to be the authorities of English language usage based on numbers alone.

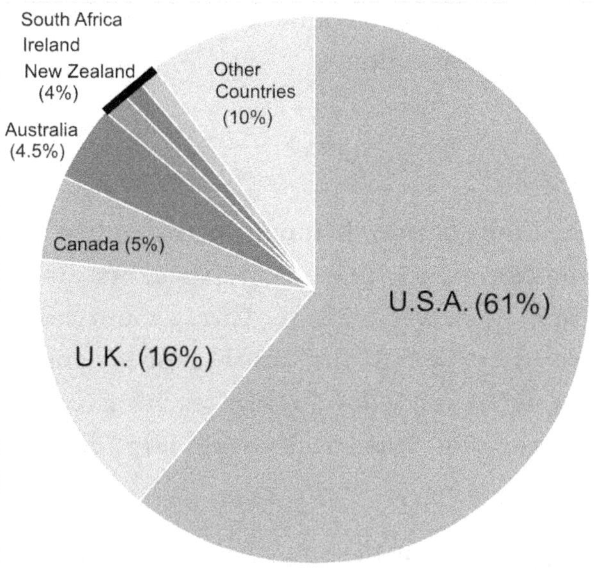

Luckily, these arguments are no longer relevant. Even without a global authority for English usage, a standard has developed for written English, largely because publishers needed a norm that ensured comprehensibility worldwide (§79). Beyond this, many countries are creating materials for their own localized use; e.g., dictionaries for Singaporean and Indian English.

Nevertheless, the Inner Circle still remains dominant in norm setting simply because these countries spend much more time, effort, and money in researching the use of English and developing teaching materials than other countries. English language teaching is big business, and publishers like Cambridge University Press, Oxford University Press, and Pearson Publishing have put vast amounts of money and resources into developing dictionaries, grammars, and textbooks. The publishers in other countries with fewer resources and/or a less single-minded focus inevitably have a hard time competing. Thus, although there is now a realization that the various varieties of World English are valid, the use of

English globally is likely to be influenced mainly by Inner Circle models for the foreseeable future.

Power Point: English now belongs to the entire world, and more ESL speakers use it than native speakers. Its norms are still predominately driven by Inner Circle countries, but this is now because they spend the most money and effort in researching English and developing teaching materials, not because of claims of historical ownership or numbers of speakers.

1. This webpage is one of the sources I referred to, and has the advantage of being available on the Internet at no charge.

https://en.wikipedia.org/wiki/List_of_countries_by_English-speaking_population

2. This British Council video presents British linguist David Crystal discussing World Englishes.

https://www.youtube.com/watch?v=2_q9b9YqGRY

96

ARE PEOPLE FORGETTING PUNCTUATION?

Some commentators complain that people are forgetting how to punctuate properly. Is that true? How good is your punctuation?

Punctuation. It is a minefield. Although some punctuation marks are relatively easy to use (e.g., periods [.] and question marks [?] go at the end of sentences), others like semicolons [;] and apostrophes ['] are trickier. For some, there are no clear, universally accepted guidelines; e.g. commas [,]. We even have some language doomsayers claiming that punctuation is a dying art, and that people can no longer do it "properly" (§88). It is no wonder that many people are becoming less sure about their own punctuation ability.

One cause of this uncertainty might be the proliferation of alternative styles of writing, which each have their own (and different) punctuation conventions.

Texting is one style that immediately comes to mind. Texting originally used a minimal style of writing due to the 160-character technology limitations and the brief nature of the message content (§38-§40). Among the other modifications, much of the punctuation used in standard writing was simply left out. This minimal use of punctuation still remains to some extent, even though text length limitations are now largely in the past. This alternative punctuation annoys some language commentators, but does not affect the comprehensibility of the messages.

In fact, the lack of punctuation can be a statement in itself. In a 2014 *Slate* article, Anne Curzan (University of Michigan) suggested that a lack of commas makes messages more similar to spoken conversation and more stylistically fun. If commas are used, it seems to indicate that the writer is being more formal. Her students also reported using periods to indicate seriousness or anger, and that omitting words showed skepticism or unhappiness.

But this does not mean that texters cannot punctuate. When they engage in more formal writing, they generally can punctuate just fine. People are able to keep different styles of writing separate in their heads and can apply the appropriate styles of punctuation for each. It is a myth that school and university students are starting to write their essays in texting style (§39). It is simply not that hard to keep the styles in their own proper places.

We should not worry that some punctuation conventions are changing. In fact – just like language in general – punctuation has always been changing and adapting to users' needs (§76). For example, the following are a number of punctuation marks that are no longer in use:

⁂ **Asterism**: used to indicate minor breaks in text, and also mean "untitled"

« » **Guillemets**: now used in non-English languages as quotation marks.

∵ **Because** sign: means "because"

The following marks are so unusual that they cannot easily be typeset. However, you can see examples of them (and a few others) here:

https://www.mentalfloss.com/article/12710/13-little-known-punctuation-marks-we-should-be-using

Exclamation comma and **question comma**: gives the emphasis of the exclamation mark to commas and question marks.

Interrobang: combines the functions of question mark and exclamation mark

Snark: indicates a sarcastic or ironic meaning

Ironieteken: indicates irony

But punctuation will never disappear, because it has a purpose in language: mainly to organize and group the ideas the language is trying to convey. When we speak, we can use all sorts of intonation to package the information we are giving (e.g., stress, rhythm, and pauses). We cannot do this when writing, so punctuation marks take over the job. A commonly used example to illustrate this grouping effect is the following sentence. Depending on the comma, it can either mean (1) a pleasant urge to eat with grandmother or (2) Little Red Riding Hood's wolf's urge:

1. *Let's eat, grandma.*
2. *Let's eat grandma.*

For another example, what do you think the following sentence means?

A woman without her man is nothing.

As you can see, the meaning differs greatly depending on how it is punctuated:

1. *A woman, without her man, is nothing.* = Females are reliant on males.
2. *A woman: without her, man is nothing.* = Males are reliant on females.

The importance of punctuation is also demonstrated by an amusing picture I saw of a squirrel crawling halfway into a jack-o'-lantern's mouth.

The caption asked, "Is this a squirrel eating pumpkin, or a squirrel-eating pumpkin?" It is amazing that such small punctuation marks can have so much power over the meaning of phrases and sentences. But of course, that is why they exist in the first place.

So although there is little reason to panic about punctuation's decline, you still need to know the rules in order to use it well.

Try this short test to see your punctuation power. Answers are at the end of the chapter.

1. Which sentence refers to one boy? Which refers to more than one?

a. The boy's toys are scattered everywhere.
b. The boys' toys are scattered everywhere.

2. When I picked up the laptop, I noticed ____ screen was cracked.

a. its
b. it's

3. The eagle is the symbol of the United States [ ] it is strong and flies free.

a. [,]
b. [:]
c. [;]

4. Where are commas required?

As a child, I loved to watch the new (1) fast (2) noisy (3) planes at my local airport.

a. 1
b. 2
c. 3
d. 1, 2
e. 1, 2, 3

5. Match the sentence and meaning:

a. She was wearing a light, blue sweater.
b. She was wearing a light-blue sweater.

___ The sweater was thin.
___ The sweater was pale blue.

6. How many commas are required?

John McWhorter a professor from Columbia University suggests we could probably lose many commas from many modern texts without problem.

a. 0
b. 1
c. 2
d. 3
e. 4

Power Point: We should not be too worried about a general decline in punctuation ability. Just as with other aspects of language, people are probably just as competent today as they have ever been. It can even be argued that people are more knowledgeable about punctuation than ever because most now engage in several different writing styles, each with its own punctuation conventions.

1. This University of Sussex site written by Larry Trask answers the question "Why learn to punctuate?" It also gives guidance on a number of punctuation points.

http://www.sussex.ac.uk/informatics/punctuation/why

2. Here is a punctuation quiz from the University of Bristol, on a website with plenty of explanations and exercises.

http://www.bristol.ac.uk/arts/exercises/grammar/grammar_tutorial/page_55.htm

Answers

1. a = one boy, b = two+

   's indicates possession by a single person or thing
   s' indicates possession by multiple persons or things

2. a

   its indicates possession
   it's is a contraction of *it is*

3. c

   A semicolon [;] combines two complete sentences.
   A comma [,] separates clauses and phrases within a sentence.
   A colon [:] has several uses, but a typical one is indicating the start of a list of items.

4. d

   When there are a series of modifiers (*new, fast, noisy*) before a noun (*planes*), commas go after each modifier except the last one.

5. thin = a, pale blue = b.

When words are connected by a hyphen (-), this indicates that they make up a single meaning. In this case, the meaning of *light* modifies *blue,* and so *light*'s "pale" meaning is appropriate.

6. c, after McWhorter and University

The commas set off the clause *a professor from Columbia University*

97

IS THERE REALLY A LANGUAGE GENE?

Is language innate and hardwired into our brains?

As you read this book, I hope you are enjoying the diversity of interesting language issues, but also becoming aware of some of the complexities of language learning and use. Language is the most complex information system that children learn, and its intricacy is a challenge for even experts such as professors and grammar textbook writers to describe.

Yet all normally developing children learn their mother tongue without fail. (See §47 for a sad case where things were not normal.) They begin doing this when they are still infants and toddlers, and by the time they go to school, they have mastered basic oral communication. In fact, fetuses begin to become attuned to the sounds of their mother tongue while still in the womb, as they hear their mother speaking. Children are not typically taught their mother tongue, but seem to pick it up naturally from their surroundings. How do they achieve this amazing feat: learning an extremely complex system while they are still cognitively immature young children?

Could it be that language is innate in humans, and hardwired into our brains? This possibility was raised in the middle of the last century by Noam Chomsky (MIT), who suggested that the reason young children could learn such a complex system was because it was already there in their minds.

Chomsky believed that all children are born with an understanding of the way languages work, or at least the grammar element. He called this *universal grammar.* They would know the underlying *principles* of language (e.g., languages usually have pronouns) and their *parameters* (some languages allow these pronouns to be dropped when in the subject position). Children would need only enough exposure to their mother tongue to determine the parameter setting. For example, children in Japan would quickly figure out that Japanese allows the deletion of pronouns if the meaning can still be understood (√*He went to work,* √*went to work*), while American children would find that English does not (√*He went to work, Xwent to work*). This parameter-setting would require much less exposure and effort than a learning the whole principle (grammar rule) from scratch, and so appeared an elegant argument for how children learned language so quickly.

However, it soon became clear that this explanation was too simplistic. In the early 1970s, Dell Hymes (University of Pennsylvania) pointed out that language knowledge consists of more than just being able to form grammatically correct sentences; it also entails knowing how to use them appropriately in particular contexts. Similarly, Michael Halliday (University of Sydney) demonstrated that language was not just something in the learner's mind but rather is a cooperative and dynamic operation between people communicating with one another. Clearly, the environment also affects language acquisition and use.

Later research in the field of genetics has made some of the most astonishing findings of all. It has been demonstrated that genes are related (at least partially) to many different traits, such as intelligence, violence, and creativity. Could it be that language is part of our DNA, and a "language gene" could also be found? There has been some recent discussion of the gene FOXP2 being such a language gene, but language is far too complex for any single gene to control it all. Ann Graybiel (MIT) explains that FOXP2 is clearly connected with language, but it seems to work by facilitating the transformation of experiences into useful information. She gives the example of hearing the word *glass* when shown a glass of water, and the creation of a nearly automatic association of that word with objects that look and function like glasses.

There is much more to learn about the relationship of genes and language, but the eventual answer will almost certainly be that 1) language is a combination of nature (genes) and nurture (effect of the environment), and that 2) the nature part will be controlled by more than one gene, probably a great number of them. Our DNA most likely puts in place the physiological and mental apparatus that makes language learning possible, but the environment supplies the input and language examples that directly drive that learning.

So if language is not innate, then how is this complex system learned by young children? Chomsky was certainly right that humans have a unique ability to learn and use language, as no other animal has the ability to communicate with anything near the complexity and flexibility of human language (§93).

But he was almost certainly wrong about the mechanism. Rather than being innate, the strong consensus is now that the answer lies in people's amazing ability to extract recurring patterns from input, usually unconsciously. These patterns exist in the largest to the smallest components of language. For example, at the level of discourse, every reader would expect some type of Introduction-Body-Conclusion organization in an academic text. At the sentence level, the typical pattern in English is Subject-Verb-Object (*Birds eat worms*). At the word level, words co-occur together in patterns called *collocations* (*heavy rain* but not *strong rain* or *powerful rain*) (§80). But this patterning exists at even much smaller levels. For example, some graphemes often cluster together in English (*spl – splatter, split, spleen*), while others rarely or never do (*zlf*). Also, affixes attach to stems in systematic ways (*re- + play = replay*).

Current thinking is that the human mind is very good at extracting these various patterns and using them to build up a picture of the system of a language. This pattern extraction facility is not reliant on intelligence or cognitive maturity, and so this explains how children can begin learning language at a very young age.

In addition, the more frequent the pattern, word, or other linguistic feature, the more exposure the child will receive, and the sooner the child will learn it. For example, children typically hear utterances like *Put the plate on the table, Put the shoes near the door,* and *Put the toy in the box* very often, and eventually come to understand the underlying structure of *Put the ___ [preposition] the ___*. This makes it easier for them to understand a new instruction which they have never heard before, like *Put the keys on the table.* Thus, frequency of exposure is a major factor that drives language learning (§86).

~

Power Point: Genes certainly play a part in giving the human mind the capacity to learn and use language, but do not contain the actual language itself. Human minds are amazing data analyzers and can efficiently extract the patterns of language from the language input they receive. This process of pattern extraction begins very early, even before birth, as children get used to the sound patterns of language in their mother's womb.

1. These webpages give two perspectives on FOXP2, sometimes referred to as the "language gene."

http://news.mit.edu/2014/language-gene-0915

https://www.europeanscientist.com/en/research/genome-study-provides-new-insights-into-how-language-evolved-previous-beliefs-about-the-foxp2-gene-are-proven-to-be-false

2. This webpage discusses how families can maximize language input for children, which supports oral language and vocabulary learning.

https://eclkc.ohs.acf.hhs.gov/sites/default/files/pdf/big5-strategies-parents-families-oral-language-eng.pdf

98

THE INUIT AND MANY WORDS FOR SNOW: DOES LANGUAGE AFFECT THE WAY WE THINK?

I've heard that the Inuit peoples have many more words for snow than English has. Does this language difference affect the way they think about snow?

You probably have heard that the Inuit peoples of northern Canada (formerly called Eskimos) have a large number of words for snow, many more than English does. This idea seems to stem from over-enthusiastic interpretations of Franz Boas' investigations of the language and culture of the Inuit of Baffin Island, which was published in a 1911 book. The idea was later challenged most famously by Geoff Pullum (University of Edinburgh) in his 1991 book chapter "The Great Eskimo Vocabulary Hoax." He concluded that the Inuit language Central Alaskan Yupik has about a dozen or two words relating to snow, which is not that far different from English, which has words like *snow, slush, sleet, blizzard, powder, avalanche,* etc.

So why the discrepancy? There are several reasons, but the main factor comes down to how you count vocabulary (§81).

English is a language where many distinctions in concepts are expressed by compound words or phrases, such as *snowstorm, snowdrift* or *a light dusting, heavy snow*. Inuit languages tend to use base words (root forms) and add affixes to modify meaning. An example of this word building method comes from Steven Jacobson's 2012 *Yup'ik Eskimo Dictionary*: "blizzard, snowstorm" = *pirta*, and "for there to be a blizzard" = *pircir*, while "for there to be a severe blizzard" = *pirretpag*. Inuit languages have very many of these affixes, and the possible word+affix combinations concerning snow could reach many hundreds. So while there may not be many more base words for snow in Inuit than in English, the possible affixed combinations will be a very large number indeed.

In northern Scandinavia, Ole Henrik Magga (Saami University College) explains that the languages of the Saami peoples of far northern Europe have a rich terminology for snow (as well as ice, reindeer, etc.). Thus, on balance, it is probably right to say that the Arctic peoples have a relatively large number of lexical items (whether words or word+affix combinations) to describe snow-related concepts.

The snow words controversy is interesting, and certainly serves to illustrate the difficulties in counting vocabulary. But it is part of a weightier issue: does our language determine the way we think? Does a large snow vocabulary affect the way Inuits think about snow? This is called *linguistic relativity*, although it is more popularly known as the *Sapir-Whorf Hypothesis*.

The answer is not a black-and-white Yes or No. There are simply too many factors that affect the way we think for language to <u>dictate</u> our thought, but it certainly seems to <u>affect</u> it.

Lera Boroditsky (University of California, San Diego) describes some of the ways where language influences thinking. One concerns location. While English speakers tend to report position relative to themselves or some object (*Put the fork to the left of the plate*), speakers of the aboriginal language Kuuk Thaayorre in northern Australia use cardinal directions (i.e. north, south, east, west: *He is standing south of my sister*). Since Kuuk Thaayorre speakers must know directions in order to talk about everyday positioning, they seem to be much better at knowing where they are in terms of direction than speakers of languages that do not require this knowledge to such an extent (e.g., English). Of course, English uses directions, but tends to use them mainly for large-scale positioning (*The sports store is south of town, Kentucky is north of Tennessee*).

Languages also seem to affect the conceptualization of time. English speakers tend to portray time linearly from left to right, while Hebrew speakers portray it from right to left, which follows their respective writing systems. Interestingly, Kuuk Thaayorre speakers work from east to west. Time can also be thought of in terms of front-to-back. English speakers refer to the past as *behind* them, and the future as *ahead* of them, while the Andean language Aymara works just the opposite.

Language also appears to relate to how well some things are remembered. Boroditsky and her student Caitlin Fausey asked English, Spanish, and Japanese speakers to watch videos of people doing things; e.g., spilling drinks, either intentionally or accidentally. Speakers of all three languages reported the intentional actions with active sentences (*The man spilled his wine*), and all later remembered the details equally well. But while English speakers also typically used active sentences to report the accidents, the Spanish and Japanese speakers tended to use passive sentences

(*The wine was spilled*). The English speakers remembered details of accidental incidents better than Spanish or Japanese, suggesting that eye-witness memory is affected by a language's preference for active vs. passive reporting.

Power Point: The number of "words" that Arctic languages have for snow misses the point. The key issue is that Arctic languages have a wide range of vocabulary available (regardless of the word-creation mechanics) to refer to the extensive variety of snow conditions and snow-related situations they encounter. Language and life experience is clearly interrelated. Overall, languages are shaped by the world they need to describe, but once in place, they also affect the way people think about the world.

1. Here are two views of the Inuit snow issue. Read them and decide for yourself. The first (not so many words for snow) has the entire "Great Eskimo Vocabulary Hoax" chapter, originally intended to satirize writers who report and inflate scientific findings without any understanding for the sake of a popular story. The second site gives Pullman's rebuttal of a *Washington Pos*t article suggesting that Arctic peoples do have a large snow vocabulary. The second view (lots of words for snow) is presented in an accessible blog that outlines *polysynthesis* and concludes that Inuits actually do have a relatively large number of word+affix combinations for snow.

https://cslc.nd.edu/assets/141348/pullum_eskimo_vocabhoax.pdfhttp://languagelog.ldc.upenn.edu

http://languagelog.ldc.upenn.edu/nll/?p=4419

https://readable.com/blog/do-inuits-really-have-50-words-for-snow

2. This site is a YouTube video by Lera Boroditsky outlining how the languages we speak affect our perceptions of the world.

https://www.youtube.com/watch?v=RKK7wGAYP6k

99

LANGUAGE TRIVIA QUIZ #1

I want some catchy facts and trivia for the next time I get together with my friends. Is there anything interesting about language?

Here are some language facts and trivia you can use to entertain and amaze your friends. It is in the form of a quiz. Some of the ideas have been explained in the book, but most are new information. Make sure you do not look at the explanations below until you have answered the questions!

1. About how many languages are spoken in the world today?

a. 1,000
b. 4,000
c. 7,000
d. 12,000

2. What is the most widely-spoken first language in the world today?

a. Chinese
b. English
c. French
d. Spanish

3. Which country has the most languages spoken?

a. India
b. Indonesia
c. Nigeria
d. Papua New Guinea

4. Which language has the most letters/sounds in its alphabet?

a. !Xóõ
b. English
c. Khmer
d. Korean

5. Some languages have clicks, particularly the Khoisan languages. Where are these languages mainly spoken?

a. Southern Africa
b. Southeast Asia
c. Australia
d. Central Brazil

6. Which consonant sounds appear in the greatest number of world languages? (The slashes indicate a sound.)

a. /b/, /s/, /l/, /p/, /v/
b. /k/, /p/, /t/, /m/, /n/
c. /b/, /m/, /d/, /r/, /w/
d. /k/, /h/, /g/, /f/, /p/

7. What are the most common letters in English?

a. e, t, a
b. s, i, d
c. i, o, s
d. a, n, t

8. How many languages are spoken in Africa?

a. about 125
b. about 345
c. about 700
d. more than 1,000

9. English has an alphabet of 26 letters, which represent sounds. Conversely, Chinese uses characters, which represent meanings (e.g. 女 = female). How many characters are necessary to read a newspaper?

a. 250-500
b. 500-1,000
c. 1,000-1,500
d. 2,000 or more

10. Which country has the most official languages (i.e., those given legal status)?

a. Indonesia
b. Zimbabwe
c. Singapore
d. Luxembourg

Answers

1. c. Although no one knows the exact number, 7,000 or thereabouts is a commonly accepted estimate (§2).

2. a. Mandarin Chinese is spoken by about 921 million native speakers. Spanish is second with 471 million, then English (370 million). However, population figures are constantly rising, and so these figures (and others like it in this book) will inevitably soon become out-of-date. Nevertheless, the relative relationship between the languages (i.e., 1st, 2nd, 3rd) looks to remain stable for the foreseeable future.

3. d. There are about 840 languages spoken in Papua New Guinea, 706 in Indonesia, 520 in Nigeria, and 453 in India.

4. a. The Guinness World Records gives !Xóõ (spoken in eastern Namibia and southern Botswana) the prize with 130 consonants + 28 vowels + 3 tones to give a total segment inventory of 161. In comparison, English has far fewer: 27 consonant sounds + 13 vowel sounds = 40.

5. a. Most 'click' languages are spoken in southern Africa.

6. b.

7. a. The 10 most frequent letters are *e, t, a, o, i, n, s, h, r, d.*

8. d. Africa is very diverse linguistically, with easily more than 1,000 languages and perhaps as many as 2,000 or more.

9. d. The BBC states that it takes 2,000-3,000 characters to read a newspaper in Chinese, but many other commentators suggest that the figure may be much higher (4,000?) in order to read with good comprehension and without constantly stopping to look up unknown characters.

10. b. The Guinness World Records reports that Zimbabwe has the most, with 16.

Here is a site with some interesting statistics about language.

http://www.vistawide.com/languages/language_statistics.htm

100

LANGUAGE TRIVIA QUIZ #2

How about one last quiz to finish up the book?

Here are ten more items, with a liberal inclusion of records from Guinness World Records.

1. There are numerous writing scripts in use in the world today. Match the name of each script with its characters.

1. _____ Arabic	a. Α, Θ, Φ, Ψ, Ω
2. _____ Cyrillic	b. ب , خ , ض , ف , ك
3. _____ Latin	c. ㄱ, ㅁ, ㅅ, ㅊ, ㅎ
4. _____ Hangul	d. A, B, C, D, E
5. _____ Greek	e. А, Б, Д, Ж, И

2. It is uncertain when the earliest writing began. But how old is the earliest archaeological evidence of writing?

a. 1,000 B.C.
b. 4,000-5,000 B.C.
c. 10,000-12,000 B.C.
d. ~100,000 B.C.

3. When was the smiley first used? :-)

a. 1978
b. 1982
c. 1988
d. 1992

4. What is the highest-grossing foreign language film of all time in the US market?

a. *Amélie* (French)
b. *Crouching Tiger, Hidden Dragon* (Chinese)
c. *Life is Beautiful* (Italian)
d. *Pan's Labyrinth* (Spanish)

5. Many English words have more than one meaning (polysemy). Which word has the most meanings?

a. set
b. run
c. look
d. cool

6. The MGIMO University (Moscow State Institute of International Relations) teaches the greatest number of languages

full-time to advanced levels. How many languages are taught?

a. 22
b. 36
c. 53
d. 68

7. Which other language is the most similar to English?

a. Icelandic
b. French
c. German
d. Frisian

8. In 1977, NASA launched the Voyager probes, which later flew by the outer planets and into deep space. A recording of greetings was attached to the spacecraft. How many languages were these greetings recorded in?

a. 25
b. 35
c. 45
d. 55

9. How long is the longest English word that does not repeat any letters?

a. 11 letters
b. 13 letters
c. 15 letters
d. 17 letters

10. Many English words only have a single vowel (e.g., *boy*, *slap*), but most of these are short. How many letters does the longest single-vowel English word contain?

a. 5
b. 7
c. 9
d. 11

Answers

1. b 2. e 3. d 4. c 5. a. Cyrillic is used to write Russian and other Slavic languages, and Hangul to write Korean.

2. b. According to Guinness World Records, the earliest written language discovered so far is on a piece of pottery from China, dated to 4,000-5,000 BC. 100,000 B.C. is a ballpark estimate by many scholars for when man began developing spoken language.

3. b. Guinness World Records attributes the first use of a smiley to Scott Fahlman in Pittsburgh at Carnegie Mellon University, on September 19, 1982.

4. b. According to Box Office Mojo, the highest grossing foreign film is *Crouching Tiger, Hidden Dragon,* with takings of $128,078,872 (as of April 2022). *Life is Beautiful* is second with $57,247,384.

5. a. Guinness World Records gives the award to "set," based on its 430 meaning senses listed in the second edition of the *Oxford English Dictionary* (1989).

6. c. Guinness World Records confirms this is the most languages taught by any institute.

7. d. Frisian (a language spoken in northern Netherlands and Germany) is commonly considered to be the modern language closest to English.

8. d. In addition to the 55 languages, the probes also carried 115 analog-encoded photographs and 90 minutes of music.

9. c. Lexico suggests that there are two words with 15 letters: *uncopyrightable* and *dermatoglyphics.*

10. c. According to Guinness World Records, the longest single-vowel English word is *strengths,* with 9 letters.

One last website with facts and trivia about language.

https://www.factmonster.com/features/speaking-language/language-trivia

NOTES

1. Many linguists disapprove of the term *native speaker,* because they feel it carries political and ideological biases. Also, in today's multicultural, multilingual world, it is not always easy to distinguish between native and nonnative speakers. Nevertheless, I feel that it is a term that will be widely understood by the non-specialist audience of this book, and using circumlocutions would sometimes make the book less readable. I use *native speaker* to mean a person who speaks a language as their mother tongue. I also use the term *first language* as a synonym for mother tongue. Note that people can be native speakers of more than one language if they were raised in multilingual environments.

2. This dialogue was originally recorded by Patrick Byrne and Barrie Long, and appears in their book *Doctors Talking to Patients* (pp. 132-133).

3. This dialogue is based on clinical data presented by Elliot Mishler in his book *Discourse of Medicine: Dialectics of Medical Interviews* (pp. 133-134).

4. This post is taken from the article 'Legitimacy, Authority, and Community in Electronic Support Groups' by Jolene Galegher, Lee Sproull, and Sara Kiesler appearing in the journal *Written Communication*, Volume 15, p. 495.

5. The Mullany extracts are taken from her PhD research:

Louise Mullany. (2003). Identity and role construction: A sociolinguistic study of gender and discourse in management. Unpublished PhD thesis: Nottingham Trent University. pp. 108 & 136.

6. This *Wikipedia* extract is courtesy of a Creative Commons Attribution-ShareAlike License 3.0: *https://creativecommons.org/licenses/by-sa/3.0/*

7. My friend and colleague Zoltán Dörnyei developed the test from which these items are extracted.

8. I made this test based on the methodology from the following journal article:

Goulden, R., Nation, P. and Read, J. (1990). How large can a receptive vocabulary be? *Applied Linguistics*. Volume 11, Issue 4. Pages 341-363.

9. Different research studies report slightly different percentages, and I have synthesized the various results into these graphs. They should provide a good general sense of the interactions between frequency and text coverage.

10. Norbert Schmitt and Richard Marsden. (2006). *Why is English Like That? Historical Answers to Hard ELT Questions.* University of Michigan Press. p. 111.

11. I adapted the letter length/frequency table from the following journal article:

Bengt Sigurd, Mats Eeg-Olofsson and Joost van de Weijer. (2004). Word length, sentence length and frequency – Zipf revisited. *Studia Linguistica,* Volume 58, Issue 1. Table 1, page 39.

12. This figure comes from the 2006 book *The Atlas of North American English* by William Labov, Sharon Ash, and Charles Boberg (page 148). Permission to reproduce it is courtesy of De Gruyter Mouton Press.

13. These figures come from the personal collections of Dennis Preston, and I am grateful for his permission to reproduce them here.

14. This extract is taken from the story 'Countries with the Highest Single and Family Income Tax Rates' by Amy Fontinelle, appearing on the *Investopedia* website, updated March 24, 2022.

15. This figure illustrating Kachru's model is adapted from a figured in the book *Why is English Like That?* by Norbert Schmitt and Richard Marsden, page 179, published in 2006 by University of Michigan Press. It is based on the discussion in Braj Kachru's chapter "Standards, codification, and sociolinguistic realism: The English language in the outer circle" in the 1985 book *English in the World* (Randolph Quirk and Henry Widdowson, editors, Cambridge University Press).

ACKNOWLEDGMENTS

In order to ensure the accuracy of the information in this book, I asked a number of experts to review the sections relating to their various specialties.

Special mention goes to my wife Diane Schmitt, who read the entire draft manuscript and gave many useful suggestions for improvement, as well as being virtual co-author for Section 51: Talking to Your Child's Teacher about Reading.

Also, my grateful thanks to Ronald Carter and Kelly Sippell, who commented on the content and organization of an early manuscript version.

Several colleagues and former colleagues from the University of Nottingham gave useful advice, including Kathy Conklin, Zoltán Dörnyei, Kevin Harvey, Louise Mullany, Ana Pellicer-Sánchez, and Michael Rodgers.

My former Ph.D. students also provided helpful comments: Mélodie Garnier, Beatriz González Fernández, Benjamin Kremmel, Marijana Macis, and Laura Vilkaitė-Lozdienė. Colleagues from other universities and institutions include Kees de Bot, Marjolijn Vespoor, Wander Lowie, Pauline Foster, and Frances Connor.

My nieces and nephews Kelsea Shook, Justin Shook, and Jesse Schmitt gave me an important reality check on the language of young people. Anna Roderick gave me helpful early advice about how to publish *Language Power.*

Special thanks go to my editor Dorothy Zemach and other staff at Wayzgoose Press who turned my manuscript into this book.

I would like to thank everybody else for their insightful input and help, and apologize that I forgot to put them on the list.

I have taken advice and input from a number of sources, but the final product represents my personal understanding and presentation of the language issues covered. I hope you like it.

This book is dedicated to Ron Carter and Zoltán Dörnyei, great friends and applied linguists from whom I learned much.

www.ingramcontent.com/pod-product-compliance
Lightning Source LLC
LaVergne TN
LVHW010625110826
845149LV00014B/2781

* 9 7 8 1 9 6 1 9 5 3 0 8 6 *